FIGHTING FOR ANDEAN RESOURCES

VLADIMIR R. GIL RAMÓN

FIGHTING FOR ANDEAN RESOURCES

EXTRACTIVE INDUSTRIES, CULTURAL POLITICS, AND ENVIRONMENTAL STRUGGLES IN PERU

THE UNIVERSITY OF
ARIZONA PRESS
TUCSON

The University of Arizona Press
www.uapress.arizona.edu

ISBN-13: 978-0-8165-3071-7 (hardcover)

Cover design by Leigh McDonald
Cover photo by Vladimir R. Gil Ramón
Interior design and typesetting by Sara Thaxton
Set in Adobe Caslon Pro (text), Abolition, and Futura PT Condensed (display)

Library of Congress Cataloging-in-Publication Data
Names: Gil Ramón, Vladimir R., 1970– author.
Title: Fighting for Andean resources : extractive industries, cultural politics, and environmental struggles in Peru / Vladimir R. Gil Ramón ; foreword by Enrique Mayer.
Description: Tucson : University of Arizona Press, 2020. | Includes bibliographical references and index.
Identifiers: LCCN 2019050455 | ISBN 9780816530717 (hardcover)
Subjects: LCSH: Mineral industries—Peru. | Mineral industries—Peru—Finance. | Mineral industries—Environmental aspects—Peru. | Mineral industries—Social aspects—Peru.
Classification: LCC HD9506.P42 G55 2020 | DDC 338.20985—dc23
LC record available at https://lccn.loc.gov/2019050455

Printed in the United States of America
∞ This paper meets the requirements of ANSI/NISO Z39.48-1992 (Permanence of Paper).

To my parents, Isabel Ramón de Gil and Oscar R. Gil Irigoyen

CONTENTS

ILLUSTRATIONS

Figures

Maps

Tables

FOREWORD

IT IS A PLEASURE TO PRESENT VLADIMIR GIL RAMÓN'S MAGNIFICENT BOOK, WHICH ANALYZES how to understand the conflicts that take place when new mining is promoted by modern extraction techniques and markets associated with a fundamental transformation in the organization of mining companies. I learned a great deal from Vladimir's study of the Antamina transnational mining project, with which he completed his doctoral degree in anthropology at Yale University. This publication should be required reading for those interested in the neoliberal transformation of countries like Peru.

From colonial times up until the present day, mineral extraction has marked the country in an unequal relationship with the metropolises that consume our metals. Mining has always been notorious for its abusive labor practices and the contamination of its surroundings. This new phase of extraction is associated with the globalization of capital investments tied to financial circuits and adjustments in relations with governmental regimes, as well as contradictory oversight and control mechanisms. For these reasons, the case of the Antamina megaproject in Ancash is very illuminating. The World Bank guaranteed the investment, conditioned on fulfillment of its own requirements in regard to the treatment of affected populations. It also demanded that the company comply with restrictions imposed by new environmental impact–evaluation processes. The emergence of the multinational Antamina marked a turning point in the shift to privatization of Peruvian mining and the return of foreign investment.

The study includes a detailed analysis of the environmental impact assessment, which, as Vladimir shows, has become, without the critical attention it deserves, the fundamental instrument of mediation between international corporations vis-à-vis local groups and their surroundings.

What stands out in Vladimir's study is how this whole process is a long path of learning for all the parties involved. With admirable meticulousness, the author recounts the interests of the actors from different perspectives. There is the company, in conjunction and contradiction with different branches of the state and globalized civil society; the indirect beneficiaries, and also those who wish to benefit but are unable to; and of course, the perspective of the victims. The main point of the book is how these parties in conflict manage to compromise in spite of having very different values and goals. We see the environmental nongovernmental organizations (NGOs) convincing Antamina's financiers to transport the ore by pipeline instead of crossing roughshod with hundreds of trucks through Huascarán National Park. But the fact that the apparent conflict was mitigated and that all parties negotiated does not necessarily mean that everyone is content.

Using political ecological approaches combined with tools from cultural anthropology, this study observes how parties negotiate under asymmetrical conditions, and how incommensurable values can be reconciled. The reader will see how complicated it is to understand such bandied-about concepts as the "development" that mining could bring to a region, and whether it is true that "Antamina contaminates." Different discursive registers are used, contrary feelings are mobilized, and support is recruited from local, national, and international sectors in complicated strategies, all of them minutely documented in this book.

Antamina presents itself as a responsible company, and for that reason the study is extremely valuable in recording the company's often pompous statements. These are assessed in a measured way, together with the loud protests of those claiming to be victims or to have been deceived. The author carefully avoids winning applause from any of the parties, and, without neglecting to criticize where he should, he brings us a book that deserves to be praised for its rigor and balance. The main lesson, I repeat, has been to document how, in the process of becoming established, all parties have learned a great deal from their faults and errors, as well as their respective achievements, availing themselves of diverse strategies. And the learning—although not yet accompanied by a better and more just redistribution of benefits from the mine—also includes steps forward on the long road that implies the building of citizenship for those Peruvians who were previously invisible and helpless.

Herders in the high punas, displaced from where there is now an immense hole in the ground, community leaders, mayors, and members of committees from neighboring towns also learned how to negotiate, how to take advantage, with whom to ally themselves, and how to force the company to be more responsible for that which it had itself initially committed to. And thus, without blindly taking sides either for or against today's supercapitalist companies, reading this book teaches us how it might be possible for new mining to avoid simply extracting wealth in the midst of so much poverty, as the industry has been doing since its colonial beginnings.

Enrique Mayer
Emeritus Professor
Department of Anthropology and
International & Area Studies
Yale University

ACKNOWLEDGMENTS

THIS BOOK TAKES AS A STARTING POINT THE VOLUME *ATERRIZAJE MINERO: CULTURA, conflicto, negociaciones y lecciones para el desarrollo desde la minería en Ancash, Perú*, based on my dissertation at Yale University (Gil Ramón 2009, 2005). Thanks to those efforts, this work benefits from the invaluable contribution of the protagonists interviewed, who still had fresh memories of the beginning of the most recent large mining expansion in Peru. Here I have rewritten and updated relevant information, including selected data produced in subsequent years, and have adapted approaches and terminologies to facilitate an appreciation by an international reading.

Like most research efforts, this work is a testimony to individual and collective generosity. Among the innumerable recognitions of indebtedness, I would like to highlight the residents close to the mining areas and the professionals associated with these impacts, who shared their time and ideas to enable me to understand the complexity of the conflicts and negotiations with mining corporations. In San Marcos, I especially thank Mito Vásquez, the members of the Local Communities of Health program, the Huaripampa and Ango Raju de Carhuayoc peasant communities, and the mayor of San Marcos, Francisco Vargas. The staff of the Chavín de Huántar archaeological complex shared valuable testimonies. Particularly attentive and collaborative with the study were, in Huarmey, Karina Morante and Jaime Zevallos of the environmental committee and Mayor Juan Pacífico, and in Huallanca, Mayor Luis Barrenechea. In Huaraz, the Mountain Institute, especially Raúl García and Director Jorge

Recharte, have my thanks for their generous support. In Lima, Manuel Glave of the Group for the Analysis of Development and Martin Scurrah, former director of Oxfam America, shared valuable advice and experience. I would also like to thank the following personnel of the Antamina Mining Company: in San Marcos, I thank the staff of the Office of Community Development—Agustín Vásquez, Raúl Urbina, Rosa Ocaña, and Iván Vega. In Lima, Steven Botts, then vice president of Environment, Health and Safety, was particularly receptive to my questions.

At Yale University I was fortunate to have exceptional mentors and faculty who supported the central work of this book. Enrique Mayer, always generous with his vast knowledge and warm support, gave me a great lesson in free thinking. His encouragement and understanding of my project, through his moral and intellectual support, have been fundamental in my studies and beyond. Michael Dove stimulated the analysis with sharp observations, suggesting innovative ways to approach and understand the interactions between nature and human groups, thereby helping me to move toward new ways of approaching research. Many thanks also to the members of the Dove Doctoral Lab, directed by Michael Dove. Eric Worby was an important motivating figure through successful questioning and recommendations for the analysis of political and social issues. James Scott, David Graeber, William Kelly, Helen Siu, Harold Scheffler, Arun Agrawal, Carol Carpenter, and Andrew Schrank taught me novel ways to both engage and question social theories in the field. At the Yale School of Forestry and Environmental Studies, Sheila Olmstead was very generous in sharing her knowledge in natural resource management, while Charles Dana Tomlin introduced me to the value of geographic information systems.

Parts of the text have benefited from the insights of participants in different academic forums, including meetings of the Latin American Studies Association, the New England Council of Latin American Studies, and the American Anthropological Association, as well as seminars at Yale, Columbia, Dartmouth, and the New School for Social Research. The anthropologists Freda Wolf and Mieka Ritsema contributed with substantive commentaries in early versions of the manuscript. I thank Caitlin Purdy for the contribution in chapter 3. The generous assistance from translator Alex Jefremov was essential to the completion of this work. I thank the anonymous reviewers of the manuscript who provided constructive comments. Amy Maddox carefully copyedited the manuscript. Geographers María Luisa Mori and Jose Barreda designed the cartography. I would also like to acknowledge the support of Carlos Iván Degregori, Mercedes Dioses, Mario Popuche, Marcos Cueto, and Víctor Vich of the Instituto de Estudios Peruanos for sections of the book in different versions.

Research for this book was possible thanks to Yale University's Program in Agrarian Studies, the George W. Leitner Program in Political Economy, the Graduate School of Arts and Sciences (Dissertation Writing Fellowship and John F. Enders Fellowship), the Council on Latin American and Iberian Studies, the Yale Center for International and Area Studies, and the Department of Anthropology (Mellon and Williams Funds). The postdoctoral work at the Earth Institute at Columbia University, with the support of its then director, Jeffrey Sachs, and Geoffrey Heal, director of the Center for Globalization and Sustainable Development, was the fundamental intellectual space for the writing of this research. I thank this center, the Earth Institute Center for Environmental Sustainability, and the Earth Institute for the resources that contributed to this publication. The book also benefited from generous conversations with scholars from different fields at Columbia University, in particular with Upmanu Lall, Paige West, Lex van Geen, Alex Pfaff, and Macartan Humphreys. The Central European University's Visiting Fellowship Program, supported by the Higher Education Support Program of the Open Society Foundations, allowed me the final intellectual space to review and finish the book. I would like to acknowledge the financial support of the University of Arizona Press for the publication, in addition to the many generous grants from its staff, led by editor Allyson Carter. I also thank the support of the Fulbright Commission and the Consorcio de Investigación Económica y Social del Perú for their contributions.

My siblings, Miluska, Richard, and Sally, and especially my parents, Isabel and Oscar, my first teachers, continue to be an inexhaustible source of energy and motivation. Friendships beyond a possible list—of different nations, cultures, and disciplines—illuminated my writing time in New Haven, New York, Budapest, and Lima, for which my recognition is monumental. To all those who helped me in some way, I hope that the lessons are deservedly reflected in the text that I share. Of course, the conclusions, opinions, and statements of the book reflect those of the author, without compromising the aforementioned organizations. Everyone deserves credit for the successes and, of course, no reproach for any possible omission.

FIGHTING FOR ANDEAN RESOURCES

Introduction

The Struggle for Andean Rocks

"NOT SINCE THE ARRIVAL OF THE SPANIARDS HAVE OUTSIDERS SHOWN SO MUCH INTEREST in Andean rocks," proclaimed the *Economist* (1995) in its article "South American Mining: The New El Dorado," in reference to the boom in mineral prospecting in the Andes of Peru, Chile, Bolivia, and Argentina during the 1990s. More than half of these explorations were for copper and a quarter for gold, both of which led to the increase in international mineral prices.[1] Following the collapse of communism in Europe in 1989, the World Bank began to promote neoliberal reforms in many countries, encouraging the lifting of restrictions on foreign investment and changes in mining codes to deregulate protections for the environment, labor, and displaced persons (Danielson 2006; Kirsch 2014). New mining codes in South America aimed to emulate the success of Chile in attracting foreign capital following its 1981 introduction of a mining law, which occurred eight years after the coup d'état that had toppled the socialist government of President Salvador Allende and ushered in neoliberal economic policies. Their legislation put an end to treatment considered discriminatory by international firms. The aim was to introduce "more stable and generous tax treatment and allow repatriation of profits" while the governments speeded up the granting of exploration permits (*Economist* 1995). The openness to foreign investment coincided with a period of environmental pressures and reduced resources for mining in so-called developed countries, such as Australia, Canada, and the USA, that combined to make the industry increasingly difficult and expensive (Kapelus 2002:277).

Development is an elusive notion. It can be seen as either an ideal imagined future to which investment efforts should be directed, or as a destructive myth: the "evil twin" of anthropology (Ferguson 2002:160), constituting for some an infamous chapter in the history of Western modernity (Edelman and Haugerud 2004; Escobar 1995). Although analyses point to improvements in human well-being, in practice a political and technical debate has yet to occur that defines what such improvements would be, the best way to achieve and measure them, and how to integrate dimensions such as sustainability and equity. As this book will show, many conflicts arise from an inability to reconcile the definitions of development. Many confrontations have arisen from frustrated expectations, environmental impact claims, and a state apparatus virtually absent in the locations where new projects emerged. In Peru, although mining investment has been presented as necessary for national progress, it has brought environmental costs, left unfulfilled hopes for development, and led to an increase in conflict, becoming a principal source of confrontation. At the center of mining confrontations are unmet development expectations, forming part of broader welfare discourses. This book discusses the role of the exploitation of nature in development in the context of the growing demand for civil participatory practices and the incorporation of the concept of sustainability.

While mining has been Peru's main source of foreign currency over recent decades, its benefits fail to meet the expectations of different groups, especially in rural areas in the Andes, where poverty and mining coincide. Despite certain strengthening of government regulations and the state's own environmental organizations since the early 1990s—mostly promoted by international entities and drawing on some national support—mining continues to be a notable source of risk for environmental degradation. The placement of colossal mines close to human settlements that are dedicated to agriculture or grazing and dependent on affected resources—such as water and soil—coupled with mining's low demand for local labor, creates a sensitive context prone to disputes in which the protagonists are local communities, the mining companies, and the state, as the promoter of the extractive activity. At the center of local defiance is an emerging environmental awareness and a set of older demands for development, within the context of great distrust in state supervisory authorities. The study of the political culture of pollution and risk illustrates how groups shape their claims through cultural and political filters, and how tensions are alleviated—at least in the short term—through participatory scenarios.

The national patrimony condition of natural resources generates expectations of benefits on the part of the citizenry. Under extractive models perceived as near enclaves that fail to generate local jobs or production chains, confrontations have increased between the mining companies and their neighbors, who do not receive the expected benefits. Local concepts and social structures are unknown or ignored by companies. Apart from the cultural differences at the core of the hostilities, there is an immense asymmetry of power between billionaire mining companies and local residents. This book examines the dynamics existing between the social actors, unveiling the rationale behind their behavior and discourses. The study highlights the sociotechnological apparatus of international investment projects, including regulatory systems and social networks, as well as conflictive behavioral patterns.

The relationship between extractive industries and neighboring populations has led to an increase in conflicts in Peru, accompanying the expansion of the mining frontier in the Andes and of the oil industry in the Amazon.[2] The demands for environmental protection and development—including basic services such as potable water systems—are at the heart of the struggles with mining companies such as Antamina, which presented itself, and was recognized by some relevant groups, as a model of openness and at the forefront of so-called corporate social responsibility. The arrival of a mine to a certain extent conditions its later relationship with local residents. There can only be one first impression. Conflict in Antamina dates back as far as 1996, when the concession for the project was granted. It includes disputes over evictions, obstruction of grazing routes, failure to fulfill promises of jobs and other benefits, and environmental degradation. The processes studied involve the environmental impact assessment (EIA) construction and its rhetorics, the analysis of environmental risks and protests, the resettlement of families, and empirical discussions of the meanings of development and demands for citizenship.[3] Those displaced by the operations provided a unique opportunity to focus on an immediate effect of the mine. A comparison of the decision-making processes of neighboring communities when using the funds obtained from the sale of their land revealed their preferences in improving their living conditions, analyzed as development choices. In addition, clues found in an examination of contamination complaints enabled an assessment of environmental degradation protests. I seek to identify the causes of the conflicts and the forms of resistance and negotiation. In this empirical account that begins with the opening of Antamina—a mine

FIGURE 1 Graffiti in Ango Raju that reads "Antamina liar, long live the regional strike!" 2002. Author's photo.

that until recently was the single largest project of the Peruvian mining boom that began in the 1990s—I track clashes and negotiations from the different perspectives in order to understand behaviors and strategies.

To understand the tactics employed by groups, the analysis includes local grievances and the rhetoric that is used as a negotiation resource by the company and other actors, such as NGOs.[4] If the underlying dilemmas associated with the capitalist mode of production are only partially resolved through different forms of renegotiation (Kirsch 2014:3), the investigation of resistance to, struggles around, and stratagems for the benefits of natural resources also help us understand the extent of everyday articulation of a state and nation under the mantle of neoliberal policies. I argue that, as a mining tactic, the rhetoric of mineral extraction models for development seeks to counterbalance the demands for real political participation. The book shows that the conflictive processes caused by the opening of a mining project can provide opportunities to extend the citizenship status of some excluded groups through the reappropriation of democratic state discourses and participatory schemes, which themselves emerge as an unanticipated consequence of precisely those same contentious processes.

Neoliberalization and Mining Struggles

The shift toward neoliberal economic policies in Latin American countries entailed deregulation and the privatization of state enterprises, affecting local relationships that frequently became conflictive (Sawyer 2004). Countries such as Ecuador and Bolivia, whose recent governments have been self-proclaimed critics of neoliberal models, have nevertheless promoted extractive activities that have led to social conflicts. Peru reached the 1990s affected by the anti-export macroeconomic policies of the first government of Alan García, implemented from the mid-1980s, and the closure of several mining projects. During the 1990s, the authoritarian regime of Alberto Fujimori led the expansion of mining through incentives provided by reforms that included rules promoting foreign investment, the sale of state enterprises, the simplification of concession purchasing, and modifications to environmental and tax regulations. Many of these transformations were promoted by the IMF (International Monetary Fund) and the World Bank (Li 2015). These changes, in the context of a rise in international mineral prices, meant that mining in Peru came to constitute, on average, 10 percent of the gross domestic product (GDP) over the last two decades. In this respect, Peru resembles Chile and Bolivia, whose extractive industries represent the largest percentage of GDP in Latin America (Dargent et al. 2017). Neoliberal reforms include the privatization of natural resources, deregulation of social and environmental safeguards, as well as significant social and biophysical transformations, especially in the communities neighboring mining operations.

Peru was one of the last Latin American countries to establish an environmental authority and a regulatory framework for national environmental policy. These changes began in 1990 when the Fujimori regime approved a strict environmental code, revised the following year with other decrees to promote private investment.[5] Prior to this, Article 123 of the 1979 Constitution was the only one devoted to environmental issues. The amendments contained in the decrees diminished state regulatory capacity by handing over jurisdiction on environmental issues in each sector, including the preparation of EIAs, to the responsible ministry. These decrees reduced environmental standards and established advantageous legal stability agreements for companies (e.g., special tax regimes and free availability of foreign currency and remittance of profits). In parallel, Legislative Decree 708 granted additional benefits for investment (e.g., administrative, tax, and exchange rate stability). The decree also defined the instruments that sought to restrict contamination, leaving a limited and mostly technical role for the state, such as the introduction of the EIA (Glave and Kuramoto 2002). The system reproduced governmental centralism and gave limited responsibility for subnational governments while empowering private consulting auditing.[6] The stability regime could not be legally altered for up to fifteen years.[7] Most of the more than eight hundred environmental regulations have been approved since 1993.

In 1992, the Rio Declaration on Environment and Development, produced at the UN Conference on Environment and Development (or Earth Summit) left an impact on Latin America. Many countries established national environmental commissions or ministries. Two years later the Peruvian government created CONAM (Consejo Nacional del Ambiente, or the National Environmental Council) to coordinate environmental policies among the ministries. Trade unions and peasant or Indigenous federations lacked representation, although the government did expand the public right to information and so-called consultation on environmental issues.[8] The 1995 Land Law, law no. 26505, allowed peasant communities to sell their land and defined the concept of *servidumbre* (easement), which obliged owners to sell their land to a mining company and be compensated in cash.[9] Subsequently, the government further extended the incentives for large extractive projects, giving rise to massive profits for businesses and speedy tax collection. Government pressure to promote mining activity by deregulating the precarious mechanisms for labor (in order to weaken unions), for environmental protection and for access to Indigenous lands, was apparent from the 1990s (Gil Ramón 2014). Only at the start of the new millennium—with the creation of MINAM (Ministerio del Ambiente, or the Ministry of the Environment) and its absorption of CONAM to comply with the free trade agreement with the USA—did a limited process commence for the consolidation of institutions for a more autonomous environmental oversight.

The privatization process in South America was leading to generalized discontent, primarily due to threatened increases in tariffs for basic services, such as electricity and water, which were to be sold off. Disillusionment led to protest. In Bolivia, following protests against high prices in 2005, the government canceled its contract with a subsidiary of French Suez for the provision of residential water services (Forero 2005). In Peru, the 2002 revolt in the city of Arequipa, or Arequipazo, was the first major mobilization against the sale of a state-owned electrical company based on the fear of massive layoffs. It would be followed seven years later by the catastrophic incidents of the Baguazo in the Amazon town of Bagua.[10] The conflictive privatization illustrates the confrontation of perceptions of local costs or damages versus purported national benefits when there is the attempt to exploit public resources without the consent demanded at the local level.

The citizenship conflicts over the mining expansion stand out as asymmetric encounters in rural areas involving marginalized sectors, which are relegated from access to private or public opportunities and modern state services. The contemporary demands for citizenry rights can be connected with longer assertion processes from marginalized sectors, especially in rural scenarios. Among the most significant citizenship battles in Peru over the last decades, we can identify both violent manifestations, such as land seizures that preceded the Agrarian Reform of 1969, and more peaceful examples, such as the large migrations to urban centers since the 1940s. The top-down agrarian reform redrew Peru's social landscape, ending cruel labor conditions for Indigenous peoples, who were converted into precarious citizens.[11] In the mining struggles, rural citizens seek transformations, especially in prevention or remediation of mining damage, and rights to greater participation in benefits and modern services. The battles are located within strains of exclusion and class-based historical privileges, as evidenced through the sharp concentration in the capital of the state and its major investments, frequently oblivious to demands from outside the metropolis.

The Antamina clashes reflect public concerns over the privatization and neoliberalization process in the region since the 1990s. The Peruvian mining boom since this decade has generated colossal income for companies but unequal gains and losses for the state and neighboring localities. The underfinanced and historically indebted Peruvian state sought funds through the sale of national companies and concessions, many of which operated in nonrenewable resources. Following this globalized exchange, the *Economist* (2005a) magazine showed that in real terms, the prices of the main industrial goods in the middle of the first decade of the twenty-first century only represented 30 percent of their value in 1845.[12] Optimism about the privatizations of the early 1990s was replaced by disappointment about their modest contribution to the generation of employment, not to mention the uncovering of government and business corruption.[13] While governments present mining as a source of development, residents question its real benefits and complain about environmental costs. Big mining—or "megamining," as many activists refer to it—with its colossal scale that starts with the exposure of deep subterranean layers in order to establish an open pit, and the clearing of vast amounts of waste rock material each day, presents serious risks for nature, organisms, and livelihoods.[14] This book focuses on conflicts with large mining projects, using Antamina as a case study, while addressing issues that relate to extractive activities in general.[15]

Examining Resource Battles

This book researches mining as one of the most powerful contemporary agents of change. Indeed, there is now much discussion about the need to define a new geological era—the Anthropocene—to describe human impact on the earth's ecosystems, reflecting global processes of socioenvironmental interconnection and disintegration. Contemporary mining reflects the current phase of the globalization of capital flows and environmental concerns (Barham et al. 1994; Bunker 1985; Escobar 1995, 1998). Discourses on natural resources, development, and power frame distributive processes about the environment, as in the case of extractive industries (Blaikie and Brookfield 1987; Bryant 1992; Escobar 1991; Peet and Watts 1996). The opening of transnational mining projects is a notable opportunity for observing "glocalization"—global-local linkages reflecting north/south, poor/rich, and West-and-the-rest encounters and disencounters—where more capitalist and urban-based actors confront populations that are Indigenous, vulnerable, marginalized, and poor.[16] I examine mutual influences between local and international relations in these contentious scenarios.

The increase in mineral prices throughout the late 1970s and early 1980s sparked a boom in mining exploration, particularly in the largely underexplored Asia-Pacific region. As a result of more advanced exploratory technologies, the majority of these new projects were located in the world's most remote frontiers, inhabited by marginalized populations, including Indigenous peoples. Economically and politically vulnerable people were located at the hub of these mining discoveries (Ballard and Banks 2003). New conflicts arose in these far-flung corners. Examples of these tensions can be found in industrialized countries, such as Canada, as well as poor ones, such as Indonesia and Zambia. Conflict intensified in politically centralized states with weak institutions.

The interest in socioenvironmental conflicts over recent decades emerges primarily from social resistance studies, showing how marginalized groups develop strategies to respond to threatening situations (e.g., Comaroff 1985; Guha 1989; Martínez-Alier 1990, 2002; Ong 1987; Scott 1985). In Rowstonian theories of modernization, culture is seen as a homogeneous "traditional" arrangement of coherent norms, almost mechanically obeyed by the community, constituting an obstacle to modernization (Edelman and Haugerud 2005:30). Ethnographic evidence shows how individual motivations and conflicts between groups shape strategies that change according to the dynamics between agents. Affected residents can create mechanisms to present their identity as local or Indigenous. Disputes over political and economic resources can become struggles for cultural representations (Dove 1999; Pigg 1997).

Sociologist Louis Kriesberg (1999:122) states that a social conflict can be understood as "a perspective in which conflict permeates and shapes the aspects of human interaction and social structure, or one of innumerable specific fights or struggles, such as wars, revolutions, strikes, and uprisings." Numerous battles were fought over expectations for development, the displacement of families, disputes over the definitions of property systems, and legitimate compensation for the opening of Antamina. I examine the fundamental assumptions to understand the causes of the conflict and the proposed renegotiation of disputes. Drawing on political ecology approaches, I use discourse analysis to understand the underlying behavioral motivations, rationales, representations, and practices of groups in conflict as manifested in acts, testimonies, and documents (Dove and Kammen 2015; Escobar 1991; Ferguson 1994; Foucault 1980; Grillo and Stirrat 1997; Orlove 1977; Peet and Watts 1996; Schmink and Wood 1992).[17]

Evidence shows that countries dependent on extractive industries often perform worse than their peers with fewer resources (in terms of economic development and good governance)—the so-called resource curse. The first studies that developed this concept were based on Latin American countries (Auty 1993; Humphreys et al. 2007; Sachs and Warner 1995). In addition, it has been found that the dependence of countries on the mining and oil industry is "strongly associated with unusually bad conditions for the poor" (Ross 2001:4). As president of Peru, García (2007) developed a discourse that attributed this fate to local residents, especially Indigenous associations and communities, together with—who he claimed presented themselves as—protectionist "pluralistic and patriotic anti-mining" groups and "environmentalists." He articulated this position in several op-eds. According to this rhetoric, the aforementioned groups, by denying others with greater capacity or capital to exploit the natural resources that they themselves don't use, act in a way that is akin to the fable of the "Dog in the Manger." In a televised interview he called Amazonian Indigenous Peruvians "not first-class citizens," accusing them of promoting "irrationality" and "primitive setback" for opposing a decree that permitted extractive industries in their territories with neither their proper consultation nor consent.[18] The discourse harks back to an observation attributed to the nineteenth-century Italian naturalist and Peruvian immigrant Antonio Raimondi (1824–1890) and aimed at sectors of the population hindering national progress: "*El Perú es un mendigo sentado en un banco de oro*" (Peru is a beggar sitting on a bench of gold).

The absence of adequate institutions and public policies—a kind of institutional curse—has been identified by research that provides more detailed explanations of the relationship between natural resource dependency and economic growth (e.g., Auty 2000; Humphreys et al. 2007; Karl 1997; Ross 1999, 2001, 2007). Evidence about socioenvironmental conflicts demonstrates institutional apparatus—legal, financial, bureaucratic, and technoscientific—perpetuating scenarios of domination (Brosius 1999). Transnational mining projects bring together colossal globalized extractive forces and "corporate social technologies" (Rogers 2012), including governance regimes designed to manage their relations with the public, aiming to mitigate concerns by stimulating uncertainty and doubt (Kirsch 2014).

This book investigates the behavior of large extractive corporations, including multilateral agencies, to understand the social dynamics of multinational capital beyond corporate culture (Rouse and Fleising 1995), examining the impact of corporate policies that seek a more environmental face for mining when pressured by civil society and international organizations such as the World Bank. Demonstrating the significance of the capacity of organizations to enforce regulations, extractive industries in regions with weak local institutions frequently lead to greater environmental degradation (Bunker 1985; Martínez-Alier 1990, 2002). The boom in these industries has weakened institutions, especially where governments lack transparency and accessibility (Ballard and Banks 2003; Karl 1997; MMSD 2002; Ross 1999). Empirical studies point to a relationship between natural resources and conflicts, highlighting the impact on state capacity or democracy (e.g., Ross 2006). In some cases, mining has damaged institutions, producing a direct relationship with civil conflicts (MMSD 2002). Countries whose macroeconomic well-being depends largely on the export of primary products have a high propensity for civil violence (Collier and Hoeffler 2000; Humphreys 2005; Ross 2006).

The importance of institutions to influence the quality of sustainable development has been addressed from the governance of natural resources to achieve sustainability (e.g., Agrawal 2005; Humphreys et al. 2007; Martínez-Alier 2002;

North 1990; Ostrom 1990). The mechanisms to ensure environmental quality and human development from mining frequently have been weak, contributing to social confrontations, especially when the mining expansion precedes the necessary institutional adaptation (Bebbington and Bury 2009; Muradian et al. 2003). The timing of the creation of effective institutions to control the arrival of extractive industries contributes to the degree of benefit or harm to the environment and society (e.g., Karl 1997). Negative impacts can generate conflicts even when regulations are implemented (Gil Ramón 2014). Institutional deficiencies explain a good part of the environmental conflicts generated by mining, which are catalyzed when it becomes impossible to channel fears and legitimate demands (Bebbington and Bury 2009; Gil Ramón 2009).

Approaches with a more institutional-cultural orientation reveal the importance of examining competitions for power, participation, and political tactics between groups. These studies identify who defines a change in nature as a risk and contributes to a recognition of the rhetorical tools in environmental degradation discussions (e.g., Douglas and Wildavksy 1982; Fortun 2001; Oliver-Smith 1996). Debates about the role of human impact in nature show how the environment is constructed, symbolized, and contested by different subjects (Brosius 1999). In response to environmental criticism and because of international pressure, the EIA process appeared as a tool that sought to reconcile negative mining impacts. I examine the rhetoric that claims that through an EIA all the environmental and social "footprints"—a term used by an Antamina official—would be predictable, manageable, and able to be mitigated. The EIAs draw on a rhetoric of prevention with little predictive power, as demonstrated by the study led by mining engineer James Kuipers in the USA. EIA discourse proclaims its authority based on the supposed technical and scientific objectivity of the experts that construct it. The evidence discussed throughout this book helps us understand how the natural sciences and technology are embedded in globalized political contexts, impacting new forms of social mobilizations (Ballard and Banks 2003).[19]

Social Research on Mining

Due to lower transportation costs in the 1960s, mines were located away from consumers and processing centers. As mines grew and the technological processes became more complex, the specialized mining labor and equipment was increasingly found outside mining localities. A global pattern was established: multinational companies, the purchase of inputs outside the mining region, and the geographical dispersion of the projects. As a result, regional economic ties decreased with respect to the time when mines were smaller and located near industrial centers (Eggert 2001:34). Higher proportions of inputs were purchased outside the extractive area, processing near the deposit decreased, and multinational companies managed their revenues away from the mining region. Tax payments more clearly benefited national governments, rather than the regions or localities neighboring the mine. The mining companies built settlements and supported infrastructure that was mainly focused on the direct needs of the mine and its workers. National governments and mining companies tended to make decisions without considering neighboring communities. The enclave and its few links with the national economy had only a slight impact on internal development (Edelman and Haugerud 2005; Scott and Marshall 2005a).

The term *enclave* was propagated in the 1960s through dependence theories, which highlighted the problems of countries on the "periphery" that based their economies on exports to countries in the "center" controlled by foreign capital. The historian Alberto Flores Galindo (1993:33 [1974]), in his study of the Cerro de Pasco Copper Corporation (or La Cerro), defines the mining enclave as "a company whose origin was abroad, where its decision center and the destination of its production were also located."[20] Historians Contreras and Cueto (2007:210–213) inquire into the general historiography, criticizing the purportedly scarce production chains from these large mining centers, at least for a large part of the twentieth century. According to these authors, the critique mostly apply to oil projects, which worked under relative isolation, whereas large mining centers, when accompanied by significant local salaried jobs, presumably contributed to dynamizing peasant agriculture in several regions. From the perspective of neighboring communities or the region, a mine becomes an enclave when it isolates itself from nonmining activities, especially in poor countries.

Underground mines hired large unskilled labor forces during the 1970s. The social sciences focused on mining in the Andes—especially in Peru during the 1970s and 1980s—concentrated on regional economic development (e.g., DeWind 1987; Long and Roberts 1984). These scholars detailed the extent to which peasants became unionized proletarians (e.g., Dewind 1975; Flores Galindo 1993 [1974]; Godoy 1985; Mallon 1983; Nash 1993 [1979]; Taussig 1980). The anthropological research into the mining industry highlighted studies focused on labor and modernity, especially from the perspective of union conflicts and local development, where the range of impacts reflected the scale of operation and type of mining (Ferguson 1999; Godoy 1985; Nash 1993 [1979]; Kirsch 2014; Taussig 1980). Nash and Taussig exemplify the works of historical, symbolic, and ethnographic political economy to understand processes of social resistance.

Working conditions improved after the appearance of open-cut mines in the 1950s and their subsequent gradual global expansion. However, this system occasionally meant temporary or subcontract labor regimes. These mines led to a fiftyfold increase of waste rock by comparison with underground mining. Labor conflicts continued, however, their political importance diminished (Dore 2000; Kirsch 2014). The neoliberal reforms in Peru during the 1990s—the reform of mining codes, the lifting of restrictions on the investment of foreign capital, and the privatization of state industries—heralded new relationships between mining transnationals and impoverished neighboring populations. In this book I also show how a large-scale mining project affects the population and the surrounding environment in different ways according to the stage of the life cycle of the mine, arguing that these new mines can be perceived locally as near enclaves, independent from other economic processes in the contiguous and impacted areas. Yet the aggregation of activities of different mines and mining-related enterprises could have a significant impact on a region. Historically, diverse scenarios account for mining activity integrating regions in a single economic sphere (Assadourian et al. 1980; Godoy 1985:207–208).

There was a shift from a process of "accumulation by exploitation" in the confrontations, with workers complaining of labor exploitation during the 1960s to 1970s, to a greater "accumulation by dispossession" brought about by privatizations (Harvey 2003). This process led to new concerns about environmental impacts, particularly manifested as threats to the subsistence agricultural activities of residents close to the open pit (Kirsch 2014). Emblematic cases in Peru included the fumes produced by the La Oroya refinery, the impact of water from the Yanacocha gold mine, and the threat to agriculture posed by the Tambogrande mining project. Research began to be conducted to understand the social dynamics of conflicts and resistance in marginalized contexts, highlighting the competition between mining and agriculture (e.g., Bebbington and Bury 2013; Bury 2004; Caravedo 1998; Gil Ramón 2005, 2009; Golub 2014; Kirsch 2014; Muradian et al. 2003; Scurrah 2008). This competition has generated particular contentious scenarios when basic resources such as water or soil are affected, leading residents, especially those of Indigenous communities, to perceive mining as incompatible with their local livelihoods (Arellano-Yanguas 2011; de Echave et al. 2009). An issue that continues to require further in-depth study is how these imposed EIA sociotechnologies affect the negotiations and interactions between various confronted groups (Gil Ramón 2005, 2009). Beyond utilitarian conceptions of natural resources, this book addresses transformations and impacts, departing from the disagreements over the opening of a mining project. The study examines the negotiations and demands for participation in environmental evaluations, using the study of the EIA assembly, established as a sociotechnological tool for approaching the impact of mining. Demands for participation are useful for understanding the questioning of the environmental "matters of fact" proposed by the mining company, replaced by a broader discussion of "matters of concern" (Latour 2004), referring to the networks between subjects and information in order to establish diverse environmental knowledge and meaning.

The anthropologist Roy Rappaport (1993:298) criticized the way in which the economy supplied contemporary societies with their "dominant social discourse" to the detriment of fundamental ecological issues. There is a growing need to study the interface of how ecological problems are economized (i.e., translated into economic terms) frequently using national development labels. By taking into account cultural contexts, an analysis of impact evaluation guidelines and the causes of conflict—examining how populations evaluate their participation in and expected benefits from mining projects—provides elements for understanding how to strengthen institutions, reform aspects of equity, and reduce negative externalities.

Expectations of Citizenship

The abundant narratives about contemporary globalization celebrating international interconnections—generally reflecting unequal exchanges—are insufficient for understanding contentious scenarios. The economist Amartya Sen (2002) prefers the term *globalism* over *globalization* to denote the current asymmetric exchanges of capital and information, where the individual has restricted capacity to cross borders for employment motivations by comparison with multinational corporations that are able to mobilize as truly globalized subjects and are welcome to work virtually in any country.[21] Changes in regulations, including the deregulation of environmental safeguards, have promoted the presence of international mining in poor countries (Evans et al. 2002).

In Latin America, the notion of citizenship that has emerged is linked to processes of democratization that have occurred since the 1980s, especially in countries with authoritarian regimes (Dagnino 2006). This panorama has generated debates about the meaning of political participation and the dynamics of state formation in relation to claims against domination and demands for legitimacy (Krupa and Nugent 2015; Scott 1976, 1985, 1998). Over the last several decades, most of the Andean region has been witness to major restructuring that has produced a particular historical conjuncture of governmental contraction and expansion associated with violent redistributions of social, political, and economic rights, as well as obligations between the public and private sectors. The beginning of the mining boom of the 1990s led to sustained macroeconomic growth in Peru for the first time in many years, something that continued into the new millennium. The word *opportunity* appeared frequently in publications, conjuring up images of an auspicious expansion of mining and favorable economic scenarios.[22] Not properly considered at first was that the Peruvian Andes now had a large population—certainly much larger than at the start of the Spanish Conquest—consisting of vulnerable and marginal citizens, with an important Indigenous presence, who were survivors of the war between the Shining Path and the state during the 1980s and 1990s.[23]

I offer consideration to discourses and practices relating to citizenship that are broadly regarded as an unstable, contextually constructed, and continuous series of transactions and sets of relations between persons and agents of a given state, in which each has rights and obligations while experiencing encounters in political terrains and where everyday economic processes and power relations are mediated and contested over access and political participation (Gregory 2008; Tilly 1995). The citizenship approach used transcends the current status and is more a "legitimating political and cultural field" (Krupa and Nugent 2015:6), constantly restructured against promises and popular clamor, applied not only to the state but also to the disencounters of citizens in the face of corporate apparatuses and regimes. I also evaluate how conflicts can be interpreted as a demand by excluded citizens who seek social participation rights for concrete benefits and safeguards against the exploitation of a "national patrimony" (Article 66 of the Peruvian Constitution), such as mineral resources. Participation by all seeks to end the "political alienation"—paraphrasing anthropologist Eric Wolf (1971)—and find paths toward a national liberation.

Peru's eminent historian Jorge Basadre distinguished between two versions of Peru—*país legal* (the state; literally, "legal country") and *país profundo* (the nation, composed of its people)—remarking that the history of a country presupposes state and national narratives. The notion was popularized as a division between the urban and the rural. In 1943 Basadre used the phrase *Perú profundo* (deepest Peru) for the first time. It pointed to groups closer to the informal sector, at the margins of the mercantile system and the cities (Mayer 1992:192). The anthropologist Arjun Appadurai (2001) proposes to examine "deep democracy" to understand social tensions in broadening the definitions of politics, as a consequence of the denationalization of older governmental spaces.[24] Depth also refers to impoverished populations establishing alliances with more powerful groups—urban, regional, national, or multilateral. This notion frames local demands and the appropriation of government discourses (such as citizenship) for local development in relation to the increase of connections between local and international networks, sharing ideals of inclusion, participation, transparency, responsibility, and activism. Citizenship is not confined only to the limits of relationships with the state but is also with the society itself, as shown in this case with the interactions with powerful corporations (Dagnino 2006).[25]

The demand for direct participation, by civil society and social movements in spaces and decision-making processes normally left only to the state, has become one of the keystones in the redefinition of citizenship, based on the transformations in the power relationships of Latin American societies (Dagnino 2006:26).[26] This book examines a citizenship from below, seeking to ally with a "grassroots globalization" while evaluating the discourses and intentions of the participants (Appadurai 2000; Dagnino 2006). To this end, I recount perceptions about compensation for damages from the opening of a mine, including the expectations for development, highlighting the formulation and deployment of the EIA, as well as the implementation of multi-stakeholder *mesas* (negotiation roundtables) and *comités de monitoreo* (environmental monitoring committees) (Escobar 1995; Ferguson 1999; Peet and Watts 1996; Rahnema 1992; World Bank 1996). In general—although sometimes the roles overlap—a *mesa* could be a *mesa de diálogo* (dialogue roundtable) or *mesa de concertación* (agreement roundtable) for addressing a more urgent conflict, and a *mesa de desarrollo* (development roundtable) for evaluating local needs for social services or programs. The widely used expression *participación ciudadana* (citizen participation) implies the right to participate in public affairs but does not clarify conditions, meanings, and the status of the act (Dagnino 2006:28). Based on the deliberative policy model of philosopher Jürgen Habermas (1996), I examine in this book the degrees and ambiguities of real political participation, contrasting offers with practices, and the extent to which actors can modify an agenda at specific points in time (Allison 2003). The mining conflicts allow empirical discussion of the competition for access to and benefits from nature, reporting cultural imperatives of behaviors and strategies assembled as practices with individual motivations, establishing citizenship as a configuration of action to participate. Becoming an active citizen entails one's transformation into a political subject, aware of one's rights and with the capacity to fight for them (Dagnino 2006:28).

Ballard and Banks (2003) demonstrate how multiactor approaches contribute to understanding mining conflicts by considering contexts with new and rapid interactions, highlighting how NGOs with national and international networks are able to establish negotiations with transnational corporations, such as mining companies. I explore unexpected collaborations (e.g., NGOs and mining companies) that maintain the "friction" (Tsing 2005) of globalized scenarios, articulated more as networks of "enunciatory communities" (Fortun 2001:11) with a changing nature and based on particular interests. I also explore a sector that has received insufficient attention in studies of mining conflicts: the media, especially mass communication systems and their influence on social interactions in contentious scenarios. I examine the role of these agents in creating expectations and channeling local demands. Their performance is important, given the growing public demand to know the details of the plans and policies of extractive projects.

Excavating Research

This book reflects my long-term commitment to socioenvironmental concerns, which stems from my being a born-and-raised Peruvian citizen. This led to approximately two years of ethnographic research conducted between 2000 and 2004, followed by further fieldwork in prioritized mining areas in 2014. Archive research was followed by interviews and informal conversations. I aimed for a data collection process in order to identify an inductive conceptual framework to understand the research questions based on key local issues, subjective norms, and cultural schemas related to the impact and conflict arising from mining expansion. Subsequently, I cross-checked information from different sources and discussed my ideas about the main factors causing conflicts so as to select optimum scenarios for the answers while remaining focused on a central case study. By examining events and processes, my approach sought to identify emerging patterns. Given the breadth of the Antamina project, I opted for a multisited approach. The fieldwork was empirically grounded close to the mine site in Ancash while also tracking the evidence about the impact in various localities, but most particularly in three towns: San Marcos, Huarmey, and Huallanca. From San Marcos I visited the neighboring communities of Huaripampa and Ango Raju de Carhuayoc. I also included Lima, where state institutions, NGOs, and Antamina headquarters were located (see map 1). In each locality I posed the same set of questions about the impact of mining and then contrasted responses.

A multiactor approach contributed to the examination of the polyphony of discourses around the subjects and cultural imperatives that lay beneath the causes of the conflict.[27] In a dispute context, the multivocal approach reflected the diverse positions and changes that were framed in interests and rationalities, all revealed when processes collide. The cross-checking of several types of data meant conducting more than three hundred interviews and collecting dozens of reports with more quantitative information. Maps, songs, photographs, and hundreds of news stories, among many other sources, were also consulted. The central questions for the research guided me as I traveled to the various localities. Since I was trying to understand the causes of conflict, I started at the sites first impacted by the mining project. For this reason, I began working in the district of San Marcos.[28] Interviews with displaced families provided a wealth of information about a social change directly produced by the mining project. During encounters with the residents, I began to discover a particular opportunity to compare the revealing negotiation and change processes experienced by the communities of Huaripampa and Ango Raju de Carhuayoc, considering also that many displaced families were either from these communities or moved there. I later compared the initial experiences of development, examining the decision-making process of these communities—among other populations—for the allocation of the funds obtained from selling their land. My assumption was that the funding choices would reveal the cultural concepts underlying the preferences for improving their well-being. During my fieldwork I also traced complaints about contamination. These grievances enabled the analysis of social structures and cultural patterns for the comprehension of the environmental degradation claims.

Huallanca offered a rich comparison with San Marcos. I heard many testimonies about the favorable impact in Huallanca of a direct relationship with the

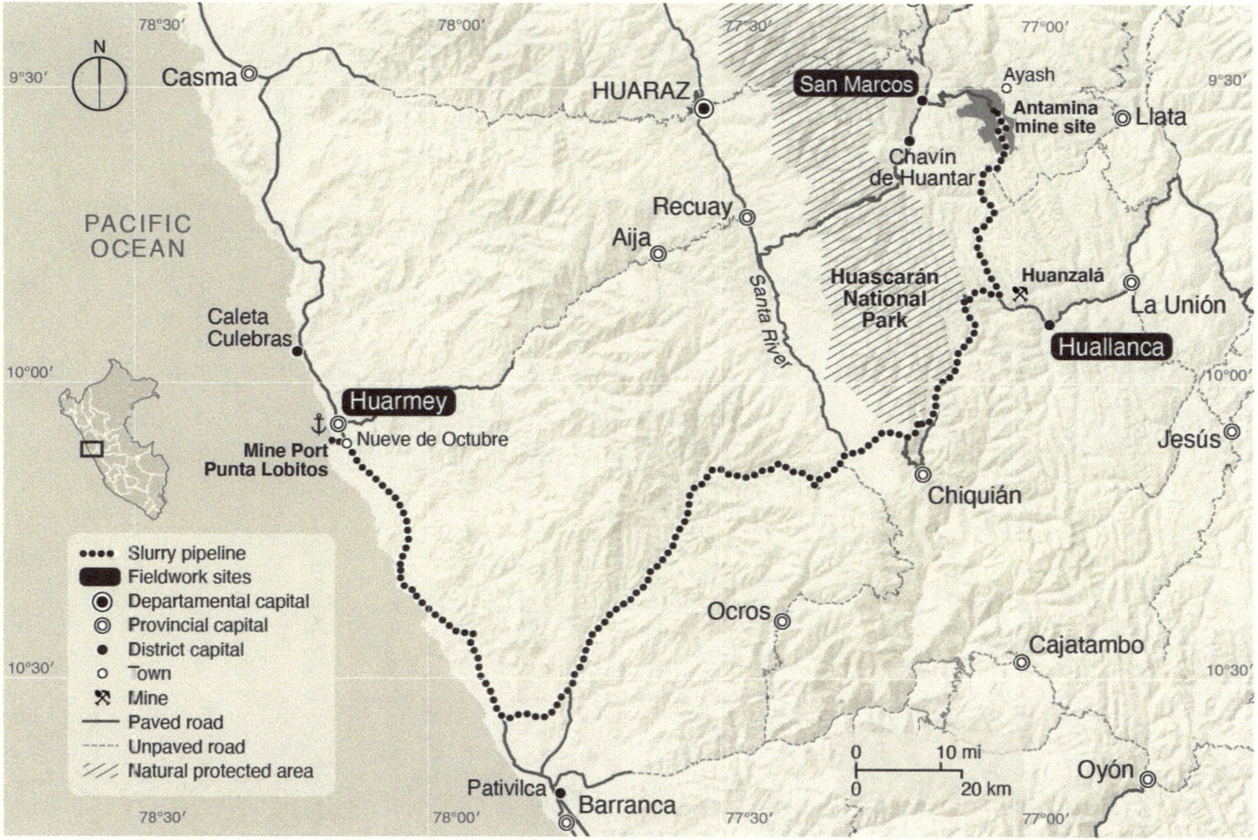

MAP 1 Antamina project map and fieldwork sites. Prepared by the author on the basis of the National Geographic Institute of Peru, CMA (2006e), and KS (1998a). Cartography by Grupo GeoGraphos.

mining company and a compensation that was perceived as fair. This condition was something the people of San Marcos resented. As the mine site was located in their district jurisdiction, the residents expected clear benefits from the outset. Although these Andean towns had much in common, from the perspective of the people of San Marcos, the experience in Huallanca came to be seen as a kind of inverted mirror because of what they perceived to be positive results that the arrival of Antamina brought. Although the urban architecture of Huallanca was directly impacted by the transportation of machinery for the construction of the mining operations area, it was San Marcos that suffered from pollution caused by the mine opening, which visibly affected aquatic bodies. While San Marcos had families complaining about displacement for the construction of the operations, Huallanca was temporarily invaded by the workers constructing Antamina's infrastructure. With advice from the municipality, several families in Huallanca provided temporal lodging, which meant temporary income. Probably the most visible collective difference between the initial impacts in these two towns was the "big gift"—in the shape of a large coliseum and reconstruction of its main square—that Huallanca received from Antamina as a compensation for the damage to its urban architecture. Huarmey, the coastal town where the Antamina pipeline terminates and from where the concentrate is shipped (see map 1), was another particularly important site, due to protests that arose there reflecting fears about environmental degradation. These protests would have wide resonance and ultimately lead to the involvement of national-level authorities. Examining events there allowed the documentation of renegotiation mechanisms mediated by direct actions, providing material for a contrast between coastal and mountain scenarios.

This book takes on the shape of a long trip, uncovering trails based on the footprints of contentious changes caused by the mining project. In the introductory chapter, by examining the most recent mining boom in the Andes following the privatization process within a neoliberal legislative apparatus during the 1990s, I focus on the context that sowed the contentious scenarios. Departing from a case study centered in the mountains of Peru, I also lay out conceptual analytical tools to address mining conflicts within a context of demands for development and citizen participation.

Since the book emerges from an inquiry of the micropolitics of negotiations, in chapter 1 I present the narrative for the impact of the initial phases of the Antamina project while tracing the main paths and footprints produced. Starting with ancient legends, I proceed to describe the background of the mining apparatus, including the concession contract and consortium evolution, which contributes to understanding the behavioral routes from the mining company's organizations. My examination of social changes introduces the EIA process as the main instrument for intermediation between nature and society. The description of the infrastructure and the main rhetorical mining tools for delimiting the extractive impact rationalize the selection of the main research sites presented. In order to save the reader from a cultural shock from the immersion into the Andean and international micro- and macropolitics of negotiations, I introduce the cast involved in the mining expansion, which lays the ground for understanding their pathways followed in the book.

In chapter 2 I examine local disputes caused by the displacement of people living at the mining site. The investigation unveils dilemmas with the communication internal to the company and with residents. By scrutinizing the debates between different parties about cultural notions and regimes of value, time, space, and land tenure rights, the chapter displays the corporate sociotechnologies that provoke marginal residents' responses to participate, reap benefits, and obtain compensation.

Through an analysis of the social groups contesting the risk evaluations by referring to the use of space—in this case, around a natural protected area—chapter 3 introduces the cultural politics of technical reports and the evolution of EIAs. It examines strategies employed under the leadership of a small NGO based in the USA, the Mountain Institute (TMI). In its efforts to diminish risks posed to the Huascarán National Park, this organization negotiated directly with the mining company's financial investors, promoting a redesign of the route and method for ore transport from the mine to the coastal shipping port in Huarmey. Many inhabitants of Huarmey had high expectations of benefits expected to accrue from the arrival of a new road. These included better opportunities for their agricultural products and the prospect of providing services to the drivers of heavy vehicles. When a pipeline option was chosen instead, Huarmey groups protested and resorted to arguments about potential contamination. By providing a cultural examination of the politics of power and place and unpacking the evolution of the behavioral patterns displayed by the confronted groups, the chapter demonstrates how ground debates over environmental impact can promote political participation, even prompting for unanticipated dialogues and alliances.

In chapter 4 I examine the meaning of development as a contentious resource for different groups. The historical overview of development myths in mining since colonial times sets the framework for understanding more contemporary expectations and demands for participation of mining benefits. I follow the route of monetary compensation obtained from land sales or compensation paid by the mining company and other fund transfers that emerged as a byproduct of the extractive activities. The interpretation of the results analyzes the "big gift" and the "corporate social responsibility" regime in order to understand behavior practices in conflict situations. The evidence shows that when abundant resources become available over a short period of time, the aim for development comes to imply a negotiation of multiple concepts in motion by different subjects. An analysis of reciprocity in the Andes helps us to understand the behavior of local residents when confronted by a large mining company and its rhetoric of voluntary corporate social responsibility. Local expectations of development through economic participation can be better understood as part of a larger demand for citizen participation in the recent history of claims for benefits from mining.

In chapter 5 I analyze the clash of cultures and the power strategies that address environmental risks, as well as the conflicts based on disagreements over the process of hazardous changes in nature brought about by the mining project. The unpacking of rhetorical battles provides elements to understand behavioral schemes in the claims and negotiations about contamination, especially regarding demands for participation in environmental risk definitions.

In the concluding chapter, I provide a review of the research approach while reexamining connections not previously highlighted, especially regarding the repertoire and dynamics of stratagems. The book concludes with thoughts about the extent of the tradability of mining claims, and with a reflection on future challenges for research on institutional regimes to understand contentious mining scenarios while considering mobilizations and their ability to redefine political landscapes and citizenship.

CHAPTER 1

Mining Apparatus

THE NAME ANTAMINA IS FORMED FROM THE QUECHUA WORD *ANTA* (COPPER) AND THE SPANISH word *mina* (mine). The Antamina Lake was located in an uninhabited rocky space mostly unsuitable for agriculture or grazing, both widespread across the region. This aquatic body and its surroundings were privately owned or in the hands of peasant communities. There had been several mining projects in the area prior to the arrival of the Antamina company. Neither the banks nor the lake had been used, although according to local legend, the lake was home to giant serpents who lived side by side with fighting bulls.[1] Marcos, a farmer from the Huaripampa peasant community, told me the lake was the site of mythical bullfights during the full moon. He grew up near Antamina Lake before migrating to Lima, the capital. At the age of sixty, he still remembered the aridness of the place and his fear of the lake with its mythical inhabitants:

> Below is a cave, a large well. We stayed away from it because we were afraid. Golden bulls have been seen there. . . . It is said of Antamina that there was a golden snake inside. . . . Some gringos were exploring. A diver went in, a gringo, and came out dripping blood. It is no story [fantasy]. We were grazing our livestock when the ambulance went by and several more cars. Later they appeared and said, "The gringo has died." . . . Nobody could live in this lake. Besides, Antamina is rocky, there is no grass, nothing. My mother said when she was a child . . . with a catapult you would throw salt into the lake and a large

FIGURE 2 Antamina Lake. 1999. Photograph courtesy of Tecno Fast S.A.

> wave would rise up and it would begin to hail. It was wild. . . . The site was all rocks, unpleasant, difficult, completely mineral.

Alejandro Espinoza is a native of Chavín de Huántar, a town neighboring San Marcos. He worked in the archaeological complex for which the town is named—one of the oldest Andean ceremonial centers. For him, the beliefs about Antamina were inscribed in the legends about the water sources.

> We have many beliefs here about lagoons, rivers, and *puquial* ["spring" in Quechua] waters whose sources are in the hills, and about giving a *pagapu* ["offering" in Quechua] to the *apus* in the hills.[2] We offer a *pagapu* to the *puquial* so that is does not dry up. . . . It is believed that within that lake [Antamina] there are bulls, bulls made of gold. The *pagapu* is mostly given to them [those types of aquatic bodies]. When the bull leaves, the lake will follow it by emptying. An avalanche will start. . . . Our ancestors believed very much in our nature, in the lakes, in the *apus*.

The thirty-two-hectare lake was drained because most of the mineral body was located under its waters (Love et al. 2004). In popular imagination the foretold avalanche and the mythical fighting bulls conjured up disputes in this mining region, embodying conflict by alluding to the dangers present in its waters, capable of drowning strangers. The poverty present in this rural landscape cohabits with ancestral livelihoods and rich symbolism about nature, quite different from icons in more urban settings. These juxtapositions are something the mining entrepreneurs were not fully capable of or willing to understand, as this book details.

This chapter offers a prelude of the sociotechnological mining apparatus assemblage landing on the main impacted socioenvironmental scenarios. It also delineates issues fundamental to understanding the power of the main social actors in the conflicts that are developed in the next chapters. It provides a preparatory overview of the mining concession, the consortium evolution, the infrastructure and its extraterritoriality, and the institutional framework of the EIA. By outlining the main elements of the conflictive orchestras, including the socioenvironmental settings, this section announces the corpus of the main cast and the tone to appreciate the complex processes dissected in the following chapters.

Background and Benefits

References to mining in and around Antamina date back to the mid-nineteenth century and start with the small Taco and Rosa projects (KS 1998a). These had also been worked by pre-Hispanic residents. In 1952, Cerro de Pasco Copper Corporation—La Cerro—owned concessions, was the first company to conduct exploratory work, and had completed a feasibility study; however, political complications postponed exploitation indefinitely (CMA 2005a). By 1971, with Peru under a military government, many of La Cerro's concessions over Antamina had expired. Control reverted to the state under the administration of Minero Perú (AMIDEP 1997a). In 1973 Minero Perú and the Romanian company Geomin agreed to develop the mine. They formed the Empresa Minera Especial Antamina, rehabilitated more than 3,200 meters of underground work, and developed approximately 900 meters of exploration. Financial problems led to the dissolution of this company in 1981 and return to state control, via the state-run mining consortium Centromin. The consortium originated from the expropriated possessions of the Cerro de Pasco Corporation in 1974. Its projects in the area had little financial success, and in 1996 the government launched a tender process (KS 1998a).

The most vivid mining experience in the collective memory of residents of the district of San Marcos was that of the Sociedad Minera Gran Bretaña in the 1980s, and its extraction of minerals in Contonga, five kilometers from Antamina Lake (see map 2). The company went bankrupt during the 1990s (it

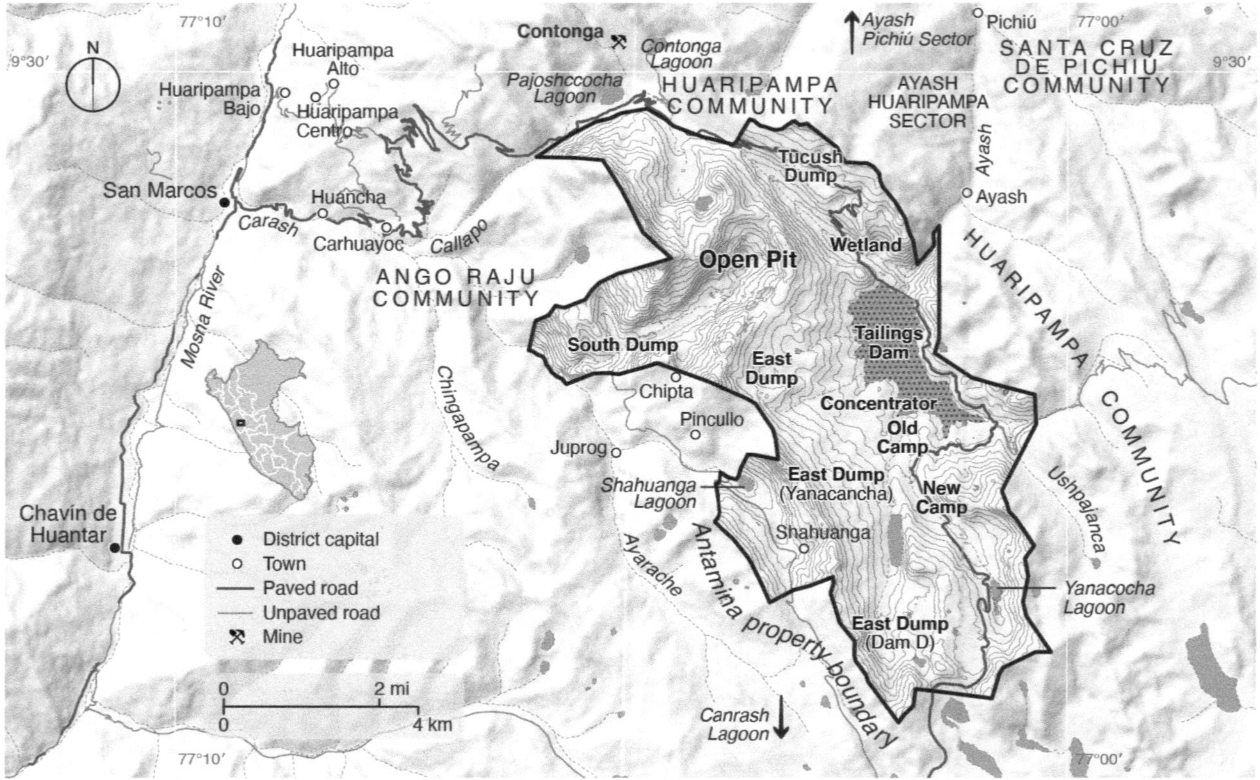

MAP 2 Antamina area of property, mine site facilities, and neighboring populations. Author's elaboration based on CMA (2006c), Ecometrix (2005), J.C.V., and Beak. Cartography by Grupo GeoGraphos.

would reopen in 2004), leaving exposed tailings in the Pajoshccocha Lagoon. The Antamina project was bombastically presented by the Peruvian media as one of the largest in the world (see chapter 2). Understandably, residents imagined the possibility of an abundance of new jobs and the opportunity to sell products, just as they had done to Contonga personnel. These old mines were a benchmark in the popular memory, setting the parameters for the expectations of development detailed throughout this book.

Political economist Albert Hirschman (1958, 1978) laid out the central logic of the power of large companies when policy makers seek to provide them with stability and protect them in the hope that they will generate employment. If companies fulfill this promise, they produce popular well-being, which in turn attracts votes for the reelection of the government. The Antamina contract contained generous incentives. The Antamina concession must be understood in the context of the stimulus provided by the Fujimori regime to attract international capital, which was a response to the internal armed conflict sparked by Shining Path and policies of the mid-1980s that had alienated foreign investment. The capture of Shining Path's leader in 1992, coupled with the legislative reforms of the decade, promoted macroeconomic stability and led to colossal profits for international investors. The government included the mining concessions belonging to the state enterprise Centromin—and, by extension, Antamina—in a decree that declared of "national interest the promotion of private investment" in state-owned companies.[3]

Through an international public tender in 1996, the government evaluated domestic and foreign bids to develop the project, which consisted of forty-five concessions, a *petitorio* (claim), support facilities (camps; *galerías*, or "levels"; and *cruceros*, or "crosscuts"), and information about exploration (CEPRI-Centromin 1996:260). Many of these concessions sat over the land of peasant communities and private individuals who lacked legal formalization of their titles. Rights of usufruct were, however, customarily recognized. Moreover, the sale of mining natural resources and privatization do not involve local prior consultation. As there is not a complete cadastre of Indigenous communities, nor is this condition verified before a private entity obtains a concession, it is common for concessions to cover territories belonging to these communities (Dargent et al. 2017; IBC 2015). The possession rights for natural resources affect the expectation of benefits, something which in turn contributes to understanding the conflicts.

Other than a few localities within countries such as the United States, Canada, and some old Spanish concessions in Colombia, mining rights around the world belong to the state (Johnston 2007:68), which manages access to the resource on behalf of the nation. Occasionally, when the minerals are part of the surface ownership, the state establishes regulations. In South Africa, for example, the (subsequently replaced) Minerals Act required the issue of a license for exploration or mining activities.[4] The ownership structure contributes to the understanding of local expectations of development. Understandably, a citizen—especially a neighbor to a mine—expects benefits from the exploitation of a resource that is both national heritage and a public good. In accordance with the Peruvian Constitution, given that natural resources belong to all citizens, the state administers them on behalf of the nation. The term *concession* only implies a right to natural underground resources that do not affect the surface. These superficial lands frequently lack legal title, although there are owners who use the terrain, sell it, or pass it down to the next generation. Some bidders for the Antamina tender expressed concern about this condition, since they understood they were also acquiring a conflict. As one former Antamina employee commented when we talked almost a decade after the company obtained the concession: "When it comes to a privatization project and the state grants mining rights . . . what is being given when the surface belongs to others? The idea that the project could fail due to lack of agreement with the owners of the surface land almost did not enter into our risk analysis. . . . It is very difficult for a company today to put a mine where people do not want it."

The management of surface rights for Antamina was left to the new concession holder. The contract released Centromin from "all clear title obligations," other than eviction (CEPRI-Centromin 1996:529; Corvetto 1996:499). The establishment of clear title required hasty work by PETT (Proyecto Especial de Titulación de Tierras y Catastro Rural, or the Special Land Titling and Cadastre Project). Established in 1992, and originally financed by the World Bank, PETT began under the Ministry of Agriculture before being absorbed by the Ministry of Housing in 2007. Included among its functions was the physical and legal clear titling of private rural land and of peasant and native communities. The state recognized its absence during a possible mediation between the concession buyer and the land surface owners or groups settled in the concession area. Although visible in negotiating the concession and for land titling, the state's presence was otherwise scarce at the time of Antamina's arrival. This increased the risk of conflict. Farmers with limited time resources and training in complex regulations had to negotiate directly with a billion-dollar transnational mining company.

The tender documentation promoted the use of state-of-the-art technology, which inevitably excludes low-skilled local labor. Tenderers had to propose a "base price" (or minimum amount) to be disbursed for the concessions and the "minimum investment commitment" to develop the project. The winner promised to invest $2.52 billion, plus $20 million for the option of the deposit. The commitment generously included many expenses or costs (e.g., feasibility studies and offices) counted as investment, which appeared to generate benefit for the company rather than the country. The tax security requested by some bidders meant an *estabilidad jurídica* (legal stability) contract consistent with prevailing legislation. The Antamina investment contract did not require the employment of a minimum number of Peruvian workers or local residents, nor did it mention how the project would directly benefit the adjacent populations. The contract ended when Antamina paid the $111.5 million penalty applied because it failed to meet the agreed minimum investment commitment (see chapter 4).

Predatory Consortium

The Antamina consortium has evolved as a creature sitting at the top of the food chain. It has opportunistically devoured the smaller organizations that previously owned the concession. The Antamina concession was won by a consortium consisting of the Canadian companies Rio Algom Limited and Inmet Mining Corporation, which in 1996 formed a Peruvian subsidiary—Compañía Minera Antamina S.A.—to execute the project. The exploration stage confirmed reserves 25 percent greater than those previously estimated, and Antamina announced that there would be twenty years of production, extracting seventy thousand tons of concentrate per day (Schmidt 1999). A subsequent expansion of operations would extend the life of the mine until the year 2029, a total of approximately thirty years.

The parent firms would change during the life of the project. The junior partner Inmet withdrew before the approval of the EIA in 1998 because it was unable to finance its part of the proposal development. Noranda Inc. and Teck Corporation, also Canadian, joined Rio Algom through the purchase of Inmet's share, giving the project a greater international dimension. Officials of the three companies visited the mine, reviewed the environmental impact statement, and replaced some employees in order to improve the project's environmental and social dimensions (Schmidt 1999). The changes were probably influenced by

Noranda's history of air and river environmental breaches from 1983 onward, which had included eighty-seven violations and fines exceeding $1.2 million by early in the new millennium (Greenpeace 2003:5). Rio Algom, the majority partner, was also involved in disputes with environmentalists and neighbors at sites in Canada and the United States. Its CEO, Pat James, stated in a speech in 1998, "If our industry cannot effectively combine social, economic, and environmental goals, then we will gradually find ourselves unable to operate" (Schmidt 1999:55).

While financing was being arranged, Mitsubishi Company of Japan also joined. At that stage share ownership of the consortium was as follows: Rio Algom (33.75 percent), Noranda (33.75 percent), Teck Corporation (22.5 percent), and Mitsubishi (10 percent). In 2000, Noranda made a hostile takeover bid for Rio Algom, forcing the latter to look to the British giant Billiton. The following year, Billiton merged with the Australian mining company Broken Hill Proprietary Ltd. (BHP) to form, at that time, the world's largest mining company. At that stage, the consortium consisted of the Anglo-Australian BHP Billiton (33.75 percent), the Canadian companies Noranda (33.75 percent) and Teck Cominco (22.5 percent), and the Japanese-based firm Mitsubishi Corporation (10 percent) (CMA 2002). In 2004 Falconbridge absorbed Noranda, which in turn was absorbed by Xstrata, a Swiss-based mining corporation. In 2013 the latter was absorbed by the Anglo-Swiss Glencore commodity trading and mining company, considered the third largest copper-zinc producer in the world. By mid-2018, the shareholders in Antamina were BHP Billiton (33.75 percent), Glencore (33.75 percent), Teck (22.5 percent), and Mitsubishi Corporation (10 percent).

The Canadian companies were welcomed by Peruvian media organizations following the announcement of the tender result. By contrast, another Canadian mining company, Barrick, which was exploiting gold elsewhere in the Ancash Department, had been criticized for its environmental record. Antamina stated its intention to avoid the criticisms that had been directed at the Yanacocha project, the largest gold mine in Latin America. A joint venture between the U.S. company Newmont (51 percent), the Peruvian company Buenaventura (43 percent), and the IFC (International Finance Corporation of the World Bank) (5 percent). Yanacocha was the first large international mine of Peru's recent boom. This project has been characterized by its conflictive relationship with local residents and by struggles that have included mercury spills in Choropampa, clashes over the proposed drainage of lagoons for the Conga mining project, and protests that led to the cancellation of a planned expansion into

Cerro Quilish. As in the conflictive scenarios of socioenvironmental disputes of Noranda and Rio Algom, BHP-Billiton withdrew from Ok Tedi Mining at Papua New Guinea in 2002 after long and costly court disputes and lawsuit settlements, some of which continued afterward (Golub 2014; Kirsch 2014). I argue that these expensive episodes marked the consortium's rapacious instincts toward investments and their accompanying socioenvironmental issues, generating internal debates that reflected in actions, strategies, rhetorics, and lessons that are examined through this book.

Project Cycle

With the transfer contract signed, the consortium began exploration to confirm the size of the deposit. Antamina contracted Klohn Crippen—SVS S.A. Ingenieros Consultores to prepare the environmental impact statement.[5] This firm, which had been constituted as a Peruvian company during the privatization of Antamina in 1996 (KS 1998a), in turn subcontracted an NGO that presents itself as specialized in social issues—AMIDEP (Asociación Multidisciplinaria de Investigación y Docencia en Población, or Multidisciplinary Association for Research and Teaching in Population) (AMIDEP 1997a). The environmental impact statement was primarily based on government information and an environmental baseline that had been established by Klohn Crippen—SVS S.A. Ingenieros Consultores in collaboration with several other firms, including Graña & Montero, one of the country's largest constructors (Pratt 2001).

In practice, the EIA process unfolds mostly as a privatized transnational business, since it is commonly based on baselines and data collected by international consultant firms hired by the same mining project, restricting the distance necessary for a proper and more realistic preventive analysis of risk. These counsel enterprises have the incentives to confine the evaluation to the minimum legally required elements, such as limiting the amount of potential affected human population, minimizing details of the stages to be considered, or simply ignoring a topic or vulnerable population that might appear as endangered by the mining process but could be left out of the scoping since it could compromise or delay the approval of the EIA. There is a conflict of interest when a consultant firm has to illuminate the risks of a project at the same time that its payment highly depends on the governmental approval of its diagnosis, which should assert a controlled low-risk project, not to mention the restricted role of the state agency, SENACE (Servicio Nacional de Certificación Ambiental para las Inversiones Sostenibles, or National Service for Environmental Certification for Sustainable Investments), assigned to evaluate the approval of the EIA, which does not gather its own field data to contrast with the information proposed by the mining consultant firm. The invisibilization of potential dangers impacts the purported preventive objective of an EIA, as we shall appreciate in the following chapters (e.g., chapter 3).

A number of activities coincided with the conduct of the feasibility study: Antamina's environmental assessment, the purchase of land, and the obtaining of government authorizations (KS 1998a). The feasibility study entailed one hundred thousand meters of exploratory development to define the extractable potential. By the time AMIDEP (1997b) presented the social baseline at the end of 1997, the exploration had been completed, and the MEM (Ministerio de Energía y Minas, or Ministry of Energy and Mines) approved the EIA in March of the following year. It was then that the construction phase began. Operations began three years later, followed by the first shipment. Antamina identified five stages of the project: design, construction, operation, closure, and postclosure of the mining site (KS 1998a). Although the environmental impact statement mentions the land purchase processes, relocation, and communication of the report's contents, Antamina did not formally include the exploration phase, probably due to the use of temporary contractors.

This start-up period sets the tone for future relationships between a company and its neighbors. Antamina later admitted that it should have "behaved responsibly from the outset: this applies particularly to all those involved in exploration activities," because "you only have one chance to make a good first impression" (CMA 2001b:18). In the subsequent chapters I examine the early processes of a mine's development—such as exploration, land purchase and resettlement, and the issuing of permits by local authorities and the purported consultation associated with the EIA—none of which were sufficiently detailed at the EIA and all of which took place prior to the operation phase. These series of events implied contentious impact resulting from local expectations created by the sale of the concession.

Mining Infrastructure

Antamina operates in three principal sites (mine, pipeline, and port) in the department of Ancash (approximately one million inhabitants in about six thousand square kilometers). Its main facilities are located in the provinces of Huari (San Marcos), Bolognesi (Huallanca), and Huarmey.[6] The facilities at the deposit (4,300–4,760 meters above sea level) in the district of San Marcos occupy land that previously was home to crops and natural pastures belonging to peasant communities and some individual owners. The rugged topography finds reflection in the winding roads. The site is 35 kilometers (10 kilometers as the crow flies) from the town of San Marcos (elevation 2,970 meters), and 482 kilometers in ascent from the northeast of the city of Lima (270 kilometers as the crow flies). Antamina constructed 210 kilometers of road (map 1).

The mine is operated as an open pit. Its infrastructure consists of the concentrator plant, the mill, the tailings deposit, three waste-rock dumps, the mining camp, the access roads, the pipeline, the transmission lines, the mining port in Huarmey, and a housing complex of more than three hundred homes in El Pinar (Huaraz), about 165 kilometers (55 kilometers as the crow flies) away (see maps 1 and 2 and figure 3). San Marcos residents would claim that the El Pinar complex should be built in their town in order to boost the local economy. However, Antamina preferred the tourist city of Huaraz because of the level of services it offered. It also felt that the more ready access to the coast and Lima would facilitate travel, especially for the workforce, many of whom would work under a two-for-one schedule: fourteen consecutive work days (two weeks), followed by a break of seven days (one week). This system—common in the mining sector—assumes working days of twelve hours. Other employees work shifts of ten days followed by another ten days of rest. Antamina also has administrative offices in Lima and Huaraz. By the end of 1998, the company opened the Office of Community Development—housing the Community Relations team—at sites in San Marcos and, in 1999, in Huallanca, and another three years later, in Huarmey. These offices would channel development projects and jobs to the mine and receive complaints.

The mining facility was a territory apart. The mining camp was a "bachelor camp"; cohabitation of couples and families was not permitted, nor was alcohol consumption. Consumption of coca leaf, the ancestral Andean energizer that helps to alleviate hunger, cold, and the effects of altitude, was also prohibited. This ban seems to replicate the confusion that has long existed between the ancient use of the leaf in the Andes—including in rituals considered sacred—and modern Western abuse of cocaine, its industrially produced relative (Mayer 2002). Entry was restricted to operational employees, unless other individuals held a pass obtained in Lima (Robles 2003) (see figure 4). There was no entry or

FIGURE 3 El Pinar Urbanization, housing for Antamina employees in Huaraz. 2007. Photograph by Nadia Mora.

exit of vehicles after five o'clock in the afternoon, in an effort to avoid accidents at times of reduced visibility. The restrictions were also aimed at preventing sabotage or theft. The services and amenities were closed to local residents, who were also deprived of access to an ancient grazing and exchange route that links San Marcos with the towns of La Unión and Llata.

The deposit contains mineral reserves that include copper, zinc, silver, and molybdenum. During preproduction 110 million tons of material were extracted (CMA 2005a). Antamina Lake was emptied and eight Andean peaks were reduced by 292 meters in Peru's highest mountain chain (Greenpeace 2003:25) (see figure 4). The mine operated continuously using shovels and giant dump trucks that remove more than 346 thousand tons of waste every day (CMA 2006f:18). Mineral processing increased from 94 thousand to 130 thousand metric tons per day (CMA 2013:13). The quarry started with a width of two kilometers and a depth of 750 meters (Pratt 2001). The ore was transported from the deposit by huge trucks, nicknamed *ticos* after a brand of small taxis that were common in Lima. These trucks transported the minerals to a primary crusher and then along a conveyor belt to the concentrator plant. The waste rock was delivered to three dumps. The copper and zinc concentrates were produced by a flotation circuit in the plant. The replacement water came from a dam and groundwater wells. The plant produced five hundred million tons of tailings—finely pulverized material that lingers after the treasured ore is extracted—that were stored in a reservoir in the inlet of the Ayash Ravine. The 232-meter deep reservoir held two million cubic meters of water and acted as the primary source of industrial water for the concentrator plant.

FIGURE 4 Entrance to the operations area of Antamina. 2002. Author's photo.

The concentrate (63 percent solid paste) was transported through a pipeline of 304 kilometers from the site to the port of Huarmey. There the water was filtered and used to irrigate some forests. The concentrate was moist, and this supposedly prevented it from escaping as dust when placed on ships. The port is located to the south of the city of Huarmey and includes a concentrate-discharge station, a filtering plant, a warehouse, and a dock for loading the concentrate onto the ships. The site also comprises a camp, auxiliary facilities, and forestation areas. The original plan included an access corridor to the port, transporting the concentrate in trucks crossing a national park (see chapter 3). The final piece of infrastructure is the connection to the national electricity system. Antamina built 58 kilometers of transmission line to connect the operations with the Huallanca substation (KS 1998a).

Delimiting the Impact

The spatial limits demarcated the mining company's responsibility. The environmental impact statement circumscribed the area of influence to a zone that included approximately two hundred thousand people (*El Comercio* 2006). Since the report was prepared by a private firm hired by the mining company, it is unsurprising that the boundaries proposed reflect a minimum possible scale for the client. It defined three "affected areas": localized impact, immediate impact, and extended impact (KS 1998a).[7] Given human mobility, social networks transcended the districts or localities that the company considered. A cultural perspective of territoriality better reflects the spatial flexibility during the evolution of the project and the multiple interactions.

The proposed "localized impact" area covered the operations area of the mine site (seven thousand hectares), including the mining camp. This space was previously inhabited by approximately eight hundred people (commoners or individual owners). The camp housed some four thousand workers during construction, a figure that reduced to one thousand once operations began. The concept of localized impact in the environmental impact statement does not address other implicit relationships outside this operations area. The formulation excludes networks of kinship and reciprocity in pasture management (see chapter 2). Likewise, it does not consider the impact of expectations on localities neighboring the project.

The scope of the "immediate impact" proposed was contiguous to the "localized impact," covering four districts (San Pedro de Chana, Huachis, Chavín, and San Marcos), including some thirty thousand people in villages and towns (Yanacancha, Juprog, Ayash Huaripampa, Centro Pichiú, and Cambio 90) and peasant communities, such as Huaripampa, Ango Raju de Carhuayoc, and Santa Cruz de Pichiú—the communities most recognized and contiguous to the mining site (see map 2). The peasant economies managed multiple ecological zones, from the valleys to the high punas (approximately 3,900 meters in altitude). The vertical model of simultaneous management of multiple ecological gradients in production zones covering ecological complementarity has antecedents that go back to macroscale patterns in pre-Hispanic times (see figure 5).[8] Ayash Huaripampa, Cambio 90, and Centro Pichiú raised cattle and cultivated tubers and cereals. The wool growers of the high puna pastures traded their surplus wool with farmers in lower areas, such as Ango Raju. The herders of Yanacancha and Juprog raised livestock and established relations of reciprocity and exchange for their lands, giving grazing rights to the inhabitants of Carhuayoc and Yanacancha and smallholders from Juprog and other *caseríos* (hamlets) in the valley (GRADE 1999). Many sold land to Antamina or were displaced from the operations area (see chapter 2).

The "extended impact" area described by the environmental impact statement included the city of Huaraz and districts of the province of Bolognesi, as

FIGURE 5 Agropastoral zones in the district of San Marcos. 2002. Author's photo.

well as the district of Llata (department of Huánuco), totaling approximately one hundred thousand inhabitants.[9] In order to become more realistic, the EIA could have included an indirect impacted area composed of urban centers to include the port in Huarmey, the El Pinar (Huaraz) condominium housing complex, political centers (e.g., Huaraz and Lima), the cities that would most benefit from the mining canon (e.g., Huaraz and Chimbote), other districts neighboring the operation, and the settlements affected during the construction of the road to the mine crossing Huallanca.[10] It should also have considered the entire Ancash Department, given that the canon was to be distributed according to the demographic weight of the region, and an estimated 25 percent of the labor force would come from there. The entire country was part of the area of influence through the impact of taxes, purchases, and employment (see chapter 4). Because falling within the impacted area brought benefits, some groups demanded inclusion. The guide for preparing the EIA was quite general, leading to subsequent debate between provincial and district mayors about the way the area of influence had been delimited. The municipality of Chimbote claimed to belong to the area of influence when development funds became available from a contract penalty incurred by Antamina (see chapter 4). These considerations help to understand the expectations the region had about the project's benefits.

A Mined Field

To understand the causes of the clashes over the Antamina mine, I traveled to the first places impacted by the project. I prioritized localities based on the level of conflict. Three towns stood out: San Marcos, Huarmey, and Huallanca. Because of the sale of its lands, San Marcos included the contiguous communities of Huaripampa and Ango Raju de Carhuayoc (map 2). Located in valleys, San Marcos, Huari, and Chavín are important urban centers, connected along an active commercial axis. Problems in San Marcos District arose from contamination, demands for development, and the displacement of people by the mine (chapters 2, 4, and 5).

Known as the Magnolia Paradise, San Marcos is a resting point along the road to Huari, the provincial capital. During the 1980s, Shining Path would pass through San Marcos on its way to hideouts in the Amazon. According to the 1993 national census, the district of San Marcos was home to 11,647 people

(INEI 2018). The majority (76 percent) were considered rural dwellers living in small communities and hamlets located between intermediate and higher valleys. The remainder lived in the town, located in the valley.[11] San Marcos was weaker in terms of the language resources to negotiate either with the governmental or the mining social apparatus, both mostly composed by monolingual Spanish *limeño* (from Lima) speakers. Quechua was the mother tongue of most (72 percent) people in San Marcos, according to the 2007 census. This figure contrasted with 23 percent in Bolognesi Province—where Huallanca is located—and only 13 percent in the province of Huarmey; the latter is not surprising given the coastal location.

Agriculture, livestock, and some fishing were the principal activities in San Marcos. They occupied two thirds of the population. In Huallanca and Huarmey, only one-third of their populations worked in agriculture. The San Marcos District was characterized by dispersed vertical smallholdings, an Andean common pattern that limits large-scale production and decreases agroclimatic risk (see figure 5). Above 3,500 meters, sheep were the principal livestock and enabled families to meet basic expenses. According to the environmental impact statement, around half of farmers had twenty head of sheep and only 10 percent had more than one hundred. In the intermediate and low valleys, farmers planted potatoes and cereals for the small local trade, and fruits and vegetables for self-consumption. The economy of San Marcos town was based on trade. The farmers sold their agricultural products at the Sunday fairs.

Mining San Marcos

"This district is very rich in minerals. . . . [The] sparse vegetation and the consequent lack of resources, make San Marcos a wretched place. The work of its inhabitants is reduced to sowing fruits. . . . A few use their mules for transport and work in the mines." This is how Antonio Raimondi (1873:55) described the paradoxes of the area toward the end of the nineteenth century. The first time I arrived in San Marcos at the turn of the millennium, prior to Antamina's full operation, it gave me the impression of a typical quiet town of its size in the Peruvian Andes, with its enchantments and weaknesses. As usual, the few symbols of national connection—mostly through services—rested around the old main square. Apart from the governor, the state presence in San Marcos was limited to just a few agencies, such as a health center, a police station, an office of the Banco de la Nación (the state bank), and an office of the Ministry of Agriculture. Huari was the only town with banking services. All commercial banking occurred in Huaraz, the departmental capital.

National indicators have long seen the district of San Marcos classified as poor. These cold numbers assemble a vulnerable portrait that contributes to conceiving the sharp contrast with the arrival of a billionaire extractive project. Temporary and permanent migration were strategies that helped to alleviate the burden of overgrazed and parceled lands. Many people had seasonal work in fields on the coast or in the Amazon. *Poverty* and *malnutrition* are terms frequently used to describe the people of the Peruvian Andes. In 1993, three years before the Antamina concession, the department of Ancash was ranked sixteen out of twenty-four on the governmental national poverty ranking of unsatisfied basic needs, and approximately 62 percent of households suffered at least one unsatisfied basic need. In Huari Province the figure rose to 91 percent, while San Marcos had 89 percent of homes (2,316 out of 2,587) or 91 percent of the population (10,658 out of 11,647) under this condition (INEI 2018; KS 1998a:chapter 8, p. 12). In this district, 24 percent of families lived in overcrowded conditions, 85 percent of housing lacked sanitary facilities, and 10 percent had children not attending school (INEI 2018:annexes I.3A, II.1A, II.2A). This vulnerable situation held for most households in the localities described in this book, especially in the highlands (see table 1). Residents of San Marcos probably never felt as poor as when the grandiloquently announced billion-dollar Antamina project arrived and shiny large pickups began traversing their rough and dusty roads.

Antamina quickly discovered that political dynamics in San Marcos were marked by longstanding family conflicts between former landowners or foremen of haciendas and medium-sized landowners.[12] These confrontations became heightened during municipal electoral campaigns. The medium-sized landowners' group gained power for the very first time at the 1999 municipal election, after the vote of the former hacienda landowners was divided between competing candidates from within their ranks. This election probably shaped the unfolding of some negotiations portrayed in this book. The mayor and the first environmental committee in San Marcos, along with their sympathizers, were not as many nor as purportedly antimining advocates as multiple rival family members in the opposition. This scenario presumably contributed to more dialogical actions where persuasion and seeking for allies—even external—had more room when facing a dispute.

TABLE 1 Percentage of population with one or more unsatisfied basic need in prioritized districts and Peru, 1993, 2007, and 2017

DISTRICT	1993	POPULATION	2007	POPULATION	2017	POPULATION
San Marcos	91.5	11,647	64.0	11,204	36.9	11,476
Chavín	93.9	9,256	74.6	8,997	49.2	7,721
Huallanca	79.0	7,673	63.9	7,098	38.5	5,567
Huarmey	52.6	17,487	41.3	21,183	37.0	24,140
Peru	56.8	21,801,654	40.7	27,057,199	25.3	28,574,337

Source: INEI (2018).

The peasant community was the most important rural organization in San Marcos. It regulated labor and collective benefits (e.g., communal lands). The *comunidad campesina* (peasant community) is a legal concept deriving from *comunidad indígena* (Indigenous community), a change in nomenclature made by the military government of Juan Velasco.[13] Located away from urban centers, the district's *caseríos* were home to smallholders not part of the peasant community. Other organizations present in areas impacted by the mine were the *rondas campesinas* (peasant patrols), fishermen's unions, religious associations, associations of farmers and livestock owners, and the *juntas de regantes*, or irrigation boards (responsible for distributing water and maintaining canals using collective labor). By regulating access to land, water supplies, and the exchange and distribution of collective labor, this range of rural institutions formed the basis of local agriculture. The defense fronts in Huarmey, Huallanca, and San Marcos formed after the arrival of the Antamina project.[14]

Because they sold collectively owned land to Antamina, the neighboring communities of Huaripampa and Ango Raju de Carhuayoc presented ideal case studies for comparing land acquisition processes and the use of compensation funds (see chapters 2 and 4). Many families were displaced from or resettled in these communities. Huaripampa was recognized as the most traditional district in the region. As one of the peasants from San Marcos told me, the town had been a "leader throughout history." Established in 1714, most of the district's territory belonged to this community. The 1969 Agrarian Reform of the Velasco military government gave three haciendas (Yanacancha, Ayash, and Pacjush) to the community. These lands were subdivided for family rain-fed agriculture. Legal recognition as a peasant community came in 1973, including the usual benefits: tax exemption and protection from land expropriation. The latter was eliminated in the 1993 neoliberal constitution. At the time of Antamina's arrival, the Huaripampa community consisted of 460 members, all of them male heads of nuclear families (KS 1998a:chapter 8, p. 16). Following the sale of 43 percent of its land to Antamina, the community was left with approximately three thousand hectares, retaining just one collective *fundo* (estate)—Pajoshccocha, in the higher lands, where cattle belonging to some *comuneros* (peasant community members) were grazed, along with a hundred alpacas belonging to the communal company (GRADE 1999; KS 1998b:38).

The name of the Ango Raju community comes from its snow-capped peak and *apu* protector. The Agrarian Reform expropriated the land of two separate haciendas and gave it to the community. The plots were distributed among the hacienda's former laborers. Recognition as a peasant community came in 1973 and contributed to the development of the small town. Three schools and a medical post were built, as well as a *trocha* (dirt road) to San Marcos and the hamlets of the surrounding upper regions. By the time Antamina launched the land purchase in 1997, the community had 152 members, with both male and female heads of household (AMIDEP 1997b:76). In 2001, following a rural pattern in which recognition and state resources are sought, the community obtained the status of *centro poblado menor* (minor town center). Its proximity to San Marcos allowed for a more dynamic socioeconomic exchange than was possible in Huaripampa. This condition has been useful for the recruitment of teachers, who prefer the comforts and better microclimate of San Marcos. Its location next to the Carash River, allowing irrigation and shorter rain-fed cycles, made Ango Raju one of the most productive agricultural areas. Prior to the arrival of Antamina, there were internal disputes over land in the upper zone and accusations of mismanagement of the communal agricultural enterprise. The communal organization fragmented at the beginning of the 1990s, with an assembly dividing the terrain while preserving collective lands (KS 1998a).

Crossing Huallanca

Since the Andean people were more exposed to the construction of Antamina, Huallanca provides a revealing comparison with San Marcos. They were the two most impacted Andean towns at the beginning. Huallanca was affected by gigantic trucks in transit for the assembling of the mining infrastructure, and it accommodated many workers during construction. The town is forty-three kilometers from Antamina on an agricultural trade route between the jungle and the coast. This cattle town has been home to Compañía Minera Santa Luisa, a subsidiary of the Japanese Mitsui Mining and Smelting Company. This medium-sized Peruvian mining firm has its largest operation in Huanzalá, eleven kilometers from Huallanca, extracting zinc and lead in a more labor-intensive operation. Discovered in 1721, the San José de Huanzalá mine was ignored until 1964, when Mitsui created Santa Luisa. By 1981 the mine was producing nine hundred metric tons per day (Crowley et al. 1997).

Just as the San Marcos community's relationship with the Gran Bretaña company operating in Contonga are revealing, so, too, the relationship between the community in Huallanca and Santa Luisa helps us understand how expectations about Antamina's costs and benefits were also influenced by the history of nearby mining (see chapter 2). During the height of mining Huanzalá in the 1970s, its camp housed some 2,500 workers and their families, a figure that had reduced to less than 1,000 by the end of the 1990s. Santa Luisa contributed services and jobs for the majority of the residents. Huallanca also had electricity and a sewerage system as a consequence of an agreement with the company. The price, however, was pollution of the surrounding river and damage to livestock production, the main economic activity.

Disembarking in Huarmey

Concentrate from Antamina flows through a pipeline and reaches port facilities in Huarmey, from where it is shipped (see map 1). Prior to construction of the pipeline, fears about the environmental risks this posed generated protests that had national resonance. The mechanisms of negotiation and direct action these events reveal are examined in chapter 3. Antamina property in Huarmey was four kilometers from the city and extended from the Pan-American Highway to the Pacific Ocean, some 293 kilometers from Lima. The site of the port was adjacent to the small fishing cove of Puerto Grande and three fishmeal factories. When Antamina appeared, the population of the cove and the settlement Nueve de Octubre numbered 285 inhabitants in seventy-one homes (KS 1998a). Huarmey, capital of the eponymous province, was a commercial town with small businesses and banking services. The city had a population of approximately ten thousand people when Antamina arrived. The main productive activities were commercial fishing, fishmeal processing, and agriculture on the banks of the Huarmey River. Artisanal fishing was conducted in small boats, mostly in the port of Huarmey near the mining facilities. The catch was distributed in Puerto Grande for domestic consumption and fishmeal factories. Industrial fishing of sardines and anchovies was supported by large ships operating up to ninety kilometers off the coast. Refrigerated trucks transported the fish to nearby cities and to Lima.

The Huarmey River—like other coastal rivers, only flows between January and April following rains in the Andes—was the only source of surface fresh water near the mining site. Groundwater was the main water source for agricultural, industrial, and domestic activities. The farmers cultivated sugarcane, cotton, corn, and bread, maintaining links with local markets. The mining area was largely without vegetation and was mostly home to rats and lizards (KS 1998a).

Social Scenarios

The main groups are located in sectors with dissimilar capacities and relative strategic alliance mobility. The business associations are quite organized and have participated in the establishment of the main environmental regulations (Gil Ramón 2014). When setting these regulations, MEM regularly consults with the mining industry body, SNMPE (Sociedad Nacional de Minería, Petróleo y Energía, or the National Society of Mining, Petroleum, and Energy). Given the fluid relationship between governments and the private sector, it is unsurprising that senior MEM officials, including ministers, can come from the ranks of mining businesses. For example, before being minister (2003–2004), Hans Flury was SNMPE president and director of several mining companies. Such associations and companies have immense resources to interpret and utilize regulations, allowing them to negotiate quickly while they exert pressure through the media, employing the discourse of capital flight.

The World Bank played an important role in the opening of Antamina through its insurer, the Multilateral Investment Guarantee Agency (MIGA). Antamina annually reported the social, environmental, and health and safety incidents to MIGA. This agency issued $106.9 million as collateral for the investment in 1999 and 2000. The financiers required it to provide experience in monitoring social and environmental standards. This is evidence that they perceived the risks to the project. The investments and loans were "covered against the risk of transfer restriction." The loans were also protected against "expropriation, war and civil disturbance" (CAO 2006:3). The financial engineering for Antamina was complex, involving commercial banks and import and export credit agencies from Japan, Canada, Germany, and Finland. The magazine *Project Finance International* considered Antamina to be the largest mining finance operation of 1997 (Kahatt 2003:274). Having the majority of Antamina's future production committed for a period similar to the repayment of the loans (ten to fourteen years) was crucial for the financial closure of the project.

There were more than two hundred NGOs and approximately twenty national networks interested in the environmental issues. Their capacities varied; some had international connections whereas others had little more than a small office. The strongest NGOs had international networks and offices in Lima. An example is Pronaturaleza, which obtained 60 percent of its funds from the Nature Conservancy in the United States. The SPDA (Sociedad Peruana de Derecho Ambiental, or Peruvian Society for Environmental Law) had ties with the World Resources Institute and the Earth Justice Legal Defense Fund, both based in the USA. Each also received funding from the European Union. Some foreign NGOs have offices in Peru, such as TMI and Oxfam America. NGOs generally lack mining environmental impact expertise, but they have played an important role in funding projects to inform local leaders and support the activities of residents. One such activity, supposedly largely financed by Oxfam, was the so-called referendum conducted by the municipality of Tambogrande (Piura), which became the prelude to revocation by the state of the exploitation rights of a mining project there in 2003. The company, Manhattan Minerals, was unable to fulfill the requirements of the contract (including a treatment plant of ten thousand tons a day and a capital investment of $100 million). The CEO and president, Peter Guest, would later claim that the company looked for a "bigger partner" to meet the conditions but failed "because the social conditions were so anti-mining that nobody wanted to participate" (Corkery 2005).

NGOs joined loosely with one another through the ANC (Asociación Nacional de Centros de Investigación, Promoción Social y Desarrollo, or National Association of Research Centers, Social Promotion and Development). NGOs with environmental interests worked through different networks, such as the Red Ambiental Peruana (Peruvian Environmental Network) or the Muqui Network, which currently brings together more than thirty organizations and has been operating since 2003. The Chavín Consortium in Huaraz brought together seven organizations. The Huascarán Working Group also emerged to monitor the impact of Antamina on the Huascarán National Park through the participation of several NGOs, state agencies, and private companies (chapter 3). International consultants are usually in charge of preparing environmental impact statements. In the case of Antamina, the Canadian firms Klohn Crippen and Knight Piésold were engaged.

If the capacity of NGOs was limited at the time of the mining company's arrival, the peasant communities were even less prepared. Until a few years ago, of the 6,069 recognized peasant communities, 5,110 had legal land title, covering 18.7 percent (twenty-four million hectares) of Peru's territory. Approximately 3.5 million people, mostly Quechua and Spanish speakers, lived on these peasant community lands during the 1990s. More recently, this figure rose to an estimated six million (Grupo Allpa 2012; Valera 1998). Usually dedicated to smallholder agriculture, this population ranks among the poorest in the nation's poverty statistics. Until the mid-1990s, peasant communities faced mining conflicts virtually without external support. The main peasant federations with national coverage (e.g., the Peru Peasant Federation and the National Agrarian Confederation) paid little serious attention to the issue (de Echave 2005:120).

Subsequently, partnerships with various NGOs strengthened the peasant communities. In 1998, under the auspices of the Lima NGO Cooper-Acción, approximately forty communities from regions with a mining presence exchanged experiences for the first time. This led to the First Congress of Communities Affected by Mining the following year, and the founding of CONACAMI (Confederación [former Coordinadora] Nacional de Comunidades Campesinas Afectadas por la Minería, or the National Confederation Body—formerly Coordinating—of Peruvian Communities Affected by Mining), supported by Oxfam America (de Echave 2005). Since then CONACAMI has been the nexus of the *frentes de defensa* (defense fronts) formed by the opponents of mining. A representative of Oxfam America told me that he defined the initial interactions with CONACAMI as a "counterpart relationship" with a collaboration "partner." He added that Oxfam Great Britain (initially) and Oxfam America (throughout) supported CONACAMI in "defense activities and capacity building," including "trips for some of its leaders." According to him, the relationship subsequently deteriorated due to a radicalization of CONACAMI's public discourse, which came to emphasize the human rights aspects of conflict between mining projects and local populations. In 2006, the Andean Coordinator of Indigenous Organizations was founded in Cusco, bringing together CONACAMI and two other groups representing Indigenous peoples in Ecuador and Bolivia. The president of CONACAMI presided over the Andean organization. CONACAMI opted for the name *confederation* in preference to *coordinating* to emphasize its Indigenous focus. This was probably a tactic in its attempts to find global allies.

In 2002 the Grupo de Diálogo, Minería, y Desarrollo Sostenible (Dialogue, Mining, and Sustainable Development Group) was formed as a forum for discussion among representatives of unions, communities, consultants, mining companies, regional governments, local governments, and public- and private-sector organizations. Some members sent only midlevel officers, and the group had virtually no CONACAMI representation. The group was criticized for being focused on dialogue rather than the generation of agreements and tangible outcomes. Its self-reported sponsors included mining companies, which prompted questions about institutional independence. The group distanced itself from antimining representatives and mostly enticed characters already amenable with mining activities. The meetings I attended reflected more the voice of consultants from private firms and NGOs. If the gatherings help to elucidate and exchange conceptual differences, it raises the question of which sectors benefit the most from the data harvest. It probably feeds more the discourses of mining companies, who generally hold expensive and more resourceful apparatuses to process information in record time. In 2011 a new group formed in Lima, the Mining, Democracy, and Sustainable Development Latin American Dialogue Group, following a regional meeting with the same title. Similar groups were subsequently formed in Argentina, Colombia, Ecuador, Brazil, and Chile.

Conclusion

The mining apparatus assembly to legitimize the project included the concession imposed on the local residents, with clear contract benefits for the mining project, and the establishment of an EIA process that minimized the size of the potentially impacted population. The latter invisibilized sensitive initial processes (e.g., resettlement) and restricted the participation of potentially affected groups. The evolution of the composition of the international mining consortium included members with significant socioenvironmental conflictive experiences before joining Antamina, all of which, I argue, helps us to understand strategies discussed in the following chapters.

With a state apparatus eager to raise funds rapidly through taxes, mining acquired privileges and laws that were adjusted in its favor, including generous tax frameworks and contracts. The tender documentation already reflected privileges for the mining consortium, including counting many expenses as investment and a legal stability agreement, while promoting the exclusion of low-skilled local labor.

The state auctions underground mineral resources to the private sector. However, this sale is limited when the surface belongs to others beyond the reach of the government contract. Considering the inapplicability of easement in certain contexts, difficult access to surface land with mining potential may jeopardize the viability of a project, as occurred in the frustrated attempt to exploit Tambogrande on the northern coast. When Antamina obtained the concession—which only implied rights over the subsoil—it also purchased a confrontation due to properties lacking clear legal title and a state mining company lacking the authority to mediate land conflicts.

The stages of an EIA have practical repercussions. Impacts that can lead to conflict should also be considered in phases. The stages up to and including exploration were only minimally addressed as part of the company's design, without considering local conditions and overlooking in particular the first contact with communities. It was only in 2004, almost fifteen years after the enactment of major legal reforms to promote private investment in Peru, especially mining, that MEM recognized the importance of the exploratory phase. As we shall appreciate in the following chapters, the social sustainability of a mining project is conditioned by the extent to which local institutions can actively participate in the decision to allow extraction or the design of that process.

CHAPTER 2

From "Involuntary Resettlement" to Displacement

THOSE AFFECTED REMEMBERED THE RESETTLEMENT PROCESS AS A TRAGIC EVENT: TRACTORS deployed against houses, and families—who were not considered residents by Antamina and were therefore not subject to compensation—wandered with their herds in the highlands and suffered material and emotional losses when they failed to find pastures to feed the cattle (GRADE 2000). Magdalena, displaced from Tranca, recalled, "Suddenly they came down on us and we were forced by guards to leave." Jeremiah, formerly living in the uplands of Ango Raju, told me, "They evicted everyone. They gave us less than a week. They burned down some houses. . . . The police, a judge, and a lawyer went up [to the puna] and I cried because I did not know where to go. This was all I had." The displacement was perceived as an eviction due to the hasty mobilization and support of state authorities.

In San Marcos the period from 1999 to 2001 was marked by conflict: lawsuits, blocked roads, attempted mayoral recall mandates, the formation of defense fronts, and letters of protest to national authorities and the World Bank. Because of the high local expectations held for the project, relations between the mining company and the people of San Marcos began well; however, these hopes transformed into disappointment during the displacement of approximately sixty families in order to open up the pit and install the mining infrastructure. Their removal began two years after issue of the concession. Although initially planned to take place as a resettlement process over one year, the operation

FIGURE 6 Protest in the central square of San Marcos. 2002. The placards read, "Association of Peasant Owners of Chipta-Pincullo and Yanacancha demands immediate resettlement of the town of Yanacancha. Life yes, pollution no"; "Enough of abuse and deception. Fulfill your commitment Antamina. Down with lying Antamina. No to land expropriation." Author's photo.

was transformed into an expedited displacement that ultimately occurred in just three months. Despite conflict, between 1999 and 2002 Antamina was repeatedly awarded for its "social responsibility" and for its relations with the neighboring community. This is evidence that competing perceptions of the situation existed. The World Bank Group's Office of the Compliance Advisor Ombudsman (CAO) of the IFC and MIGA (CAO 2001:8) even reported, "The Antamina Mine project is apparently considered highly in Peru for its implementation of social corporate responsibility."

In this chapter I explore the causes and consequences of conflicts in the so-called resettlement process. The unveiling of the mining sociolegal apparatus helps to understand cultural differences, social strategies, and lessons that explicate the outcomes of the resettlement disputes. It consists of two parts: a critical overview of the events followed by a more interpretative section titled "Deciphering Conflicts." I begin by describing the mining sociotechnologies displayed at the arrival of Antamina into San Marcos, focusing on the social baseline and the urgent land titling for purchasing land for the operations. I then portray how the mining project was immersed in national and international regulatory regimes that were applied with limitations. I continue with a detailed depiction of the individual and communal processes for land negotiations, including a comparison of two neighboring communities. Then I expose how the alteration of resettlement plans accelerated the process, producing contentious reactions. In the second part, the interpretation of the conflicts highlights the cultural roots of conflicts, especially regarding expectations of reciprocity. The study of the resettlement frictions unveils the early cultural and structural disencounters between a transnational corporation and marginalized Andean citizens while also dissecting the corporate sociotechnologies that prompt the powerless to organize, confront, proclaim concerns, and negotiate in their quest for their basic rights and expectations.

Urgent Titling

Antamina began the exploration phase in 1996 after winning the tender. Approximately thirty engineers arrived in San Marcos to dynamite the first summits. They also identified an area of approximately seven thousand hectares for operations. These workers made the first contact with the owners of the properties that were to be purchased. They were well received by local authorities and the people of San Marcos. Some mining employees were even chosen as godparents to San Marcos children. For residents of San Marcos, contact with the mining company had begun. Nevertheless, until that point Antamina had still not sent a single professional with social expertise to formally mediate relations with the community. Antamina hired Klohn Crippen—SVS S.A. Ingenieros Consultores to prepare the environmental impact statement. This company in turn subcontracted the small Lima-based NGO AMIDEP to record the social issues. In October 1997, just one month before the start of the land purchases, AMIDEP personnel arrived in San Marcos to collect information for the land acquisitions and for the environmental impact statement. AMIDEP (1997a:2) conducted a census of 564 families and a survey about expectations in the operations area. The NGO presented the result as the social baseline.

Most land for the mine site operations area belonged to people lacking property title legalized by the state or other instruments necessary for legal transactions. Their records included papers such as a will or other documents with customary validity. Community land was legally registered. It fell to Antamina to interpret local customary arrangements and make them intelligible for the national legal framework. In 1997, one year after obtaining the concession, Antamina signed an agreement with the state to finance the PETT (chapter 1), which aimed to formalize and grant legal land title to the surface area that the company wished to acquire. The state would guarantee the purchase of the land. Gabriel, a former resident of the operations area, described to me how property was recognized through the inheritance of both parents: "We did not have property titles" because the rights were recognized "by our grandparents." In a small community where relationships were more personal, social control was direct and social references sufficed, without the need for recourse to formal documents issued by the state.

The titling and registration process in Antamina proved to be quite rapid by comparison with the experience in other areas with similar challenges. The process included the right to object. As this had the potential to bog the process down for years in the judicial system, Antamina intervened directly when the need arose. In twenty-nine cases it applied a *contrato de reconocimiento de obligaciones* (obligations recognition contract) to the individuals refusing to sell their land or title. This instrument contained the promise of resettlement of the owners in equal or better conditions to those characteristic of the land to be sold and vacated. Nevertheless, the arrangement generated confusion among those who sold. PETT worked on the basis of the AMIDEP census; however, this largely excluded herders lacking a fixed abode in the area required by Antamina. Confidence was affected by the fact that the $1,500 cost of a single copy of the new title was beyond the reach of those who did formalize their rights and then disposed of their property. Suspicion was also created by the use of Antamina company vehicles by government officials working on PETT (Szablowski 2002).

Conjuring Regulations

The environmental impact assessment committed Antamina to meeting national and international environmental, social, and legal standards. The applicability of these rubrics fell under different degrees of compliance, including indefinite spaces, which allowed for the company to just conjure some of the regulations without much enforcement, especially when the level of obligation or the route to approach such generic guidelines were vague enough. Since the 1990s, the environmental impact statement had constituted the main tool for environmental management in Peru. The rhetoric held that negative effects can be foreseen, controlled, and mitigated, leading to preservation of the sustainability of nature and of its population. The Peruvian Civil Code governed the possession and purchase of land. A change to the legislation in the 1990s allowed the sale of peasant community land to external agents, such as mining companies. The 1995 Ley de Tierras (Land Law, law no. 26505) allowed a community, with majority agreement of its members, to opt to title and then sell all or part of its land.[1] This operation had previously been prohibited so as to protect the communities from expansion of haciendas. The Peruvian legal framework did not include a procedure to regulate the involuntary resettlement caused by mining projects, although some specific regulations exist in other sectors (e.g., Law on Internal Displacement). The easement mechanism, regulated by the Land Law and its amendments, indicated that the use of land for mining required prior agreement with the owner or, following compensation, application of a procedure determined by supreme resolution and endorsed by the ministries of energy and agriculture. The procedure was problematic because the requests usually exceeded those required for the operation; it was sufficient to show that a negotiation had merely been convened—without it yet having taken place—in order to request the processing, and compensation did not include lost activities or livelihoods (Pulgar-Vidal 1999). The 1993 Peruvian Constitution that was promulgated during the Fujimori regime and cemented the neoliberal economic reforms of the period also eliminated a land protection article contained in its 1979 predecessor and thereby allowed expropriation by mining companies. In this way, the state formally dispensed with the obligation to mediate between companies and populations. Although Antamina's environmental impact statement indicated that the legislation referring to "expropriation in the public interest or other mandatory resettlement is not relevant in this case," the easement mechanism was crucial during the land purchase (KS 1998a:annex SE II, p. 4).

Among the range of applicable international regulations, those of the ILO and the World Bank were preeminent in the establishment of Antamina.[2] The 1989 ILO Convention 169 on the Rights of Indigenous and Tribal Peoples was ratified by the state in 1993. The convention prioritizes information and consultation with Indigenous populations for projects or laws that may affect these groups, including extractive explorations, as well as the right to compensation, benefit sharing, and the mitigation of harmful effects (Chirif 2015). Out of the twenty-two countries that have ratified the convention, fourteen are from Latin America. However, laws to develop the definitions of the convention and adjust it to current legislation were lacking in Peru. Furthermore, later governments have enacted or preserved laws at odds with the convention.[3]

The convention (ILO 1989:article 16, item 2) states that while the moving of a population should be avoided, where it is unavoidable it should be carried out "only with their free and informed consent" and after establishing procedures such as public inquiries. In terms of compensation, it indicates, "Persons thus relocated shall be fully compensated for any resulting loss or injury" (ILO 1989:article 16, item 5). In respect of the displaced people, the convention prioritizes "land for land" compensation, seeking "lands of quality and legal status at least equal to that of the lands previously occupied by them, suitable to provide for their present needs and future development" (ILO 1989:article 16, item 4).

Because of the structure of the project's finance, Antamina was committed to complying with the World Bank's social and environmental policies and guidelines. MIGA, the bank's insurer, monitored compliance. It inspected the contract loan while the guarantors and lenders—through the insurer Export Development Corporation—selected the U.S. firm Pincock, Allen, and Holt as the "independent engineer" to oversee the procedures. This was because MIGA's socioenvironmental policies and directives only came into effect in mid-1999 (CAO 2001:3). MIGA's initial role was to ensure against political risk. The owners (the backer and shareholders) and the commercial bank lenders (i.e., Citibank and Deutsche Bank) received a guarantee even though the project was a private initiative without financing from the World Bank. In this way, the private sector achieved better insurance and surveillance, taking account of all risks, in the absence at that time of standards such as those of the World Bank. The World Bank's Office of the CAO, which was created in 1999, supervised the environmental and social performance of these agencies and addressed the complaints of those affected by the private projects these entities supported, including the claims for the Antamina project.

The displacement of people by Antamina was guided by the Operational Directives of the World Bank, which appear to draw from ILO Convention 169. "Operational Directive 4.20: Indigenous Peoples" (World Bank 1991) indicated the conditions applicable when a project affected an Indigenous population, and "Operational Directive 4.30: Involuntary Resettlement" (World Bank 1990) set the guidelines for population resettlements.[4] Compliance with these documents was necessary for the financing approval. Both directives emanate arguably idealistic goals while requiring a development and resettlement plan (World Bank 1990:1; 1991:20). These rules claimed to ensure that marginal groups (e.g., Indigenous people and women) were informed about and represented in the preparation of resettlement plans (World Bank 1990:8). The Indigenous peoples directive (15d) alleged mechanisms that would guarantee the "participation" by Indigenous people, especially at the beginning, to ensure a design adapted to local conditions. The goal's intent was summarized as follows: "The borrower must ensure that indigenous people benefit from development investments" (World Bank 1991:8, 9, 14a).

To ensure local participation, the directives demanded the employment of social science professionals in the design phase and, subsequently, experienced social, technical, and legal personnel for monitoring actions (World Bank 1991:16, 15h; 1990:25). Moreover, the directives pointed out that early collaboration with NGOs and local leaders would help identify participation mechanisms and local development opportunities (World Bank 1991:17, 15d). The involuntary resettlement directive encouraged participation in the preparation of a timetable and budget by both the residents to be relocated and the receiving population, as well as consultation and the provision of information to those affected about their options and rights (World Bank 1990:3c, 4, 8, 17, 18). It also mentioned a plan to regularize land tenure and explore new economic strategies in accordance with ILO Convention 169. A contingency plan was also required (World Bank 1991:9). These purportedly good intentions in the directives were mostly declarative, since it was not clear what the mechanisms were to enforce real analysis for grounding them, especially regarding local participation. Under the absence of Peruvian laws regulating involuntary resettlement caused by mining and the overly general level of the bank's directives, the company could merely conjure the guidelines for receiving the loans.

Lip Service: Landing the Directives

Antamina's environmental impact statement paid much more attention to World Bank's involuntary resettlement directive than the Indigenous population directive. The report lacked the analysis that ideally would have grounded the bank's guidelines, adapting them to facilitate interaction with and monitoring from local institutions, thereby addressing issues of cultural difference and social vulnerability. The report merely invoked some guidelines' topics for the resettlement with Indigenous populations, especially in terms of public participation. The statement opted for the expression *reubicación voluntaria* (voluntary resettlement) even though the bank's guidelines referred to the process as "involuntary resettlement." This term exemplified the document's optimistic tone, which sought to play down risks and negative impacts. Beyond designating the fifty-five families (286 individuals) to be resettled (and doing so without foreseeing significant environmental impact), "a consultative process," and a budget of $700,000 (for construction of residences, sanitary facilities, and compensation), the document's resettlement section failed to convince that Antamina would conduct a process with participatory supervision in the manner required by the World Bank.[5] According to Ian Thomson Consulting (1999), Antamina managers were unaware that they had to comply with the Indigenous populations directive until five months after the families were displaced.

During March and April 1998, five months after beginning the land purchases, Antamina presented the environmental impact statement at six *reuniones públicas* (public meetings): Lima (with NGOs interested in environmental development), Huaraz (with local authorities), Chavín, San Marcos, Huallanca, and Huarmey (presented as "open to the population") (KS 1998b:2). This exceeded the Peruvian legal requirements, which only demanded a single presentation, to take place in the capital. Antamina used the newspaper *El Comercio* to announce the event in Lima. However, the consensus and informed participation requirements contained in the Indigenous population guideline would prove more difficult to achieve.

Local residents had little information about the resettlement plans at the start of the project. Antamina's lack of either a clear policy for local relations or trained and experienced personnel in community relations all contributed to a situation in which people freely constructed their own expectations. Various testimonies show that the information provided by Antamina employees was inadequate. More than a few referred to mining personnel offering employment opportunities as a way of facilitating the purchase of land, including a document signed by an Antamina employee mentioning a resettlement commitment (GRADE 2001). As an Ango Raju community leader told me, "Antamina kept offering us permanent work for our children in Yanacancha when we were living there, to convince us to sell." A member of the San Marcos environmental committee assured me that "when the engineer [name] came, everyone said, 'There is the owner of the mine.' Everyone wanted to talk to him and he offered things to sign . . . [such as] support and work for the whole family."

CAO (2001:9) rated the supervision by Antamina and its contractors as "inadequate." Ian Thomson Consulting (1999:22) considered communications between Antamina's Community Relations team and its subcontractors—during the construction phase—as "deficient or non-existent." Antamina's temporary subcontracted employment regime was also unhelpful in the relationship with the neighboring community. Both the personnel employed for the environmental impact statement and the subcontractors claimed a lack of awareness of the World Bank guidelines and lacked incentives to manage the relationship with the community well. These requirements could have been included in their contracts.[6] Up to that time, there were no external organizations (e.g., NGOs in Lima) participating in the land-purchase process or the preparation of the environmental impact statement. Some institutions would become involved later, once the conflict had intensified. In sum, not only did the environmental impact statement lack a convincing analysis for complying with the bank's directives related to resettlement involving Indigenous peoples, but also the company's personnel only became aware that they had to comply with these guidelines late in the process of displacement, while subcontractors lacked both this awareness and incentives for a good relationship with the residents.

Acquiring Land

Antamina purchased approximately seven thousand hectares to build the mine and facilities, spending almost $3.5 million in the process (see table 2). The two types of lands—communal and *fundos privados indivisos* (undivided private estates)—would be subject to quite different forms of land acquisition. The purchase price of surface rights and private property was subject to the Peruvian Civil Code, where ideally the parties—through the free market—would negotiate and agree on a sum (KS 1998a). However, the process had serious limitations. The market for land was underdeveloped in the operations area; there were just a few transactions for rent or sale of plots between owners or community members. Antamina set its offer price based on the value of the *arancel* (duty), possible land uses, and the experience of other mining companies that had purchased land in Peru (see table 3). The company differentiated *tierras eriazas* (unproductive land) from natural pastures, setting a rate of $400 per hectare as the basis for subsequent purchases. The Antamina and La Tranca estates were exceptions. The rate for these properties was $1,000 per hectare (table 2) because the majority of the deposit was located in the former, and the lands of the latter were agricultural. The price exceeded that paid by other mining companies in similar situations and for small local transactions (GRADE 1999).[7] Thus, in 1998, the Huaripampa community received the unprecedented sum of almost $1 million for their land.

TABLE 2 Land purchased by Antamina

OWNER	JURISDICTION	PROPERTY OR ESTATE	POPULATION	HECTARES	AMOUNT PAID
Huaripampa community	Yanacancha	Yanacancha Huaripampa; Antamina	72	2,337.00	$934,800
Ango Raju de Carhuayoc community	Yanacancha	Yanacancha Angoraju	32	518.00	$207,200
	Neguip	Neguip	35	611.86	$244,744
Santa Cruz de Pichiú community	Ayash Pichiú	Chogopampa	0	24.00	$9,600
Communal land total			139	3,490.86	$1,396,344
Private land	Yanacancha	Chogopampa; Aselgaspampa; Challhuash	72	454.45	$181,780
	Juprog	La Tranca; Fundo Antamina*	59	1,038.00	$1,038,000
	Juprog	Shahuanga	21	750.00	$300,000
	Yanacancha	Yanacancha	33	487.02	$194,808
	Tucush	Tucush	24	817.91	$327,164
	Tucush Yanacancha	Tucush Yanacancha	0	103.00	$41,200
Individually owned land total			209	3,650.38	$2,082,952
Total			348	7,141.24	$3,479,296

Source: GRADE (1999), B&R (1998a), KS (1998a) and the San Marcos Office of Community Development.

*Antamina paid $1,000/hectare for these estates and $400 or less for the others.

TABLE 3 Duty price and Antamina offer price by type of land, 1997–1999

		DUTY VALUE		ANTAMINA VALUE (INITIAL OFFER)	
LAND TYPE	HECTARES	DUTY	TOTAL VALUE	ANTAMINA PRICE	TOTAL VALUE
Agricultural land (rainfed)	154.93	$249.5	$38,588.70	$400	$61,972
Natural pastures	4,156.42	$20.8	$87,095.50	$400	$1,678,568
Bofedales or *oconales* (wetlands)	157.81	$20.8	$3,275.30	$300	$47,343
Terreno eriazo (unproductive land)	2,473.91	$20.8	$51,137.80	$100	$246,391
Caserío, corrales (hamlets, stockyards)	7.41	$249.1	$1,845.60	$300	$2,223
Totals	6,950.48		$181,942.90		$2,036,497

Source: B&R (1998a, 1998b), GRADE (1999:87).

When it encountered opposition to selling, Antamina committed to other forms of compensation via the aforementioned obligations recognition contracts. The initial resettlement plan would have relocated families to a neighboring equivalent plot of land with compensation for the owners and others affected (e.g., herders and tenants enjoying rights of usufruct). Seeking to convince landowners to sell, mining officials organized negotiation meetings, invoking the value of the mine for local development and the easement rights, but without relying on a single version of official company policy (GRADE 1999). Antamina increased the number of resettlement cases, including nonpermanent residents of the upper zone. This would become one of the first problems. Several landowners who had agreed to sell, and had therefore not signed obligations recognition contracts, complained about the increase of the number of cases.[8]

Purchasing Land in Huaripampa and Ango Raju

Antamina's land purchase in the comparable neighboring communities of Huaripampa and Ango Raju de Carhuayoc revealed participation dynamics in negotiation processes. The purchase of land in Huaripampa began in September 1997. At a single communal meeting with Antamina, the community approved the sale of 2,337 hectares at $400 per hectare, and received $934,800. This represented 43 percent of its land, especially the communal pasture, which was mostly under private usufruct. The community retained approximately 3,000 hectares (KS 1998b:38). It simultaneously agreed to a program of public works in which Antamina would collaborate over and above the resettlement of those affected: electrification, a school, an internal road, and a medical post. Seven months later, the story in neighboring Ango Raju would be more complicated. The community sold 1,129 hectares, almost half of the area sold by Huaripampa, and received $451,944. The sale required a total of eight communal meetings with Antamina. The final agreement was the result of numerous long and heated internal assemblies to debate the proposed conditions.

At the first presentation in Ango Raju, Antamina offered improvements for the community (health, education, agriculture, and livestock) in exchange for the sale of land. The community members agreed to discuss the price and did it intensively in several internal assemblies. At the second meeting with the company, the community agreed (with a two-thirds majority) to sell the communal pastures (Yanacancha and Neguip) and appointed a negotiating commission to establish a price of no less than $400 per hectare. Huaripampa sold land while continuing to manage a communal area. As such, it remained more of a community. Ango Raju ended up with no collectively managed land. Jeremiah, a member of the Ango Raju community board, remembered the process as a threat: "The people of Antamina said that if we did not deliver [sell our land], they would use the easement mechanism." Lucas, former president of the community, reflected, "We thought that if we did not give in, the mine would not give us work and other things. They would marginalize us."

The Defensoría del Pueblo (or Ombudsman's Office) (DP 2005:25) reported complaints about pressure put on landowners where the deposits were located "to grant easement under disadvantageous conditions," criticizing the regulations for containing "characteristics of confiscatory nature for the property of those affected, without providing adequate protection of their rights." The lawyer Manuel Pulgar-Vidal (2002:73) noted that easement "weakens the property rights" of those affected, granting "clearly insufficient compensatory amounts far from the legitimate expectations of the owners." The mere mention of the mechanism constituted a threat that became a weapon in the hands of the mining company in the negotiation process. The easement was activated by the mere demonstration of the provision of an offer. In addition, the mining companies had abundant financial resources to pursue long-term legal action, even if it meant incurring costs from delays and social tensions.

The margin for negotiation in the sale of the community land was limited by the easement mechanism, which become a form of intimidation. Marcos, director of the Yanacancha Association of Displaced Persons, recalled, "Antamina did not really negotiate." They said, "We pay $400 per hectare or easement [will be applied]." Lucas was certain that the easement mechanism contributed to the lower price for the land. Thirty-four percent of land purchased by Antamina was considered "*eriazas*" (unproductive), which would have expedited the application of the easement, although it also would have increased conflicts, which have additional costs, such as delays (B&R 1998a). The right to easement had not often been used in Peru to its full extent. It generally functioned as a tool to intimidate residents, probably accelerating negotiations and reducing the land price. The mechanism was beneficial for the mining companies, where a rhetoric was in operation that privileged the national common good over the local, and mining over agriculture. For land to be expropriated, it was sufficient for a company to show that it had tried to negotiate and that the community did not accept the offer. A *justiprecio* (fair market price) was then paid to the community members, equivalent to the duty or the declared value of the land for taxation purposes. Easement was complex to interpret and risky in its application. Since the Peruvian Constitution prohibits the expropriation of property, except where it is in the public interest, something not directly applicable to mining activities, the mining easement mechanism should be constitutionally barred (Szablowski 2002).

A legal advisor hired by Ango Raju at the suggestion of Antamina to verify its land titles would subsequently urge the community to raise the land price (GRADE 2000:95). The higher amount was rejected by the company. Amid discontent among community members, who accused the adviser and the community board of corruption, the negotiation ultimately led to a community development deal. As part of the agreement, Ango Raju achieved a written pledge from Antamina that in the event the company needed vehicles, it would hire the trucks that the community planned to acquire with the money from the sale of land. The community used the agreement subsequently to pressure the company to hire the communal trucks. Ango Raju also achieved a favorable collective obligations recognition contract. Through this later agreement, the mining company agreed to acquire the Buenavista Estate for the community and the displaced. This land was forty kilometers from San Marcos and was suitable for livestock and agriculture. A former employee of Antamina claimed that this commitment came about because of the company's limited knowledge of the World Bank guidelines. On September 16, 1998, the deadline expired for Antamina to invest the $2.52 billion as provided in the contract. Prior to this date, it could have withdrawn and paid a penalty. The project started aggressively. The purchase of land in Ango Raju was completed, and the following month, with the approval of the environmental impact statement, infrastructure construction commenced. No family would move until the end of November.

At the collective level, the rapid acceptance of the offer to sell the land and the apparent misappropriation of funds in Huaripampa probably reflected a lack of experience in handling large sums of money. Pablo, director of the Ango Raju school, recalled that the community did not negotiate a better price for the land because "since they were dollars, everybody was impressed" and this conjured "an illusory sale, an illusory sum." The Indigenous peoples directive required the proponent of a project to prepare communities for socioeconomic change. Antamina proposed—but never delivered on—a Financial Supervision Committee in Huaripampa. The differences in the conditions and results achieved by Huaripampa and Ango Raju raise questions about how much the former would have gained had it applied more pressure in the negotiations. Why did Huaripampa expeditiously accept a price close to the initial Antamina offer? These similar neighboring communities adopted dissimilar strategies to negotiate the sale of their land. The differences are understandable considering the different assumptions about the concept of reciprocity and expectations in the context of a formal business transaction. Ango Raju also presented certain features that probably strengthened its bargaining power.

By comparison with Huaripampa, the community of Ango Raju was better able to negotiate with Antamina. Its leaders were better trained and more experienced and there were more dissenting voices providing a greater range of ideas in the communal assemblies. In the San Marcos District, the people of Huaripampa had a reputation for being more traditional and less organized than those in Ango Raju. Some argued that this difference was due to the fact that the former were more *indios* (Indians), an Indigenous condition that they perceived to be reflected in the use of Quechua.

"Huaripampa preserves a communal structure that is more solid and stable than that of [Ango Raju de] Carhuayoc," concluded GRADE (Grupo de Análisis para el Desarrollo, or Group for the Analysis of Development) (1999:82). It noted that Huaripampa owned more collective land and organized more communal work, while Ango Raju was "politically unstable" due to conflicts based on internal differentiation. At communal assemblies in these communities, while I observed rivalries among the leaders in Ango Raju, I also heard more discussion and exchange of ideas. In Huaripampa I witnessed communal assemblies predominantly led by particular individuals. This probably led to a less critical elaboration of collectively debated ideas. In Ango Raju, by contrast, multiple individuals debated aggressively during long communal meetings, in which there was enriched discussion.

The higher level of formal and informal education in Ango Raju meant its people were better prepared to negotiate with an external agent. Approximately 16 percent of Huaripampa's population had completed at least one year of secondary or higher education, while in Ango Raju the figure was 27 percent—the second best in the area after Carash (31 percent) (AMIDEP 1997a:26). The business experience of wool weavers and the presence in Ango Raju of many former workers of the old Contonga mine probably also contributed to the community's better preparation for impersonal commercial transactions with an urban agent. Lucas, also a former Contonga mine worker, was convinced that his work experience strengthened his leadership: "I worked for ten years in the Contonga administration; I knew a lot. At that time there were unions and I could see how all this was managed. I then had the idea of advising the community. . . . That is why they chose me."

Timing was also a factor. Ango Raju's negotiation with Antamina followed six months after the experience in Huaripampa, and the community leaders were therefore able to observe the evident asymmetries and learn from them. This probably also contributed to a better choice of lawyer. Huaripampa had chosen a lawyer native to the community with little experience in large-scale negotiations. The attorney was funded by the mining company. Ango Raju, on the other hand, chose a lawyer from Huari who had participated in negotiations with other large mining companies, such as Barrick.

The formalization of the contract was understood in Ango Raju to be a guarantee of compliance. Pablo told me how at community meetings he demanded the preparation of "an agreement, an *acta* [record], a formal commitment in front of a notary," because if the mining companies were going to operate in the community, "everything had to be with a contract." Otherwise, he added, the mining company could have evaded the agreements. Lucas underlined the inadequacy of a "small verbal arrangement" by comparison with a "legal document" endorsed by a "Ministry or a public notary." He concluded that his community had "known how to get to Antamina" through "a more intelligent negotiation, proposing alternatives." The image of Ango Raju as a more organized community was consolidated locally by its more successful negotiation with the mining company and its investment of the funds in vehicles that Antamina would be obliged to use. Several Huaripampa leaders left the community under accusations of corruption after the funds obtained from the sale of the land had been exhausted. In the process, the community also lost a leadership cadre.

Initial Displacement

In September 1997, more than a year after obtaining the concession and only two months before beginning the land purchases, Antamina hired a single part-time employee to be responsible for the project's social dimensions, or "public relations," to use the language of the company. The San Marcos Community Relations team would form more than a year later. The team's initial mission was to resettle the residents of the properties purchased by Antamina. The first problem was the shortage of nearby land available to resettle residents under the "land for land" scheme recommended by the World Bank directives. The lack of productive agricultural lands was a generalized problem across the Andes because of an increase in demographic pressure on agropastoral land, notwithstanding mass migration to the cities. Testimony from former residents reflected the problems associated with labor reintegration following loss of the basis of their livelihood and the scarcity of land: "We wanted land equal to the land we had, because we are peasants and we eat from the *chacra* [field] all year round. But who would want to sell their land if everyone here lives from what our *chacra* produces?" (AMIDEP 1997a:45). A Quechua-speaking woman told me, "For me, more land would have been better, because you do nothing with money."

Antamina defined the resettlement plan guidelines through two consultancies subcontracted to the company Barrenechea and Rosemberg Asociados (B&R 1998a, 1998b). The consultants followed the environmental impact statement's recommendations to look for sites with similar environmental conditions to those being vacated. It also extended the list of affected families and investigated possibilities for agricultural development for these households (KS 1998a). It initially selected adjoining spaces within the boundaries of land acquired by Antamina. Accessibility issues and low productive potential led to further assessment, with sites in Juprog, Shahuanga, and elsewhere coming into consideration. The consultancy firm concluded that by improving pastures and developing other activities (e.g., ecotourism), twenty-five families could move. Another forty-one families could move to land near Canrash Lagoon, on the assumption that they would be able to take advantage of the fishing opportunities available there. However, the residents rejected three of these properties because they considered them too distant from the economic circuits (thirty to forty kilometers).

Antamina began the transfer of some families to temporary housing in the Huayco Gorge when the rainy season began at the end of 1998. This would later be transformed into permanent housing. Intimidation and other friction with inhabitants of Huayco—one of the sites for resettlement—were alleged to have occurred during the initial transfers. The initial resettlement plan included moving families in the following dry seasons (i.e., April to October of 1999 or 2000). The time initially contemplated to complete the transfer was estimated at one year. Simultaneously, negotiations began with the families close to the Yanacancha blasting area for the clearing and removal of the vegetable layer. Many families claimed that Antamina offered them fully serviced cement houses at locations of their choice rather than temporary homes in the designated sites. Additionally, to ensure the safety of their animals, residents asked to wait until the full effect of the rainy season, by which time pastures in the relocation area would have been ready for grazing.

A Rushed Move

Toward the end of 1998, one month after the start of implementation of the resettlement plan contained in the socioeconomic annex to the EIA, Antamina made fundamental changes to its construction plans, included in addendum 3 of the environmental impact statement (K&H 1999a). These altered the schedule and increased the exploitable reserves from 500 to 576 million tons. This meant that Antamina "would need the relocation of the families that live in the entire property faster than previously planned" (Ian Thomson Consulting 1999:9). In addition, land that Antamina had previously allocated for resettlement (i.e., Huayoc and Matará) was now urgently required for mining operations, even though some families had in fact already relocated to Huayoc. The importance of the land being free of residents increased because of the high daily costs of labor and machinery. Other modifications also altered the priorities for vacating areas, and this affected other families (GRADE 2000). However, the aforementioned addendum did not assess the impact of the design changes on the resettlement plan, even though they made access to certain places that were originally planned for resettlement impossible and drastically shortened the time frame. The first volume of addendum 3 to the environmental impact statement contained just a couple of paragraphs titled "Socio-economic Aspects" for the "Changes in the Antamina Project" section, without mentioning the resettlement plan in the document (K&H 1999a:4.3.3, 4.4.3). The executive summary optimistically claimed, "The proposed modifications to the mine plan will not bring additional environmental impacts to those specified in the initial environmental impact study and there will be no negative socio-economic impacts as a result of these modifications" (K&H 1999a:E-4). The second volume of addendum 3 contains a small reference to the land-for-land World Bank guidelines in case a family would need resettlement (K&H 1999b:4.3.4.1).

Three months after the transfer of the first families began, Antamina released the Accelerated Resettlement Plan for fifty-three families over a maximum of ninety days, down from the twelve months originally planned and taking into account the effects of the rainy season. The absence of usable land around the area of operations limited the possibilities for resettlement nearby. The land-for-land policy also shifted toward monetary compensation, with Antamina claiming to implement a follow-up plan and advising each family on how to invest the money, via the NGO Colectivo Integral del Desarrollo. This guidance began late, four months after the compensation started, and not necessarily under ideal conditions (GRADE 2000).

The pressure to vacate became significant. This is evident in the text of the resettlement offer provided by Antamina to the residents at the start of the accelerated resettlement phase: "Taking into account that resettlement is essential for security reasons and because of the high costs that the delay in the disoccupation could generate (a single day of stoppage could affect the integrity of the project), if the families do not freely and voluntarily agree to vacate the land, Antamina will be forced to enforce its rights according to law so that the said resettlement becomes effective immediately" (CMA 1999b:2). This stands in stark contrast to the tone of the environmental impact statement of a year earlier. At public hearings Antamina had asserted, "Resettlement is voluntary. No individual can, or will be forced to move" (KS 1998b:38).

The Accelerated Resettlement Plan was executed over a period of just two months (March–April 1999). Antamina required families to leave even while it was still looking for resettlement sites and building houses. The mining company presented three alternatives. The first was an allowance of $500 per month for lodging and food for up to six months. The other two possibilities required the families to move to one or more prefabricated houses in the town of San Marcos, with a monthly stipend of $200, for six months. The residents chose the first option because of the higher allowance and because some could find accommodation with family members or friends, while others could use properties they already owned.

Because of a lack of trust, families chose not to move based on the mere offer of resettlement. Antamina then presented two further proposals. The first was insurance of $30,000 (the estimated price for the purchase of land and construction of the house) to be deposited in a bank trust account in the name of the affected party. If, after six months, Antamina had not complied with the resettlement, that sum passed to the affected party. The second was to receive an immediate $30,000 for resettlement plus "subsequent technical assistance to the affected party to establish themselves in a sustainable activity" (GRADE 2000:11). The latter proposal implied the transformation of the originally recommended land-for-land resettlement scheme into financial compensation. Antamina signed resettlement agreements for $33,000 ($30,000 for resettlement and $3,000 as a living allowance over six months) with fifty-three families regarded as suitable for resettlement. The $30,000 was the sum of three items, each valued at $10,000: purchase of land, construction of a house, and improvement of the productive base. In the end, sixty-eight families received money because of the problems of allocating resettlement rights (GRADE 2000:11). Antamina also committed to developing a postresettlement assistance program. The affected families moved in less than three months.

The dizzying set of changes to the original plans for resettlement marked a turning point in the relationship between Antamina and the local residents. The transformation from land-for-land to monetary compensation caused a loss of credibility for the company and diminished trust among the locals (CMA 1999c; GRADE 2000; Ian Thomson Consulting 1999). Ian Thomson Consulting (1999:20) reported loss of confidence due to personnel changes, poor communications, and incoherence in the community relations policy. For CAO (2001:8), the modification of the agreements "greatly accentuated problems associated with the disruption to the community." Levi, a native of the town of San Marcos and member of the environmental committee, told me that "the people, having not seen their expectations fulfilled, lose confidence in the mine, they see it as an enemy." In this changing context, the residents' preference for immediate cash compensation was understandable.

Government officials and mining companies in Peru use the expression *apagar incendios* (put out fires) in reference to the resolution of mining conflicts. The metaphorical flames evoke a phrase of Mao Tse-Tung, which in turn alludes to a Chinese proverb: "A single spark can set fire to the whole prairie." Antamina's Community Relations staff frequently complained that the Operations personnel failed to listen. Some representatives jokingly recalled that the only way to elicit a timely reaction from the company was to repeat the mantra *se nos viene el pueblo* (the people are coming for us). The fear of the "burned prairie" would encourage executives to allocate resources to local relationships. An employee of the Lima consultancy Social Capital Group assured me that it had the power to stop a mining project and make a company negotiate with the residents. The task of putting out fires was known as *paga yuca* (yucca pay), in reference to the tuber, which is invoked in national slang to refer to a big problem or difficulty. The experts provided to help with extinguishing the collective fire would be GRADE from Peru—at the suggestion of MIGA—and Ian Thomson Consulting from Canada.

For Ian Thomson Consulting (1999:6, 22), Antamina's "lack of experience in resettlement" and the "breakdown of communication" between the operational staff and the Community Relations staff implied noncompliance with the original resettlement plan. The procedures and the objective of the initial design were transformed (GRADE 2000). The process revealed the limited bargaining capacity of the Community Relations personnel within Antamina. The precarious state of internal coordination was revealed in February 1999, about three months after the beginning of the accelerated transfer, when Operations personnel informed the Community Relations staff of an invasion on mine land. An eviction commenced with heavy machinery and police. The revealing surprise came when Community Relations staff confirmed that the usurpers were in fact families included in the resettlement plan, transferred under supervision to land that Antamina had later decided to use (Szablowski 2002). The world seemed upside down.

Reactions and Complaints

The complaints about the displacement process reflect its complexity and the level of conflict. Two years into the process, Antamina had accumulated 151 formal complaints, some lawsuits, and notarized letters. The majority (101) related

TABLE 4 Type of complaints about land acquisition and displacement, 1997–2000

TYPE	QUANTITY	PERCENT
PETT (titling issues)	28	18.54
Damage by contractors and road construction	25	16.56
Other	19	12.58
Money for resettlement	14	9.27
Reciprocity	7	4.64
Obligations recognition contracts	6	3.97
Money for house	2	1.32
Total complaints for land acquisition	101	66.89
Money and/or resettlement	35	23.18
Obligations recognition contracts	8	5.30
Damage (house, livestock, and one case of "brutal eviction")	7	4.64
Total complaints for displacement	50	33.11
Totals	151	100.00

Source: Prepared by the author on the basis of Antamina information in GRADE (2000).

to land acquisition and almost one-third (50) were about the displacement (see table 4). Most of those related to land acquisition arose as a result of the hurried titling and PETT registration processes. A typical example was that of a family claiming ownership by inheritance of land that PETT had not titled (GRADE 2000). There were complaints about the behavior of contractors, primarily associated with construction of the road to the mine. Typical claims included animals hit by vehicles or damage caused to pasture or cultivated land. There were fourteen claims from people seeking to be included in the displacement compensation scheme or requesting better reparation conditions. Seven complaints sought favors from Antamina (reciprocity complaints). Examples included job applications or loan applications, such as to purchase a tractor. As a private company, Antamina would normally have felt no obligation to address these unless a contractual commitment applied. A further category of complaints derived from the obligations recognition contracts. Many families sold their land with the offer of resettlement. It is worth remembering that under such deals, Antamina promised to purchase the land and relocate the family under equal or better conditions.

The local categories of use and ownership of the land included *precarios* (squatters) and *pastores* (herders) residing on a permanent basis in the concession area for operations. A squatter used the land without having legal rights or any agreement with the owner to do so. The herders cared for the animals of the owners and nonresident community members (GRADE 2000). These herders tended the cattle at the request of the owners through arrangements of reciprocity and family ties, or through other forms of affinity. The owners of land generally referred to the herders as *mi cuidador* (my caretaker) or *mi pasteador* (my herder). The possessive adjective highlighted both the relationship of reciprocity and an asymmetry of power in the social hierarchy.

At first Antamina proposed to include only herders in the compensation arrangements, under the two binary categories of permanent/nonpermanent resident and affected/unaffected. Numerous claims arose from this compensation scheme because of the fact that many nonresident landowners, who also owned livestock, received smaller amounts for the sale of their land than did "their" herders for displacement. Some landowners who did not live in the area sought inclusion in the relocation compensation. They later demanded full compensation and did not consider that the herders deserved resettlement. Speaking in his office, Pablo, director of the Ango Raju school, remembered a feeling of injustice about the compensation: "They gave half to someone who was caring for my livestock. . . . What documentation was there to justify this when he did not own a single animal?" By giving "caretakers" sums of money considered to be large by local standards—at times more than that received by landowners—Antamina was perceived by the landowners to have violated a social order that they needed to preserve. Marta, who moved from Yanacancha, explained to me her concerns about the criteria used: "In Yanacancha, PETT only recognized the title of those living higher [the puna] and those who were taking care of livestock. That is, there were people who have benefited by being caretakers. . . . They gave [compensation] to those who provided care. . . . They were *pasteadores* and they were happy because money fell from the sky to people who had never had anything." Antamina's homogenized compensation challenged a local culture in which land tenure formed the basis of the social hierarchy.

The binary category used initially of affected/unaffected later proved to be inadequate. A more graded system was necessary, one that would have better reflected the range of social relationships relevant to land access in the high Andes.[9] The arrangements typified in several categories illustrate the complexity of the local institutions for access to puna grazing lands, rather common in the Andes (for an overview, see Flores Ochoa 1977). GRADE (2000:26) estimated a "net present value" of fifty-six affected families by comparing the 1997 AMIDEP census with the situation two years later, following the displacement. It found that the conditions of only thirty-six had improved, with the remaining going backward, a reflection of the vulnerability of the population. Originally lacking in property rights, the squatters and herders finished up benefiting the most, particularly those who received compensation under the arrangements contained in the Accelerated Resettlement Plan. Conditions for landowners remained unchanged. *Comuneros* were worse off.

Several accounts reflected jealousy about an alleged asymmetry between the benefits received by the displaced people and those received by the people of San Marcos. Residents from the higher areas were labeled as more "traditional" or more "Indian"—traits that carried the connotation of being unable to manage monetary compensation, exacerbated by the perception that the sums delivered were exorbitant by local standards. Ana, displaced from the upper lands of Chavín, had the painful memory of an Antamina employee, a native of San Marcos, insulting her brother: "You, who have been resettled, are good for nothing! We earn our money. And you? What are you going to eat?" The animosity would linger, as would the uncertainty about future monetary income as families moved to lower areas with less pasture for livestock feeding.

These problems led families to claim compensation on the basis of fairness or for having been excluded from the beneficiary group (see table 4). Many sent letters of protest to institutions. Correspondence sent in 2000 by the municipality of San Marcos and the Yanacancha Association of Displaced Persons (ex-owners) had the greatest impact. Its addressees included the president of Peru, members of Congress, the Canadian ambassador, the CAO, and the World Bank's office in Lima. A lawyer from the municipality of San Marcos wrote the draft of the letter to the bank after learning about safeguard policies at a conference in Lima (Szablowski 2002). The only reaction came from CAO (2001:3), registering the local request that Antamina "abide by promises" contained in the environmental impact statement about development and environmental protection. The "letters alleged that the company had not been fair in its resettlement program, and had committed a number of abuses." Five months later a MIGA mission visited San Marcos to hear more about the complaints. As the supervising agency, it suggested an external evaluation be carried out and recommended the engagement of GRADE.

"Here Everything Is Money," and in the Puna, "The Pasture Is Endless"

The World Bank indicated that the compensation should consider the vulnerability of groups, such as the Indigenous people, that might have lacked legal protection against the loss of land. It stated that the "resettlement plan must include land allocation or culturally acceptable alternative income-earning strategies to protect the livelihood of these people" (World Bank 1990:16). It also argued that this plan should design measures for "improving or at least restoring the economic base for those relocated," preferring the provision of land for displaced farmers, given the experience that "cash compensation alone is normally inadequate" (World Bank 1990:4). The World Bank suggested the land-for-land scheme, with the land to be at least "equivalent" to that previously held, in terms of "productive potential" and "locational advantages" (World Bank 1990:13). In the absence of available land, it recommended fostering "opportunities for employment or self-employment" (World Bank 1990:4, 15). The ideal compensation in agricultural contexts means replacing the basic productive asset (i.e., land). These directives were in tune with the manifest desire of the residents registered by AMIDEP (1997a:44) in the operations area, whose preference was to receive land in addition to compensation for damages to land and animals. It was indicative that 93 percent of the displaced families (sixty-one out of the sixty-five) moved to sites near San Marcos. Closeness to their former residence contributes to the maintenance of their agricultural livelihoods, taking advantage of their expertise and the leverage of social networks based on reciprocity for the exchange of labor, especially for sowing and harvesting, while also maintaining safety networks for food or seeds for facing agro-climatic disturbances (see table 5).

The price paid by Antamina for the lands in San Marcos considerably exceeded that which was disbursed in other high Andean areas and the *justiprecio* established by the Ministry of Agriculture (GRADE 2000:9). The difference reflected the absence of developed markets in the area and the urgency of a mining company that had much to gain through the purchase. Five years earlier, the US-Peruvian Yanacocha mine, one of the first projects of the large-scale mining era that started in the 1990s, had initially paid $37 per hectare before settling closer to $1,000, in addition to compensation for some residents. The cost to avoid conflicts was internalized quite late, through the subsequent higher price, following the outbreak of conflict (GRADE 1999; Pulgar-Vidal 1999).

TABLE 5 Distribution by resettlement location, 2002

DESTINATION RESIDENCE	CASES	%
Ango Raju de Carhuayoc*	21	32.31
San Marcos	9	13.85
Other**	9	13.85
Huaripampa	5	7.69
Pacash	4	6.15
Lima***	4	6.15
Rancas	3	4.62
Chavín	3	4.62
Carash	3	4.62
Orcosh	2	3.08
Juprog	2	3.08
Total	65	100.00

Source: Antamina and fieldwork.
*Includes two cases from Ango Raju de Carhuayoc with Jato and Asga.
**One case each in the localities of Pujún, Piruro, Pincullo, Pariacancha, Llaquir, Huaura, Huancha, Hato/SM, and Ayratzin.
***Includes one case in Lima/Ayash.

The unexpected shift to an accelerated involuntary resettlement plan led to a failure to appreciate the initial social costs of the acceleration. The families that moved to lower areas confronted limitations in a more monetized culture, distinct from the customs that prevailed at higher elevations. Herders unfamiliar with lowland agriculture were also at a disadvantage. Ruth, a mother of six children, told me that she felt the money from the sale of her land was insufficient and noted that "if one is accustomed to doing business, the change to a more urban area would work. However, I had only lived in Yanacancha with my animals. I sold them and sowed, nothing more." Esdras, also displaced from the highlands, shared his reflection on the loss of exchange and self-consumption: "We lived peacefully before from agriculture; now . . . every day you have to obtain money. In the town we exchanged too. When we sold animals, they were replaced by food. And apart from this we planted potatoes. . . . We bartered potatoes, corn, wheat, and rice. In my farm I sowed everything! There were all kinds of food and with that we lived. . . . The closer to the city you are, the more education you need to do business." The problems of changing the productive matrix were aggravated by the high cost in time and resources involved in re-educating adults, especially the elderly. Gabriel's mother, seventy-five years old and now in Chavín after being displaced from the upper zone, summed up this vulnerability: "In the puna your children support you, and with the rams it is better than a bank."

The lack of pasture for the livestock of displaced families would affect their production, and approximately 80 percent of families raised livestock before their displacement (CMA 1999c). Following the move, this figure dropped to 16 percent, and agriculture became the primary occupation. A sample survey of ninety-nine families, including the sixty-eight included in the Accelerated Resettlement Plan, showed a drastic reduction in head of livestock per family between 1997 and 2000: from eighty-one to thirty-three head of sheep and from five to three head of cattle (GRADE 2000:20). Cattle farming was the main source of family liquidity, a common pattern in the economy of the Andean highlands, while agriculture was mostly oriented toward self-consumption (Golte and de la Cadena 1983; Mayer 2002). Anthropological studies documented Andean farmers highly aware of money in the sphere of *gasto* (expenditure) (Gudeman and Rivera 1990; Mayer 2002), using it carefully because of the difficulty in reproducing it and because of its volatility. The following testimony I gathered from Ana demonstrates the complexity of the change in expenditure and savings habits caused by the move from the high puna in Huaripampa to the narrow valley in Chavín, where economic relations are more monetized:

> Here the money is not enough. Everything here is money, electricity, etcetera. Up there the money lasts. Here every day you need money. In the puna, the food is covered, clothing is covered by the rams. . . . We want work for my husband. . . . We can't get anything to sell. Sometimes three cows grew each year and we sold them. Here we have just one cow for milk, but we have to buy alfalfa and it is not enough. . . . Up there in the puna it was easier. We were used to it. We didn't buy grass for the guinea pigs and the horses. The pasture was free. . . . There we just worked with the animals. There traders came to buy. For between 1,000 and 1,500 soles we would sell ten to twelve bulls. That's how we were able to buy clothes and everything else. The farm produced potatoes and we had trout, everything. . . . Here it is not like it was in the puna. It is just money. In the puna you raise rabbits and guinea pigs, and there is grass at no cost. We sold guinea pigs and cheese. The pasture was free. Everybody knew their area, it was parceled, but it was large. We had three or four hectares. The cows grazed on the hills for two or three days. . . . Now we have a cow and a small ram and we have to give them all their food.

Lucas invoked the ideal of sustainable pastures, remarking that "they are eternal, they pass through generations, they go on and they continue to be valuable even though they do not produce that much." Levi reflected on the cultural and economic shock of the change:

Levi: He [a former Antamina Community Relations officer] told me, "I can't understand why they keep bothering us, if we've given them $33,000!" "Wait," I said, "it's not about the money, it's about changing their way of life. You are taking them from one world to another. Being so close, they are so far away!"

Author: It's like if they were to give me cattle and send me up to the high puna. They can give me a thousand head, but without advice I wouldn't be able to do a thing!

L: But if you do that for someone from here, it would be the best gift in the world. The example you mention is excellent!

New ways of satisfying needs arose due to the transfer from the highlands to the valley, where the displaced people generally bought houses that lacked pastures. Rebeca had moved from Tranca to San Marcos. She told me how she relied on wood as fuel for cooking, and, whereas "in the puna everything is firewood," she now had to purchase eucalyptus. "It is worse now because my children don't want to eat what they used to in the puna. They want other food." "Now we buy meat whereas before we produced it," said another displaced person who had lived in upper Chavín. "At school my girls had [enough] and now they want a personal allowance. They want everything now! There are more expenses, everything means expenses," said Ana.

The move from the high puna to the valley also meant becoming accustomed to a more temperate climate and other conditions. The cold and dry climate in the puna facilitated food storage. The surplus production could be preserved for six months by preparing potato *t'uqush*, a dehydration process common in the department of Ancash. These tubers became affected by pests in the valley. Many herders also missed the cold climate and the sense of freedom and tranquility that came from the spaciousness of the pastures by comparison with the restrictions of urban spaces. A survey of displaced families highlighted the insufficiency of land allocation for agricultural activities and the difficulty of acclimatizing to the new environment (CMA 1999a). An individual dislocated from Antamina and now settled in Ango Raju said in reference to his father, "Up there he took his animals to graze. Here he stays indoors, bored. . . . Here is like a prison. You miss it." Although the families of the high puna lacked the means available in wealthier communities to protect against the cold, some felt nostalgia for the climate they had left behind. As Magdalena told me, "It's very hot here, but there [in Tranca], it was cold. Up high it is chillier because of the cold. Here we have been shocked by the abrupt change in the environment and the idiosyncrasy of the town."

Deciphering Conflicts

Cultural differences and differing capacities are central to understanding the disagreements that became manifest during the displacement of the population. Seven years after the resettlement began, I asked a high-ranking former Antamina staff member for a reflection on the process: "We knew we had to comply with World Bank regulations, but nobody understood how complex it would be. . . . There were a lot of problems and risks in the implementation that we had not grasped." The personnel sent by Antamina encountered high local expectations about the potential for selling services and food products. These derived from precedents set by other mining projects in the area, as detailed below. National and international regulations—observed to a certain extent during the land acquisitions—were insufficient to prevent conflict. At the national level, the easement mechanism illustrated the power of the mining sector and its links with the state. At the international level, the principles formulated by the ILO, such as the requirement for local participation, found reflection in the World Bank guidelines. Both sets of standards were applicable to the land purchase and resettlement plans. These international safeguards lacked precision for their application. "They are like the Bible," said the aforementioned former Antamina staffer, noting that there were multiple interpretations.

Cultural Translation, Catalysis, and Time

The monumental injection of resources and the changes brought about by the arrival of a transnational mining company can provoke and catalyze old conflicts, something that can be sharpened if the transformation occurs over a short period of time. Five years after Antamina won the concession, a campaign began to recall the mayor of San Marcos. According to him, the campaign reflected local appetite and the conflict that had arisen with the arrival of the mining project, together with resentment about the sale of land. It also reflected an exacerbation of historic disputes between family groups in the town.

Considering the size of the mining project, the number of families affected by construction of the infrastructure was small. "We, the resettled families, number just sixty-six. That is easy to accommodate," said the daughter of one displaced family who had moved to Chavín. Antamina's environmental impact statement identified fifty-five families to be relocated (286 individuals out of San Marcos's populations of 11,647, according to the 1993 census). Following the commissioning of a consultancy, eleven cases of noncompliance and one case of "vulnerability" (advanced age and adaptation problems) were added in accordance with the World Bank directive on involuntary resettlement (GRADE 2000).[10] According to this directive, the relocation of up to two hundred people constituted a small project (World Bank 1990:4). Ian Thomson Consulting (1999:2) concluded that Antamina had complied "extensively" with the involuntary resettlement directive and was "moving towards" complying with the Indigenous peoples directive. It also identified fives areas of noncompliance and recommended these be addressed. The presence of Antamina and the expectation of cash money from the displaced population generated local inflation, which was reflected in an increase in the value of scarce land in San Marcos (Ian Thomson Consulting 1999:11). Because of a deterioration in living standards, Ian Thomson Consulting further recommended the preparation of a development plan that would integrate both sets of World Bank directives. Given the enormous monetary investment, it is hard to believe that Antamina could not have managed its initial relationship with this small group better.

The scant understanding between the parties, exacerbated by asymmetries of resources and organization, catalyzed conflicts. The World Bank's guidelines, although nominally well-intentioned in their stated aim of addressing cultural differences, proved insufficient. They were too general and did not constitute a binding obligation on the company, especially in the context of the lack of training for employees and contractors. This was compounded by the limited information and resources available to local organizations to negotiate and monitor the process. Eliseo, a San Marcos municipal councilor, recalled the asymmetries in the purchase of land and argued that residents "should have asked us for legal advice" in the negotiation. He referred to the extant social and political distances between a more westernized and urban municipality and rural Indigenous communities.

The criticism extends to the mining company's communication policy and its relationship with the residents. Almost a year after the presentation of the environmental impact statement, the families affected by the displacement lacked precise information on the criteria to define which of them were eligible for resettlement. Antamina produced a nondisseminated document with the criteria eight months after the implementation of the Accelerated Resettlement Plan (GRADE 2000:13–14). Ian Thomson Consulting (1999:11) acknowledged the lack of foresight by Antamina was manifest in its deficient mechanism to resolve claims, despite this being a World Bank requirement. The mining company failed to anticipate this complexity and did not employ social specialists or ensure that its personnel and contractors were familiar with World Bank guidelines and understood the compliance requirements. An indicator of these deficiencies was that the Community Relations team for San Marcos consisted of just three engineers and was not formed until two years after the company's arrival. The first land purchase contacts were the responsibility of two civil engineers who had previously worked for Milpo mining company, owned by the family of Antamina's CEO between 1997 and 2003. A significant proportion of the personnel involved in the purchase of land and of the initial San Marcos Community Relations team came from Milpo (Salas 2002). They brought a corporate culture characterized by a reluctance to share information. This traditionally had been the pattern of behavior expected at old mining projects in Peru, especially those operated by nationally owned companies, which had little commitment to socioenvironmental concerns (see chapter 3).[11]

The World Bank admitted that the time variable was crucial in the relationship with Indigenous residents, who were not just vulnerable but also would be less able to find work or adjust to new occupations as they aged. Without specifying the parameters, the World Bank (1991:14g) emphasized the need for "long lead times" for the planning and monitoring of development projects for Indigenous populations. Walter Arensberg, former head of the IDB's environmental division, told me that a project to repair pipes in the Bronx in New York would require two years of consultation with the residents. Yet the time frame from the Antamina resettlement plan was reduced from one year to just three months. Time becomes a costly factor, particularly for a large modern mine located high in the mountains.

Antamina deployed technical experts for the exploration and lacked trained professionals to interact with local residents. The World Bank (1991:15h) indicated that the "monitoring units" of work with Indigenous populations should be "staffed by experienced social science professionals." CAO (2001:9–10) highlighted the lack of "anthropological expertise" at the beginning of the project required for "supervision" and "initial assessment" (World Bank 1991:19). Furthermore, Ian Thomson Consulting (1999:6) argued that only a few members of the Community Relations team were aware of the bank's guidelines and were only belatedly informed of the need to comply with them. It is therefore understandable that the division could not internally communicate the need for more time for the relocation. A former Community Relations staff member claimed that the perception of the Operations area staff was that they would arrive and find a "free and empty site." Community Relations personnel had to adapt their plans to the schedule of the Operations team. The short-term economic priorities were given greater weight than the risks presented by the untimely change of plans. This unleashed conflict. The mining company, as a social organization, had internal problems in understanding its environment, and establishing priorities, deadlines, and future costs.

Expectations of Reciprocity

"The key problem area for Antamina has been management of community expectations. There has been a wide range between what they thought they were communicating to the community, particularly regarding resettlement and distribution of benefits, and what the community understood they were going to receive and when" (CAO 2001:9). This is how CAO described the mismanagement of expectations by Antamina: a problem of interpretation that led to conflict. The people of San Marcos had assumed that Antamina would become a source of employment and a purchaser of local products that would provide sustained income to families and their descendants. There was reason to believe this. Personnel sent early on by Antamina, in particular temporary workers, had little incentive to manage the long-term consequences of their behavior. This led them to promise future employment as a way of encouraging local people to sell their land expeditiously and at a good price for the company.

The promise of work in the mine reinforced messages circulating in the national media and then echoed on local radio, the most accessible communication network in rural areas. Following privatization of the Centromin mines and the initial prospecting at Antamina, newspaper headlines fed old dreams of development and revived the myth of lifting the indigent from their golden bench, invoking the aforementioned statement attributed to Antonio Raimondi in the nineteenth century: "Peru is a beggar sitting on a bench of gold." A sample of headlines from *El Comercio*—Peru's oldest newspaper—from 1995 to 1997 shows the following: "Demand for 20 thousand new mine workers expected for coming years" (*El Comercio* 1995:E08); "Over the next ten years US$15 thousand million to be invested in mining" (*El Comercio* 1996a:A16); "Foreign investment growth in Peru of [253.91 percent]" (*El Comercio* 1996b:E01); and the celebratory "Antamina reserves almost triple" (*El Comercio* 1997: E02). The prime minister and the head of MEM, Alberto Pandolfi, summed up the hopes, stating that the mines would "generate important poles of development, a positive flow of foreign currency, improving our trade balance, generating job opportunities, and demand for products and services in their areas of influence . . . the most [economically] depressed areas in the country" (Ortiz 1997). Lucas summed up the impact of these media-fed expectations: "At the beginning, the big transaction for the Peruvian government was news for the area. . . . The population was satisfied that a private company would come and there would be work." These quotes evoke a return to an old myth of progress through mining in Peru (see chapter 4).

These offers seemed credible given the history of Gran Bretaña's Contonga mine and the exploration undertaken first by La Cerro and then subsequently by Minero Peru and Geomin in the Antamina area (see chapter 1). Contonga was the closest mining reference in local memory. More distant was the memory of the companies that explored Antamina. Many people from San Marcos had worked in Contonga and recalled that the company had purchased locally. Lazarus, former president of Ango Raju, told me, "The whole community and San Marcos have been expectant, because a mine brings development. . . . Because we had seen it previously with Contonga and Gran Bretaña, which brought work for people and business. Even bread, fruits, meat, potato [we would sell to Antamina], all these things that entered the mine [Contonga]. So we thought that Antamina would be like that too. We sold Contonga blankets, scarves, sweaters, ponchos of all kinds. . . . That was the people's expectation." Gran Bretaña workers moved to the Contonga mine with their families. In addition, at the start of operations, the farmers rented animals to transport the ore.

The environmental impact statement mentioned job offers and noted that there would "be employment opportunities, access to natural resources and public services" (KS 1998a:annex SE-II, p. 1; 1998b). Many San Marcos people recalled that job offers, occasionally written into the obligations recognition contracts, constituted a rhetoric to ensure the sale of their land: "They promised us wonders: 'You will have stable work, all your products will be bought.' So the people became excited and sold their pastures," recalled Lazarus. Huaripampa's generous welcome of Antamina and its willingness to sell land is understandable when the desire to obtain employment is added to the opportunity to sell local products. In the words of Francisco Vargas, the mayor of San Marcos, "Since the time of our grandparents there had been a lot of expectation about the mine. They knew that Antamina was a very large mine . . . and that there would be a lot of economic activity. We thought that it would provide a lot of jobs to many people, because the camp is near San Marcos and would accommodate many workers."

Huaripampa sold at the price offered by the company after a single meeting, while Ango Raju obtained a commitment under the contract with Antamina to use the trucks that the community would buy with the compensation. Huaripampa sold 43 percent of its land, including a crucial grazing area, preserving about three thousand hectares of land. Ango Raju sold all its pastures of the high puna—its entire livestock area. The residents of Huaripampa did not demand signed undertakings for the employment offered. This was surprising considering the Andean pattern of putting collective agreements in writing, which is almost a communal cult of stamped, signed, or fingerprinted paper, particularly where the other party is an external agent.[12]

When AMIDEP (1997a:11) visited Huaripampa two months before the negotiations for the land purchase, it summarized the social climate as follows: "They show a willingness to dialog and a great openness to the changes that will occur." The NGO located Huaripampa among the three locations with "better disposition to reach a concrete settlement with the company. They are willing, and have decided in a communal assembly, to cede part of their land in exchange for development aid" (AMIDEP 1997a:43). Ian Thomson Consulting (1999:20) noted that the locals "know that the mine is no Santa Claus." It is certainly true that they did not request gifts but instead sought an exchange of favors, or symbolic and material benefits. It was not due to mere charisma that an Antamina employee could come to have many godchildren in San Marcos. In the context of an expectation that the company would be an employer for several generations, a lower price for the land represented a consideration provided by the community to initiate a personalized reciprocity tie under the expectation of promised benefits sustained over time.

CAO (2001:4) concluded that the local expectations were a consequence of Antamina's "extensive consultations" during the preparation of the environmental impact study. It added, "This effort raised expectations in the local community to a high level that it would benefit directly from the mine, and set a high standard for transparency and communication." Antamina interpreted this problem as reciprocity within a negative and "paternalistic" framework. Antamina's own *Reportes de sostenibilidad* (sustainability reports), and a public presentation to investors on the principles of "community development" (May 30, 2002), highlighted the need "to avoid paternalism." It is sufficient to note here that a sample of families involved in the displacement showed that just over half (fifty out of ninety-seven) worked for subcontractors to Antamina (GRADE 2000:21). This was Antamina's way—occasionally or on a short-term basis—of fulfilling its obligation to those affected by the purchase of land, an aspect that tended to coincide with a decrease in protests. Chapter 4 examines the offer of employment and development projects to the populations close to the project. Reciprocity is in fact generally expected in exchanges and transactions that involve households and smallholders in diverse Andean contexts.

Local exchange practices coincided with business behaviors where a personalized relationship particularized through reciprocal ties prompts sustainable and secure bonds (see chapter 4). By accepting a relatively low price for their land, the people of San Marcos were offering a bond of reciprocity in the hope of special treatment from Antamina in the long term. The result, however, was no different to similar negotiations that had occurred throughout Peru's history—for example, those between the *hacendados* (landlords) and the Indigenous workers. Paternalism does not ensure the best outcome for the more vulnerable party because reciprocity and the limits of generosity reflect asymmetric power relations, where one party can fail to comply with its commitments and the other probably lacks the capacity to enforce compliance or sanction noncompliance.

The mining company behaved in a manner consistent with a contemporary, urban market operation: formally impersonal, time bound, and with a precise accounting based on the conditions at the moment of sale. Local logic, on the other hand, envisaged a long-term and personalized economic relationship. While it is possible for businesses to initiate ties of reciprocity, this condition is not implicit in formal and urban mercantile scenarios. From the perspective of the community, the land sale marked the beginning of a personalized and lasting reciprocity bond. This is not surprising for a small population more accustomed to small-scale business transactions and collective, face-to-face social control.

In a more urban and impersonal market encounter, completion of the transaction normally marks the end of the economic relationship. The legal contract indicates the terms of the transaction. The direct social bond is not implicit, although in practice an economic transaction can also initiate a social bond, including contractual renewals. Thus, local claims for "support" from the mining company can be understood, as in the example described to me by an Ango Raju community leader in reference to a communal enterprise: "In Antamina there are negative people who do not care about community development . . . and don't support us."

The low level of monetization in the Andean rural economy encouraged personalized economic reciprocity relationships, such as the exchange of labor or products. A farmer short of money depended on the labor of his or her social network for sowing and harvesting. In addition, labor- and product-exchange relationships, such as barter, operated as insurance against disasters (Mayer 2002).[13] Some economic principles regarding optimal negotiations contribute to an understanding of these negotiations. Huaripampa, the first community to negotiate, had less information than Ango Raju. Given that perfect information for a negotiation is improbable, especially when cultural distances are important, we can argue that Ango Raju had less imperfect information than Huaripampa. Changes to the resettlement plans further impoverished the information available for the residents.[14]

The abysmal asymmetry between the parties, manifest in Antamina's unilateral decision to accelerate completion of the displacement process, was better managed by the community of Ango Raju, which translated the vacuous invoking of corporate social responsibility into a commitment by the company to hire the vehicles the community intended to buy. The informality inherent in the concept of reciprocity tends to benefit the more powerful agent, which explains why the apparent offers of employment made by Antamina representatives proved impossible to enforce in the absence of a contract. Ezra, displaced from Ango Raju, expressed it this way: "They showed us a drawing of a beautiful house in San Marcos! They would give us a house apart from the money. They didn't sign anything, it was just their word. You don't need paper, nothing, they said. . . . I should have made a document" (grammar modified). As they were written commitments, Antamina did recognize the obligations recognition contracts. Although the company would subsequently consider it excessive, Antamina committed to acquire new land for Ango Raju in addition to the payment for the lands.

The Ango Raju community awoke in time to the importance of negotiating concrete formal limits to the reciprocity: "We formed a negotiation commission to see how far the land [purchase] could be negotiated. . . . We said, 'It's better not to sell,' and some of the less experienced in the community said, 'They will take the land for free, so we have to give [sell] it to them, they will take it from us.' We were afraid. [Antamina employee's name] made that threat. We signed the agreement in 1998, but the condition we set was that we would form a company in which we would work [with Antamina]. The condition of the sale was that it generate work." Written agreements are more applicable than verbal offers, especially when cultural differences and asymmetries of power are present.

Conclusion

The dramatic social change experienced by the people as a result of their displacement and relocation was exacerbated by Antamina's incomprehension of, or inattention to, the complex local system of access and landownership. The company also underestimated the vulnerability of displaced people needing to reproduce their livelihoods. The initially planned resettlement process became an accelerated, disorderly, and disruptive displacement. Changes in the speed of the resettlement plan ended up altering the nature of the program. Pressures from those in charge of Antamina's operations produced drastic changes in the design and relocation schedule. The new accelerated plan entailed modifications that distanced them from the World Bank's safeguards guidelines. This led to the abandonment of the land-for-land scheme advocated by the World Bank and its replacement with monetary compensation.

The criteria to identify who was affected, and to what degree, determined the identification of who was to receive compensation and what form that compensation would take. As in many Andean areas, access to land and pastures was embedded in the social structure, defined by exchanges and consanguinity and affinity networks. In this case, the nuclear families were grouped by consanguinity, and there were property patterns with arrangements of reciprocity between landowners and those with usufruct rights. Collective models based on social networks beyond the nuclear family reflected the multiple dynamics of work and access to land in the Andes. In San Marcos, the initial lack of definition of those who would be subject to compensation caused conflicts because of social hierarchies. When the company included landless *pastores* or *pasteadores* on the list of displacement compensation recipients, many landowners who did not live in the area claimed entitlement to the same amount of money as the aforementioned herders with usufruct rights. In order to distinguish the degree of impact and identify the subjects involved, it is fundamental to first understand the complexity in the patterns of property rights and access to resources associated with the productive organization—in this case, the highland livestock.

The World Bank provided general guidelines for preventing social conflicts but lacked real mechanisms for implementation. It recommended establishing criteria to facilitate compensation and to determine what requirements should be met by affected families in order to be able to benefit from resettlement. When assessing eligibility and valuation of different tenure types, it also recommended recognition for those with customary usufruct rights (World Bank 1990:3e, 17). The bank demanded a "socioeconomic survey" to identify the magnitude of the displaced population; the infrastructure affected; the resources, assets, and income affected; and attitudes toward relocation options (World Bank 1990:11). AMIDEP (1997a) indicated that the property rights of the land in the area were complex. The plurality of land access rights illustrated by the categorization of heads of household (individual owners, *comuneros*, tenants, feudatories, *condóminos*, and herders) proved insufficient to establish a compensation plan based on the census applied by the NGO. Given that the data was collected on just two dates, it could not reflect the seasonal patterns of some farming (AMIDEP 1997a, 1997b).

AMIDEP (1997a:6) pointed out that it was necessary to find out the local "socio-legal" reality to discover "who really lived and typically worked in the area," as well as to negotiate and establish a compensation policy for inhabitants, even if they did not own the land. It recognized that many legally "undivided" properties were, in practice, very much divided among descendants of familial "trunks." Likewise, many cultivated lands were exploited and owned in a de facto sense by each heir, but the pastures were kept undivided and all the heirs had usufruct rights. PETT state officials apparently relied on information from AMIDEP to rapidly complete the formalization of title without considering the complexities of the system. It is worth asking to what extent PETT wanted to or could have recognized this complexity.

Antamina merely followed the World Bank's recommendations at a superficial level, without really reflecting on the demands and concerns of the affected population. The resettlement plan, running to only five pages in the environmental impact statement, was a clear example. It lacked real mechanisms for implementation. In addition, temporary mining workers, contractors, and those directly responsible for preparing the environmental impact statement lacked the training to apply the bank's guidelines and felt no obligation to do so. The safeguards policies encountered serious limitations, such as a lack of available land of the size necessary to accommodate displaced families. The difference in the negotiation undertaken by the respective neighboring communities of Huaripampa and Ango Raju illustrates how cultural aspects, such as the level of organization or education (formal and informal), can account for different results. Antamina allocated insufficient time and resources to establish links with the locality and understand its complexity. This affected the outcomes and the company's ability to determine who would receive compensation and the amount that would be fair and sustainable.

Michael Cernea (2003:37) was hired in 1974 as the World Bank's first in-house "sociologist/anthropologist" and until 1997 served as the organization's "Senior Adviser for Social Policy." He collaborated in several of the bank's social safeguard policies, including the involuntary resettlement policy. Cernea has pointed out that in "developing countries," a vast number of displaced people ended up living in worse conditions than before the arrival of development projects. He shares the criticisms of compensation based on simple monetarized cost-benefit analyses and the absence of distributive evaluations of gains and losses among project stakeholders where displacement occurs (Cernea 2003). Cernea notes that one problem for organizations such as the World Bank arises from the impossibility of estimating in monetary terms the value of losses in social and human capital. He is supportive of contemporary approaches—that are not without complexities of definition and construction—that attempt to integrate fields such as economics, sociology, and anthropology in the search to conceptualize investment in the comprehensive development of displaced people, seeking to transcend mere financial compensation and aiming to reestablish their productivity and improve their livelihoods.

The evictions damaged the relationship between the company and the local people. The complaints were heard by the World Bank, leading to the arrival of external auditors that sought to dampen the local clamor. The conduct of the resettlement revealed both the lack of participation of local organizations, including the municipality or NGOs, and the absence of the state while displaying the powerful sociotechnologies of a large corporation. These corporate sociotechnologies allowed—virtually unilaterally—decisions affecting vulnerable citizens, including unconsulted changes in plans (e.g., the Accelerated Resettlement Plan) or merely conjured national regulations (e.g., easements) or international regulations (e.g., the World Bank's directives) for acquiring the land. To what extent the state could mediate and mitigate the oceanic asymmetry between the capacities of a large international corporation and those of Indigenous vulnerable or marginal citizens, through prevention or alleviation of conflicts, is something worthy of consideration. The World Bank's directives served more as an ex post resource for complaints rather than their supposed preventive purpose, due to their unclear binding or applicable mechanisms. In this case, the bank's directives acted mostly as rhetorical corporate sociotechnologies of appearance in relation to social risk prevention.

The displacement process also unveiled struggles within the company between the Operations and Community Relations areas. Staff dedicated to social issues within mining companies apparently have an increasing voice and are even able to suspend a project for short periods of time. The displacement of people, the problem that Antamina itself most clearly recognized during the initial phase of the project, led to external evaluations that contributed to understanding the complaints. These events taught Antamina several early lessons about cultural differences between a mining corporation and a local community. This social process demonstrated the complexity of resource-access systems and property rights and the vulnerability of local livelihoods, both insufficiently understood or recognized by Antamina. This chapter evidenced how imposed and unbalanced development can breed social actions for a learning process of political maturation. We shall follow these patterns in the next chapters, where I examine conflictive events that arose through the design of the mining operations in larger socioecological landscapes.

CHAPTER 3

A Pipeline to Save a National Park

Participation in the Environmental Impact Assessment

> *[H]igh in the mountains where the air is pure and subtle, one breathes more freely, one feels lighter in the body, more serene of mind; pleasures there are less intense, passions more moderate.*
>
> *. . . as one approaches ethereal spaces the soul contracts something of their inalterable purity.*
>
> —JEAN-JACQUES ROUSSEAU, 1761

THE MOUNTAIN INSTITUTE (TMI) ANDEAN PROGRAM DIRECTOR COULD NOT BELIEVE IT. HE shook his head as he tried to imagine something he was unable to accept. "There are a lot of trucks, too many trucks," he insisted with exasperation during the dramatic first meeting with Antamina in which both parties exchanged opinions about the potential impact of the mining project. The French philosopher Jean-Jacques Rousseau (1997:64 [1761]) wrote the lyrical opening epigraph about the Alps in the eighteenth century. It also was used in the *Mountain Protected Areas Update* (Hamilton 1998b), the newsletter of the Mountain Protected Areas Network—with more than 450 international expert members—in which Jane Pratt (1998), the then president and CEO of TMI, reported the risks Antamina posed to the Huascarán National Park. Both episodes reflect environmentalists' apprehension due to the company's announcement of transporting the ore through hundreds of daily round trips, crossing this natural protected area. This chapter identifies the socioenvironmental impact options contained in Antamina's initial design for transporting the ore through the park, which first triggered the alarms of environmentalists about the reserve's conservation. It unveils the way in which these concerns were addressed and, in particular, how the company's fear of damage to its image played a key role

FIGURE 7 Panoramic view of the Cordillera Blanca from Antamina. 2002. Author's photo.

in the strategy of environmental groups. It also reveals unexpected outcomes, including local opposition at the port of shipment following modification of the project design to protect the park, and the dialogue that arose among extractivists and environmentalists.

The chapter weaves together the complex and contested actions and events that the choice of transport alternative entailed, by contrasting contentious behaviors, perspectives, and group tactics to assess the advantages and disadvantages of moving ore across a natural protected area. The review of the social construction of a national park, as well as how public participation in mining gradually became accepted globally and in Peru, including an analysis of how public hearings for mining projects become central, all speak to a key issue: the importance of unexpected alliances, environmental organizations, and mediating bodies for the negotiation of alternative approaches.

The chapter traces the contentious decision-making process that led to the installation of a pipeline for the ore transportation. The episodes expose antagonistic visions and strategies, and in the last section, titled "Enacting Strategies," I provide an interpretation of the confronted schemes. I begin by depicting the globalized recognition of Huascarán National Park as a protected area facing anthropogenic risks. I next portray the debates for the ore transportation options based on Antamina's EIA. I then delineate the geographical challenge of the pipeline while discussing the company's safety rhetoric. By zooming out to the fabric of purported public participation in mining, I open the black box of a discussion of the extent that EIAs and consultation could offer some popular involvement while legitimizing the manipulation of nature. Zooming back to Antamina's EIA, I test its public hearings limits through the Habermasian deliberative model. Then I review the tactics used by environmentalists to level the playing field in the design negotiation process. The discussion of unexpected outcomes sets out the motivations of excluded groups at the port of shipment, including the dialogues between mining companies and groups more concerned about environmental sustainability. The epilogue of the failure of a technology that was purportedly safe highlights the limits to the rhetorics of EIA. Finally, I discuss the strategies that limited or enhanced each group participation in the project design. As we shall appreciate from the contentious process analyzed in this chapter, disputes can eviscerate or push limits for political participation.

Huascarán National Park

The highest Andean mountain ranges remained underrepresented in the state's protection model (see map 3). Over the period in question for this chapter—1997–1999—the state managed fifty-one natural protected areas covering approximately 9 percent of Peru's landmass. Only seven of these protected areas were national parks. Two decades later there were seventy-seven protected areas (fourteen national parks) covering 17 percent of the national territory. Of about twenty mountain ranges in Peru, only the Cordillera Blanca (or White Range, home to the Huascarán National Park) and part of the Cordillera Vilcabamba (the site of the historic sanctuary of Machu Picchu) were considered protected areas at the beginning of the twenty-first century (INRENA and SPDA 2002:180–190).

Huascarán National Park is a natural protected area. Its 340,000 hectares represent 0.26 percent of Peru's territory. The park is located between the Port of Huarmey and Antamina, thirty kilometers to the west of the mining operations (see map 1). Named after the highest peak in Peru, it spreads across ten provinces and ranges in elevation from 2,400 to 6,768 meters above sea level. The biological and cultural importance of the park was first acknowledged in the 1970s. The Peruvian government designated the area a national park in 1975 in an attempt to preserve the Cordillera Blanca, the world's highest and longest

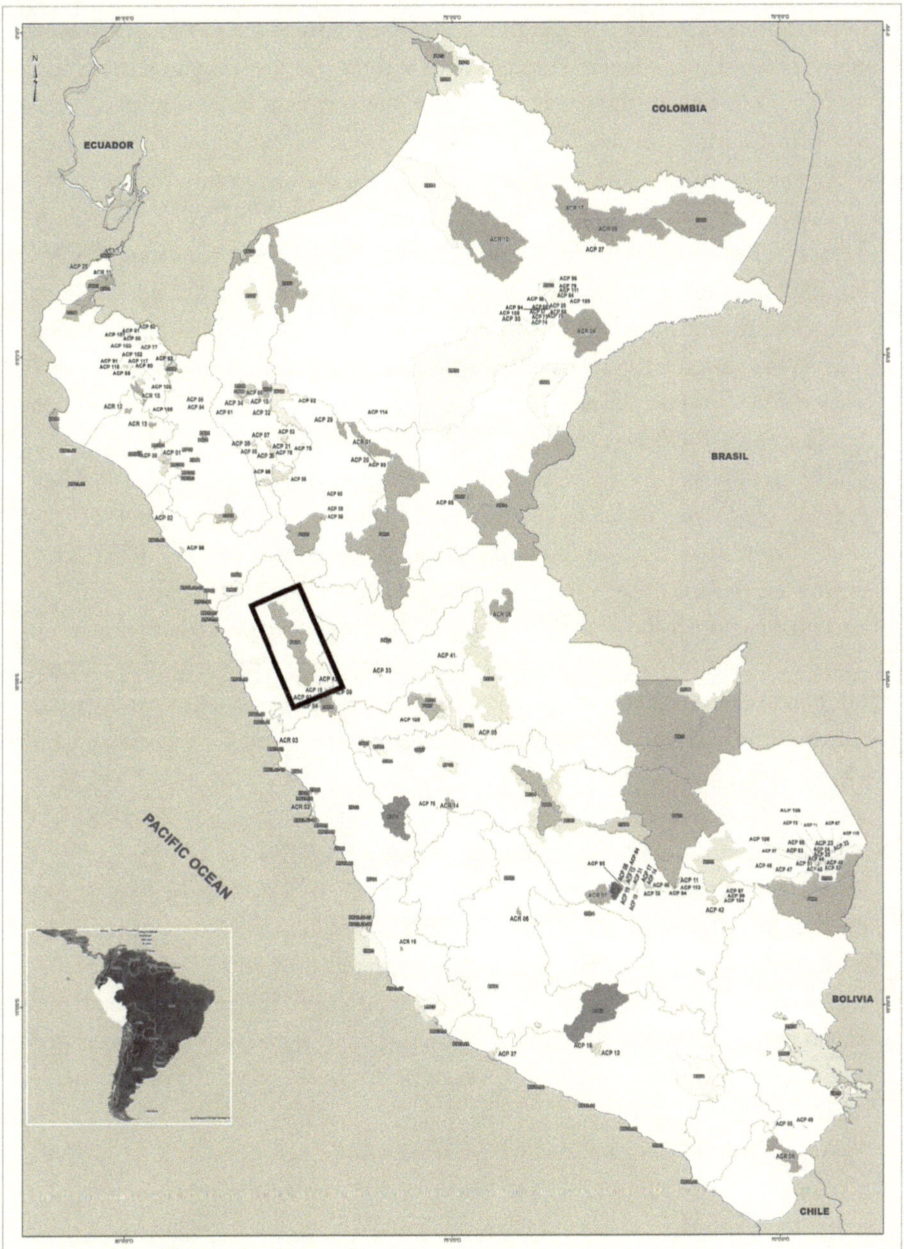

MAP 3 Natural protected areas and Huascarán National Park (box). Courtesy of the Servicio Nacional de Áreas Naturales Protegidas por el Estado (SERNANP). Source: SERNANP (2017) and INEI.

tropical mountain range. The park encompasses most of the Cordillera Blanca, which takes its name from the snow-capped peaks visible throughout the range. The state recognized the need to conserve the area's snowy peaks, archeological sites, and unique geological formations while at the same time allowing tourism to stimulate the local economy. The park was granted a second—international—layer of protection two years later, when UNESCO, through its Man and the Biosphere Programme, designated the area a biosphere reserve. In 1985 the area received a third layer of conservation, as a World Heritage site, to safeguard its scenic beauty and ecological systems. This international recognition commits Peru to protect the park's ecological resources, promote sustainable economic development in adjacent areas, and administer the site in accordance with UNESCO guidelines (K&H 1999a).

The natural beauty of the area was first appreciated by Europeans when Spanish conquistadors led by Hernando Pizarro, brother of conquistador Francisco Pizarro, saw the Cordillera Blanca in January 1533 (Ricker 1981:2). Following the capture of the Inca emperor Atahualpa, in Cajamarca, Francisco had sent his brother to speed the gathering of the fabulous gold and silver ransom offered by Atahualpa in exchange for his release. In the course of the journey, Hernando and his companions reported that "there are mines in many parts" (Bebbington and Bury 2013; Markham 1872:121). The same year, Pedro Sancho, a secretary of Francisco Pizarro, described the mountain range as a vision from a dream (Dourojeanni and Ponce 1978:62). The Spaniards scaled the peaks and placed crosses to mark their religious conquest, motivated also by a fervent secular search for mineral wealth (Echevarría 1981). Three hundred years after the first expeditions by the Pizarros, the liberator Simón Bolívar sent troops to traverse this same landscape. The rugged geography bore witness to later battles and persecutions. Andrés Avelino Cáceres, the Wizard of the Andes, exploited his knowledge of secret passageways between the craggy mountainsides in the cordillera to gain advantage over Chilean troops during the War of the Pacific (1879–1883).

Antonio Raimondi, credited with the scientific discovery of the exotic Puya plant (family Bromeliaceae) that bears his name, was the first to study the Cordillera Blanca from a more scientific perspective (Dourojeanni and Ponce 1978). He looked in detail at the cordillera's geology and flora but never visited the high alpine valleys. Systematic study of the alpine region had to wait until the twentieth century. Mountaineers attempting to scale Huascarán and other snowcapped peaks had by this time become the most frequent visitors observing the beauty of the Cordillera Blanca. The following passage, taken from a collection for mountaineers and travelers written by Canadian geologist and zoologist John Ricker (1981:1), exemplifies the lyricism that the area evokes: "Delicately corniced snow ridges and fluted ice faces make the Cordillera Blanca as fanciful in reality as in legend. . . . To view the changing hues of such ethereal snow formations is to transfigure the soul. To wander once in such enchanting surroundings is to be captive for life." Huascarán National Park's international recognition since the end of Peru's internal armed conflict in the latter part of the twentieth century can be measured by the annual number of visitors, which grew from 22,000 in 1989 to 91,000 in 1995 (TMI 1996), before reaching 123,000 by the turn of the century, and more than 180,000 in 2014 (Botts et al. 2001).

The park's geography includes 27 snow-capped peaks surpassing 6,000 meters in altitude, 663 summits, 296 lakes, and 41 rivers providing water to the farmers and cities downstream. The park's biodiversity is exceptionally rich and fragile. Its 3,000 square kilometers shelter 111 species of birds, 13 species of mammals, 2 species of reptile, and 779 flowing plant species. The latter include the extraordinary Puya Raimondi, the world's tallest flowering bromeliad. This plant reaches 12 meters in height, boasts a unique inflorescence, and only grows in Bolivia and Peru, at altitudes over 3,800 meters. Several of the species in the park are considered endemic and endangered (Pulido 1991). The park contains one of the last remaining *queñoa* (*Polylepis spp.*) forests. This native tree, which strengthens the soil and prevents landslides, covered the Andes in pre-Hispanic times. Few of the world's mountain ranges are as archaeologically rich as the Cordillera Blanca, which contains vestiges of at least four pre-Hispanic civilizations. Ancient terraces, temples, and irrigation systems are silent witnesses to great agricultural achievements. Probably the most spectacular remnant left by these ancient peoples is the archaeological complex of Chavín de Huántar, located in the town that bears its name and adjacent to the district of San Marcos—home to the Antamina mine site. It is one of the largest sites of Andean civilization and is considered one of the most important (Burger 1992).

Even prior to the establishment of Antamina, competing interests in resource use and ecosystem sustainability had generated latent conflicts in the park. The tensions included the impact of agricultural activities, intensive tourism in areas such as the Pastoruri snowfields, and the overgrazing of pastures by forty-three thousand head of livestock from neighboring communities. A lack of personnel and other resources to manage the park exacerbated this situation (Botts et al.

2001). The establishment of Huascarán National Park in 1975 sparked conflict between residents and state authorities. The first staff members were greeted with rocks thrown by inhabitants fearing state expropriation (Schmidt 1999). Three decades later, INRENA (Instituto Nacional de Recursos Naturales, or the National Institute of Natural Resources) reported the existence of sixty natural pasture–use committees who were grazing livestock and collecting firewood and medicinal plants (INRENA 2003:32). These groups chose their own authorities and were autonomous from the park. In exchange for using the protected area, the committees were required to register their cattle and contribute to reforestation by planting seeds provided by the park (Schmidt 1999). The park's response claims to harmonize conservation efforts with economic development in order "to protect world-class biological values and landscapes that are critical to the sustainable economic development of endless future generations" (Botts et al. 2001:6). The park currently maintains an inventory of archaeological sites and regulates its number of visitors.

Huascarán National Park includes the land of Indigenous communities who live in poverty and have attracted the interest of international organizations. Among the first to arrive was the University of Calgary in 1990 with Canadian government funding to design the park's master plan. Six years later TMI designed the park's tourism and recreational use plan with support from USAID and the Dutch embassy. Ultimately TMI was to play a crucial role in the design of the Antamina mine and, in particular, the choice of transport option for the ore the mine produced, as detailed in this chapter. Initially named the Woodlands Institute, TMI was founded in West Virginia in 1972 as a "conservation-based education and outdoor adventure company" for the appreciation of nature in the Appalachian Mountains. The organization evolved into an international association seeking to "advance mountain cultures and preserve mountain environments in the longest, oldest mountain ranges in the world" (TMI 2002:4). Its internationalization began with the opening of an office in Nepal in 1987 focused on protected areas in the Himalayas. The organization established an Andean program in 1994, aiming to support projects in the Huascarán National Park in collaboration with the park's authorities and local residents. TMI presents itself as a global institution that serves both mountain ecosystems and the communities that inhabit them, "supporting global networks as well as range-based programs in the Himalayas, Appalachians, and Andes" (Pratt 2001:39). In 2002 the institute established its international headquarters in Washington, D.C.[1]

Although Peruvian law prohibits mining activities inside the park, licenses granted prior to its establishment are exempt. While prior to the 1990s there were few small-scale legal mining operations inside the park, the risks from mining for the socioecosystemic viability of the park began to increase due to large mining concessions in the surrounding areas. Threats to the ecosystems, such as decades-old discarded smelting ovens and abandoned tailing ponds, had been discovered. The Japanese multinational Mitsui Mining and its Peruvian company had been operating the Santa Luisa mine to the east of the park since the 1970s, and during the 1980s had used roads inside the protected area. In 1990 six mining licenses were in use and ten were dormant. Together with overgrazing, the Santa Luisa mine had been the greatest threat to the area up until the mid-1990s. Its operations polluted the Vizcarra and Huallanca Rivers, and the mining vehicles generated dust pollution, as did tourist buses traveling to Puya Raimondi and the snow-capped Pastoruri. The establishment of the large-scale Pierina and Antamina mining projects in the buffer zone of the park's biosphere reserve in 1997 marked the start of mining infrastructure development in the Ancash Department that posed a serious threat to the protected area.[2] By 2001 there were fifty-nine mines and old prospecting sites, seventeen of which were situated within already existing mining concessions (INRENA 2003:56–57). The government was under pressure to revive old mines and issue new licenses (INRENA 2003), and several environmental organizations had recognized the need to monitor those mines established prior to the creation of the park.

Ore Transport Alternatives

In 1998, two years after winning the concession, Antamina presented the EIA. Although a pipeline would ultimately be chosen as the preferred alternative to transport ore to the port facilities at Huarmey (K&H 1998; KS 1998b), the assessment initially also considered a rail option and a road option. The company rejected the rail option, stating that it was unable to identify a feasible route—among three—"short enough to be constructed at a reasonable cost" (KS 1998b:9). According to the EIA, since trains cannot efficiently ascend slopes with a gradient in excess of 1 percent, the topography would have meant a route that skirted the sides of mountains and required the construction of tunnels and the creation of immense fill zones in the valleys (KS 1998b:9). The 304-kilometer pipeline option, which entailed transporting the ore after mixing it with water, was also initially ruled out because of the company's concerns about construction and operational costs. Antamina also considered a pipeline crossing the park to be among several "critical unfavorable environmental and operational factors" (KS 1998b:10, 11).[3]

The trucking alternative received Antamina's initial backing. It would have entailed three consecutive sections: an 83-kilometer section from Huarmey to Pativilca along the Pan-American Highway, a 122-kilometer section from Pativilca to Conococha along the highway from Pativilca to Huaraz, and a section from Conococha to Antamina. This would require the construction of new roads and improvements to secondary roads. The final section contained three possible alternatives, all departing from Conococha (see map 4): the northern route (Catac–Machac–Canrash Lagoon–Antamina), 157 kilometers in length; the central route (Antarraga–Huanzalá–Canrash Lagoon–Antamina), 146 kilometers; and the southern route (Mojón–Suyán–Huanzalá–Canrash Lagoon–Antamina), 133 kilometers (with 70 kilometers of new road).

The principal arguments against the northern route were that it traversed the park and that the steep, rugged mountain terrain made it expensive. The proposed southern route ran at elevations below 3,048 meters, but it required the construction of a highway around the park, a factor that would make it seventeen kilometers longer than the central route. The proximity to a nearby town would increase the risk of road accidents. Other factors included potential slope stability risks, the increased time to establish running operations, and the threat of landslides during the rainy season. Although it did not provide figures, the EIA report concluded that "the direct cost of capital" for the southern and central routes was "almost equal." As Antamina initially opted for the central route, it can be assumed that the small difference in cost, together with the time savings, were sufficiently important for the company (KS 1998b:14).

Antamina's design—approved by the World Bank's MIGA—involved expanding and paving an existing dirt road (*Ruta Central*, or central route), entailing the construction of a new highway that would cut through the middle of the park (see map 4). The route would first connect the mine to Huanzalá and then join the preexisting paved highway between Huaraz and Pativilca. Antamina committed to comply with all relevant environmental, health, and security standards set by the governments of Peru and Canada, and by the World Bank (Botts et al. 2001). The main risk to the park's ecosystems posed by the central route would have been the 145 daily round trips made by heavy vehicles. These would weigh thirty-five to fifty tons, depart every 7.5 minutes, and cross the

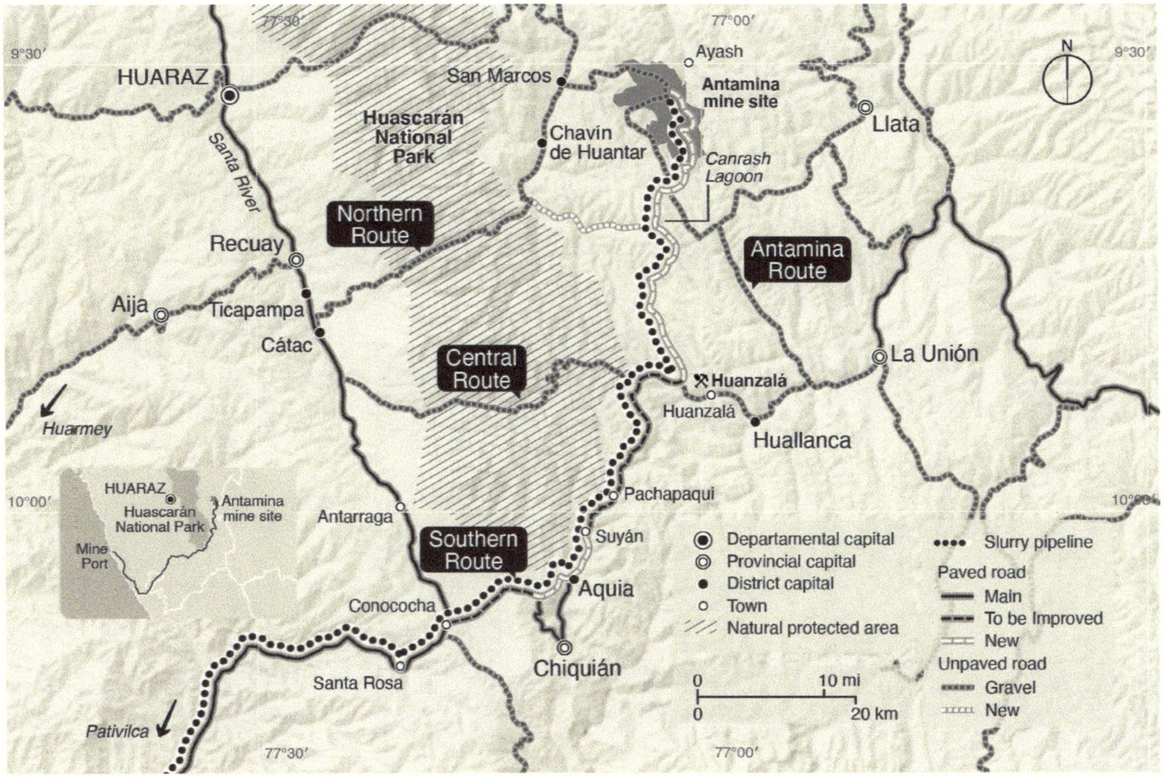

MAP 4 Possible trucking routes considered in 1998–1999 and the pipeline route ultimately selected. Prepared by the author based on information from InfoMine Inc. and Antamina. Cartography by Grupo GeoGraphos.

center of the park twenty-four hours a day. They would transport 1.5 million tons of ore annually over a period of more than twenty years. During the construction phase alone, approximately 10,000 trucks passed through the park. The company contracted around seven hundred drivers for its fleet of nearly 250 trucks (Zavaleta 1998a). The risk of accidents such as rollovers or crashes in the steep Andean slopes was high, given the frequency of trips along a route where, judging by the quantity of debris from wrecked cars, mishaps were common.[4] This option would have meant transplanting part of the remaining population of Puyas and affecting the habitat of the vicuñas (*Vicugna vicugna*) (INRENA 2003:45). It would have also entailed high maintenance and fuel costs and the risk of mechanical breakdowns at hard-to-reach points along the road. Finally, it would have sparked acts of sabotage. Antamina provided assurances that the central route "would have only minor effects in the park" (KS 1998b:14, 84).

In assessing the three ore transport alternatives (train, pipeline, or truck), the EIA aimed to "achieve an equilibrium between cost and acceptable environmental protection, health, and security standards" (KS 1998b:9). Antamina invoked and stressed the engineering and environmental costs—supposedly controlled—to justify a road through the heart of the protected area following the central route (KS 1998b:15). TMI, on the other hand, pushed for conservation of the park's ecosystems as a prerequisite for any long-term development. Lacking its own personnel to review the environmental impact statement, the NGO engaged two Canadian volunteers sourced from the Canadian Executive Service Organization. These experts reviewed—from a technical perspective—the specialized information contained in the environmental impact statement's nearly one thousand pages. TMI allocated resources from its budget for the debate process. Two team members—including the director—studied the environmental impact statement over a period of one year. While TMI favored the southern route around the park, Antamina dismissed the option, citing the slope instability that would be caused by the construction and the potential impact on the Chiquián population (KS 1998b).

Antamina also argued that a route through the center of the park would have a positive impact on tourism through the construction of parking areas and lookouts and the sealing of the road that would reduce travel times. The company stressed that paving the road would minimize the dust particles that affect flora, fauna, and glaciers. Its EIA recognized that "due to dust, among other factors, glaciers like Pastoruri, a tourist attraction, are melting" (KS 1998b:17, 18). Curiously, the EIA failed to mention that these "other factors" can include fossil fuel emissions that would have risen with the increased frequency of the transit of mining vehicles. The EIA pointed to the existence of highways in national parks in the industrialized world, such as Canada's Banff National Park. When contacted by TMI, however, the director of that park stated that its roads were having a major overall impact and causing particular problems such as roadkill. TMI's Andean director concluded that "the highway was an insult to the park" (Schmidt 1999:71). The rhetorical tone of the environmental impact statement is optimistic and plays down or conceals the socioenvironmental costs; for example, it suggests that "an indirect effect of the higher number of accidents that result in animal deaths is the possible increase of scavengers, particularly endangered species such as the Andean condor" (KS 1998a:chapter 6, p. 56). The generally confident and positive language contained in the EIA report sought to portray the company as capable of controlling major environmental changes, and to make the case that the benefits of the project greatly exceeded the potential costs.

For environmentalists, on the other hand, the permanent presence of heavy vehicle traffic would jeopardize the "future existence of the park as such or at least its World Heritage Site status" (Botts et al. 2001:11). The dust and noise produced and the potential for accidents represented a threat that would disrupt the habitat of several endangered species. Individual conservationists and organizations also feared that the central route would set a dangerous precedent with the potential to awaken latent threats to the preservation of the park's ecosystems, such as hydroelectric dams, new roads to the Amazon, and the expansion of thirteen legally operating small mines (Botts et al. 2001). For TMI the risk of environmental degradation in the region threatened the results of its five years of work. Its Andean program director, Jorge Recharte, told me during an interview, "We feel that our work, the investment of several years in Huascarán National Park, is being personally threatened." He was quick to assure that TMI never claimed its position on the central route was representative of views of the communities with whom it worked. He also claimed that as an institution, TMI sought a balance between conservation and the sustainable development of the area: "The future of the mountains is in the hands of the people. It is the local people who make the decisions and implement development processes. . . . Our ability to be able to involve communities at that time was minimal . . . but in the long term, our approach seeks to consistently strengthen local capacities. Sustainable development requires strengthening local capacities."

Thus, there were two distinct visions for the park's future. Conservation groups regarded the park's ecosystems and landscapes as development priorities and were fearful of the central route. For Antamina, on the other hand, fears about the central route were "narrowly focused on technical issues concerning the physical nature of road impacts" (Botts et al. 2001:11). The dimension and scale of impact were debated as rhetorical tools. Antamina sought to focus the discussion more narrowly, on the proposed highway's tangible benefits and the way in which paving it would produce insignificant and manageable impacts. Its strategy aimed to avoid examining the impact of mining on fragile and highly interactive ecosystems, thus minimizing responsibilities on ecosystemic levels. With careful use of language, it focused instead on a mere object—the highway—without acknowledging the multiple uncontrollable effects that major infrastructure activity generates. A rhetoric that imagined targeted and controlled change—despite the fact that hundreds of trucks would have transited close to the habitat of delicate species—is also hard to believe: "Improvements to the central route will widen the road and the shoulder. . . . These changes will cause a *localized loss* of wild habitat, and of flora and fauna. . . . Antamina proposes to transplant and/or cultivate Puya Raimondi and other species of flora and fauna. . . . No long-term impact is predicted for Puya Raimondi and other species of flora and fauna" (KS 1998b:18, emphasis added). Yet the EIA acknowledged that the central route would approach "restricted zones intended to protect the vicuña and the Puya Raimondi" (K&H 1998:58).

Ultimately, the slurry pipeline would prove to be the mining company's preferred option. Although it would carry higher up-front costs, the financial backers favored it because it was consistent with their sustainability criteria (Pratt 2001:40, 41). A former Antamina official told me how the company valued the pipeline's low maintenance cost in the long-run cost-benefit analysis: "TMI's participation contributed to the final decision: first, the use of a pipeline instead of the trucks, and second, for it to go around the park. However, this is also the most economical solution. The pipeline had a much higher up-front capital cost, but the maintenance cost is very low." Resolution of the dispute over transport options required Antamina to strategically incorporate the stated concerns of several stakeholders about the impact on Huascarán National Park into the mine design (Botts et al. 2001).

MEM expeditiously reviewed and endorsed the EIA in March 1998. Formal government approval was granted seven months later. The rapid approval suggests that MEM received no substantive objections from public consultations and that the government, more broadly, was anxious to proceed. This speed reflected the extent to which the mandatory public hearings—far from being a referendum, as demanded in later projects such as Tambogrande—were merely informative. The rapid endorsement probably echoed government eagerness to access foreign currency and begin receiving taxation income. It is a reminder of how dependent the Peruvian state is on natural resource extraction for scarce foreign exchange and revenues, and the way the legal framework is adapted to facilitate immediate exploitation.

The EIA evolved in its treatment of the spatial scale of the impacts. Antamina's initial explanation for the road relied on a discourse focused on isolated road impacts. This later became more permeable, referring instead to larger spatial and temporal dimensions. There is a clear turning point. Following a change in Antamina ownership, addendas 2 and 3 to the environmental impact statement were prepared by a different consultancy firm from the one that had prepared the main report and the first addenda. For example, the environmental impact statement initially preferred the term *concentraducto* (ore duct) instead of *mineroducto* (mineral duct). The former directs attention away from extraction activities and toward the transported material. The language intermittently changed to *mineroducto* in the latter stages of the EIA process, following replacement of the consulting firm preparing the reports (K&H 1999a). Two examples illustrate a clear progression. Firstly, toward the end of the process, the concept of *confiabilidad* (reliability) was emphasized as a key factor for the "long-term economic viability of the project" (K&H 1999b:5). Secondly, Antamina came to recognize that in environmental and engineering terms, the investment in a pipeline would bring greater long-term payoffs when viewed in a broader context. "Until recently, it was usual for mines all around the world to transport minerals by truck. . . . This method has become less viable due to the volumes of concentrate, transport distances, and capital and operational costs. With the arrival of more advanced technology . . . a pipeline is considered a better alternative to mineral transported by truck, from an economic, environmental, and socioeconomic perspective" (K&H 1999a:E5). In the end, the long term was redefined by investors to include additional risks. As TMI president Jane Pratt explained, the organization stressed the accident and operational cost risks and attempted to translate these impacts into Antamina's "own economic interest" (Pratt 2001:40). At high altitudes, fuel costs would increase, the trucks would need constant maintenance, and breakdowns would be difficult to attend.

Pipeline Challenges

The uneven topography of the Andes and the complex social setting presented unique challenges. The engineering would need to tackle dramatic cliffs and slopes, and agreements would need to be struck to avoid major conflict along the route. The environmental impact statement confirms that most of the land along the proposed pipeline belonged to peasant communities (K&H 1999b:103). Antamina purchased six-meter plots to bury the pipeline. During long meetings, the company negotiated access rights and purchase prices. It distributed written materials and photographs that sought to prepare the inhabitants for the shock that the enormous machines excavating agricultural lands might cause. Several modifications to the route were made following the discovery of archaeological sites. Some towns were bypassed because landowners either refused to sell or demanded too much money.[5] The installation included the ore tube, pipe control systems, telecommunications, obstruction and leakage detection stations, and storage tanks at the mine and the port, as well as three pump stations and four valve stations (with four wells for ore separation in case of a flow stoppage) (K&H 1999b:8).

The pipeline is a 304-kilometers long subterranean steel tube transporting copper and zinc ore mixed with water to the port in Huarmey, from where the material is loaded onto ships for export (see figure 8). It has an annual concentrate transport capacity of 2.5 million tons. A French-Peruvian consortium took one year to construct the pipeline system, which required an investment of $140 million (CMA 2000). A crew of more than five hundred employees working in several camps was necessary (K&H 1999b:13). As the pipeline traverses the Andean mountains, a pumping station is necessary to move the concentrate upward, combining with gravity to move it to the coast. Four high-pressure pumps and four valve stations were installed to reduce the force produced by the fall in gradient from the Andes to its final station at the port (CMA 2003b). The mineral duct follows the southern route from the mine to Lake Conococha and then continues beside the state highway system to the port (see map 4). Seventy percent of the pipeline is buried next to a ditch designed to protect it from Andean mudslides. The environmental impact statement stated that the route was chosen to avoid "biologically sensitive areas" and limit construction within one hundred meters of lakefronts, except where it was necessary to avoid wildlife habitats. The pipeline traverses dunes along the coast and communal agricultural lands in the Fortaleza Valley. Where the pipeline encounters a river,

FIGURE 8 The Antamina pipeline and a ship loading ore in Huarmey. 2002. Author's photo.

in most cases it runs underneath the riverbed, but in some instances it crosses the water itself.

Advanced technology was necessary, particularly for the real-time monitoring of its long trajectory. The EIA report asserted that all disaster scenarios were covered. The copper and zinc ore forms pulp for transport. A fiber-optic network runs parallel to the tube. This filament sends constant data about the passage of the ore. Antamina estimated the lifetime of the mineral duct to be approximately thirty years. It is purportedly designed to resist pressure of two hundred bar, including earthquakes up to grade eight on the modified Mercalli scale. According to the mining company's narrative, a failure at a valve station or a leakage in the pipeline would trigger an alert with the Emergency Response Team (K&H 1999b:89). Any spill generating a drop in pressure would be instantly communicated to the operator at the mine site, who could close any or all parts of the mineral duct. The EIA report also stated that residents downstream would be immediately notified of any leak. It did acknowledge, briefly, that "[a] rupture to the pipeline could have serious consequences for the receiving environment . . . particularly to agriculture, water sources, and the quality of potable water found downstream" (K&H 1999b:114–115). One of the greatest risks posed by leakage in a pipeline is the mixing of ore into water currents.

Participation in Environmental Impact Assessments

Globally, three parallel change processes have contributed to the expansion of participation by social groups in the mining industry. The first was the signature of international agreements and the creation of bodies to protect the rights of Indigenous peoples. These included the ILO's Convention 169 (1989), the UN Working Group on Indigenous Populations (1982), the UN Declaration of the Rights of Indigenous Peoples (2007), and the Organization of American States Declaration on the Rights of Indigenous Peoples (2016, drafted seventeen years earlier). The second was the rise of Indigenous movements and NGOs working to protect and advance the rights of Indigenous groups. The third was the institutionalization of EIAs for large-scale mining operations and the inclusion of neighboring communities as stakeholders in these evaluations (Vanclay and Bronstein 1995). These developments changed the previous binary relationship between states and corporations. It opened the process to populations situated over or near resource deposits who generally lack the proper skills to engage in negotiations that are typically unequal and complex. Nonetheless, the state remains a key player, regulating the entry of companies and providing standards for managing socioenvironmental impacts. The EIA is a tool that legitimizes the manipulation of nature on the assumption that controlled effects can be mitigated or compensated.

The EIA as a requirement in mining resource exploitation has its antecedents in US Environmental Protection Agency protocols, the Rio de Janeiro Declaration, and the Agenda 21 agreement. The United States formalized environmental evaluations at the federal level in 1969 through the National Environmental Policy Act. This aimed to improve the administrative procedures and the quality of environmental and social decisions (Pulgar-Vidal and Aurazo 2003). The European Economic Community adopted similar regulations in 1985. The UN Conference on Environment and Development held in Rio de Janeiro in 1992 established that environmental issues are best handled with the participation of national and international citizens. The Rio Declaration on Environment and Development (Principle 10) recognized the value of information. As part of the same event, Agenda 21 encouraged governments to expand public participation while emphasizing the delicate and interdependent relationships between the environment, sustainable development, and the well-being of Indigenous peoples. The obligatory inclusion of citizens in socioenvironmental assessment processes for mining, together with their designation as stakeholders, can be interpreted as a democratized product that also responds to the fears of investors about socioenvironmental contentions or sanctions. With an eye to its own profit motive, a mining company broadens the scope of local participation as an investment in preventing costly conflict with affected groups.

Since the 1980s, several Latin American countries have adopted legislation supporting public participation in natural resource–management issues. The institutionalization of EIAs initially responded to the fulfilment of the loan requirements of multilateral financial institutions, leading to an emphasis on the presentation of environmental impact reports rather than the procedures for broadening participation in public decision-making processes (Pulgar-Vidal and Aurazo 2003). In Peru, multinational petroleum companies began to take environmental and social concerns into consideration in their Amazon projects during the 1980s. International NGOs, such as Conservation International, also influenced the work of these businesses to avoid or mitigate the impact on nature and Indigenous populations. The evolution of environmental protection processes marked the beginning of a presence by local groups in the development of mining projects (see chapter 5). Although there was little visible national demand for these safeguard processes—apart from a few environmental NGOs, such as the ones that collaborated in work leading to the development of the 1990 Environment Code, which introduced impact assessments for mining projects—international financiers pressured for their inclusion, seeking a guarantee for their investments.

In 1991, along with the other laws to promote mining investment, the Peruvian state adopted an EIA requirement. These mandated EIA and public hearings for the development of any major new project and any expansion of more than 50 percent to any existing operation in the energy and mining sectors. They also included external audits, closure plans, and PAMAs (Programas de Adecuación y Mitigación Ambiental, or Environmental Remediation and Management Programs) for working operations (Glave and Kuramoto 2002). Under PAMAs, existing mines were given five years to meet emissions and environmental standards, and refineries were given ten. The EIA and PAMAs were instruments executed by private companies under MEM supervision; environmental monitoring was thus oriented toward privatization (Glave and Kuramoto 2002). Also in 1991, the Framework Law for the Growth of Private Investment established ministries as the competent sectoral authorities for environmental matters, raising claims due to conflicts of interest. MEM, who has the mandate to promote mining, also became responsible for dictating standards of environmental protection and control for this extractive activity and for approving EIAs. Only after about a quarter-century, late in 2015, the Ministry of Environment—through SENACE—was given responsibility for approving the EIA of mining activities.

The state presented the EIA as a tool capable of preventing major negative environmental impacts through an evaluation of physical, biological, cultural, and socioeconomic factors. The EIA seeks to establish means of preventing and mitigating impacts and to develop an exit plan following the closure of operations to avoid adverse long-term effects. EIA rhetoric aims to convince the public that it is possible to develop mining operations in harmony with the environment. An EIA has three components: a description of baseline conditions, the proposed means of prevention and mitigation of any negative effects, and an exit plan. The existing settings are characterized as follows: soils, geology, hydrology, physiography, archaeology, socioeconomic factors, terrestrial and aquatic biology, and surface and subterranean water quality. Antamina admitted that it did not aim to take a complete inventory of conditions according to these categories, but rather to identify ecosystem types and existing environmental conditions in order to apply "appropriate protection" with "environmental control and mitigation measures" (KS 1998b:4). The discourse of EIAs promises mining developing without major negative environmental effects.[6] Antamina synthesized this audit culture rhetoric, emphasizing the control of impacts through "monitoring programs" designed to prevent and mitigate environmental effects:

> To summarize, the analysis of the potential impacts consists of evaluating changes predicted in existing environmental conditions as a result of the implementation of project components. It identifies potential environmental effects during each state of the project (construction, exploitation, closure and post-closure) and compares the magnitude of predicted changes with determined criteria, which define what constitutes a significant [negative] impact. It develops environmental controls and strategies for mitigation and identifies potential residual impacts. Through monitoring programs that will begin in the construction stage and continue until the post-closure stage, it will determine if the predictions of "no significant impact" are correct. (KS 1998b:4)

The influence of multilateral financial agencies that promoted the framework for private investment helps us understand the establishment of the regulations related to public participation in environmental issues. The IMF and the World

Bank were the first multilateral agencies to encourage Peruvian policy makers to support the mining sector and increase citizen participation. The latter became a fundamental right in the 1993 Constitution (article 2). Under the principle that loans and technical assistance were partially contingent on environmental regulations, in the same year, the World Bank's Energy and Mining Technical Assistance Loan implemented a $12 million, three-year project to assist MEM in developing a clear regulatory structure for environmental protection (Schmidt 1999). This led to the creation of an environmental monitoring system, dependent on the private sector via a panel of environmental audit firms. Simultaneously, the Peruvian Congress ratified ILO Convention 169, although implementation would be delayed until the 2011 approval of Law 29785 on the Right of Indigenous or Native Peoples to Prior Consultation. Indigenous organizations, NGOs, and the Peruvian ombudsman called for approval of a consultation law following the tragic events in the Amazon town of Bagua in 2009 (see the introduction). The ILO convention empowers Indigenous groups: where underground resources belong to the state, it requires the government to establish consultation procedures prior to any exploration or exploitation of resources contained on their land and to ensure that they receive compensation and a share of the profits (ILO 1989:article 15).

In 1996 MEM formalized the requirements for public participation in the EIA. However, this was limited by four factors that did have partial advances—especially in terms of locations, concerns addressed, and prior consultation—in the years that followed. First, regardless of where the project was located, the public hearings were held in Lima, making attendance by affected communities virtually impossible. Second, only preregistered participants could receive information, which was in any case limited to the executive summary only. Third, the complete environmental impact statement could only be accessed at MEM's offices in Lima. Finally, the regulations did not clarify how the government or industry should address or incorporate concerns raised during the hearings. Three years later, the Regulation for Citizen Participation in the Process of Approval of EIA represented a step forward by requiring the public hearing to take place at the project location.[7] It did not, however, consider that the area of influence could encompass several districts. The 2002 Regulation for Consultation and Citizen Participation in the Process of Approval of Environmental Studies in the Energy and Mines Sector required the government to locate the public hearing in a place that takes into account the population center closest to the project and to time the event to maximize attendance.[8] Depending on the scale of the mine and its impact, MEM could program multiple hearings in different locations. In 2005 the General Environment Act (Law 28611, article 3) declared the universal right of citizens to "participate in the decision-making processes, as well as in the definition and application of the policies and official measures relating to the environment and its components that are adopted at every level of government." In papers, it required the state to act in concert with "civil society on the decisions and actions for management of the environment" (Law 28611, article 3). In 2008 the Regulation of Citizen Participation in the Mining Subsector required that public audiences were to be held in settlements in the "direct area of influence," the closest urban center, and the province capital.[9] Furthermore, a company would need to establish a permanent office to provide information about the project and the rights of residents. Although the company was required to acknowledge observations or questions received from citizens (by including these commentaries in the EIA approval report), the decree still did not explain how or whether the citizen contributions were to be addressed.

The aforementioned 2011 Law on the Right of Indigenous or Aboriginal Peoples to Prior Consultation, and its 2012 regulation, ratified ILO's Convention 169 and finally made consultation with communities mandatory before a project development. Unlike the hydrocarbon sector, the prior consultation for mining is required after the government grants a concession to a private entity and is related to state approval of later phases.[10] Two pro-Indigenous organizations—the Pacto de Unidad (Unity Pact) and the NGO coalition Grupo de Trabajo sobre Pueblos Indígenas (Working Group on Indigenous Peoples)—formed in 2011 in response to concerns about the participatory measures. Each sought prior consultation rights for Indigenous peoples potentially affected by mining projects. The former included Indigenous groups that were advocating for monitoring instruments to evaluate consultation agreements. The latter demanded more participation from subnational authorities.

Indigenous prior consultation on mining projects is defined differently from citizen participation in the EIA. MEM had argued that citizen participation, enshrined in existing legislation, qualified as prior consultation, a position Peru's Constitutional Tribunal—roughly equivalent to a Supreme Court—declared unconstitutional in 2013 as part of a ruling that required the ministry to fully comply with the new right (Sanborn et al. 2016). The Environmental Regulations for Mining and Metallurgic Activities of 2014 stated that the EIA must include information about the potential impact on Indigenous collective rights.[11] The first three mining consultations on projects affecting Indigenous peoples occurred during 2015. At four to six months, they were more rapid than expected; in neighboring Colombia, some have lasted a decade. The Regulation for Citizen Participation in the Framework of the National EIA System in 2017 introduced further requirements.[12] Henceforth, the environmental impact statement executive summary would have to be translated into the predominant local language and the mining company would have to present the mechanisms proposed to address the concerns about the EIA that are collected during the hearings. Above all, the state retains the right to approve or reject any administrative or legislative measure where prior consultation applies. The consultation does not grant the right of veto to populations affected by mining activities or governmental decisions.[13] Popular referendums such as the consultation organized by NGOs in 2002 regarding the Tambogrande mining project—one of the first of its type in the world—are not accepted as legitimate by the government or mining companies, since the decision for using underground resources remains constitutionally with the state.

Immersion in Antamina's Environmental Impact Assessment

The presentation of Antamina's EIA in 1998 exceeded the requirements prevailing at the time, and for this reason can be regarded as a milestone in the relationship between mining companies and communities. Although only one presentation was technically necessary—before MEM, in Lima and advertised in the government's not-widely-read official newspaper, *El Peruano*—besides the public hearing that took place in Lima, there were six town meetings within the mine's area of influence. While the strict requirement was presentation of the executive summary to MEM, Antamina distributed copies of the full environmental impact statement in several localities. Following the government approval, the environmental impact statement was placed online via the MEM website. However, an addendum reporting the participatory process, which included criticisms raised during the public hearings, was missing. By the end of the first decade of the twenty-first century, only eight mine environmental impact statements were available online.

The nature of the public hearings defines the effectiveness of communication and participation in an EIA. The hearings were by and large for informational purposes only. Antamina claimed that its participatory process across various public meetings was "prior, timely, and knowledgeable, and not based on . . . incomplete or summarized information" (KS 1998b:1). The term *participatory process* in reference to meetings with stakeholders appears repeatedly, with Antamina claiming to provide "all information . . . without restriction," while allowing the public to "express its opinions, suggestions, observations, and recommendations" (KS 1998b:1). Nevertheless, there were weaknesses. Access to the environmental impact statement was only possible three weeks prior to the hearing and only for formally registered groups. The general public could only access the executive summary held by MEM. Furthermore, the way in which the company would address the comments it received was unclear. NGOs criticized the facts that their only opportunity to consult (on March 19, 1998) with Antamina was solely informative, that hearings should have been held prior to the development of the environmental impact statement draft, and that the report failed to include the viewpoints of groups interested in the park, including UNESCO and environmental NGOs (Schmidt 1999). Although its MIGA had approved the plan for a heavy vehicle route across the park, the World Bank's CAO (2001:5) issued a disclaimer admitting that MIGA's policies and procedures had been ineffective and should have sought the inclusion of local viewpoints through "public notification and local disclosure of the EIA."

The time invested in a participatory process is also a critical factor. Where formal education levels are low, more time and human resources are required because of the technical nature of the information. The former mayor of Chavín, Emilio García, was relieved to learn that technical questions had been asked in Lima, since he considered that there was not sufficient technical capacity at the local level and the residents were left to "rely on the MEM and mines to oversee environmental management" (Schmidt 1999:69). By contrast with the process in Peru, the U.S. National Environmental Policy Act requires scoping (an iterative process that entails exploring and mapping the concerns of all stakeholders), the preparation of a draft proposal arising from the scoping, and a public hearing that leads to a final draft that incorporates comments received at the hearing (Schmidt 1999:67). This typically takes twice as long as its equivalent in Peru. Antamina was spared the prior consultation requirement, which, as noted previously, only became mandatory much later.

Real political participation is defined by the degrees to which actors can modify an agenda at specific points in time (Allison 2003). In a more cultural sense, the process demands that consideration be given to the different meanings the subjects involved assign, based on their own unique interests and capacities. A participatory design inspired in the deliberative politics model of Jürgen Habermas should provide participants with the ability to question or modify the ground rules for a decision and to set the agenda (Habermas 1996; Schmidt 1999). The deliberative model is based on an ethical discourse that emphasizes the process, where appropriate decisions can only be taken through unconditional discussions between the stakeholders affected by the decisions. For environmental policy, this idea has been implemented via discussions and participatory workshops, assuring collective representation (Dietz 2001; Renn et al. 1995).

Neither Antamina's meetings nor the aforementioned mandatory *audiencias públicas* (public hearings) met the criteria for the deliberative model. Antamina established both the format and the agenda for the meetings. Moreover, although environmental risks could have been raised at the time of the concession's sale, and some of the later difficulties thus avoided, those groups who were ultimately able to question and overturn the decision to build a road across the park were given no voice. EIA in Peru normally takes place over just a few months (a year, in the case of Antamina) with consultants hired by the mining company collecting data that rarely includes local consultation, local knowledge, or cross-checking with local organizations—all effectively excluded at the report drafting stage. This process leads to the information remaining uncontested, impacted groups underrepresented, and potential issues unidentified. This is evident in the case of Antamina's initial design, where the majority of government and World Bank representatives favored transporting the ore through the park via trucks (Botts et al. 2001; K&H 1998). Jane Pratt founded TMI and was its president when Antamina presented the environmental impact statement. Pratt (2001:43) contends that Antamina's "EIA was not up to World Bank standards as claimed." Prior to TMI, she had occupied various World Bank environmental policy executive positions—including as head of the Environmental Operations and Strategy divisions—over a period of fourteen years and "had been closely involved in designing the EIA process" and as such claims that she "knew exactly what would have constituted an acceptable EIA." The process could have been preventive rather than corrective, including better implementation of international socioenvironmental standards from the beginning and open discussions with stakeholders (Pratt 2001:40). The significant funding used for the EIA could have been partly invested instead on mechanisms to include local voices, and a substantial amount of time and money could have been saved. An earlier acknowledgment of criticism of the EIA could have led to earlier identification of risks and prevented the raising of fears, which in turn could have delayed or even halted the project.

Sufficient staffing is necessary for there to be greater participation in the EIA processes. The lack of personnel in Antamina's social and environmental divisions to cover the vast area of influence is an indication that the company was unprepared. Although reinforcements arrived later, this shortcoming compromised the EIA from the beginning. As mentioned in chapter 2, Antamina Community Relations resources consisted of a single part-time employee as late as 1997, three months prior to submission of the EIA, a situation that persisted until its presentation. According to a former Antamina officer, the EIA's social component was "very anecdotal, very repetitive and a little off-base" (Schmidt 1999:66). With just two employees, the environmental division fared little better.

Leveling the Playing Field

When Antamina chose to transport the ore by truck through the park, TMI discovered that the Peruvian environmentalists were divided. The Chavín Consortium, formed by institutions in Ancash, was complacent about the mine and assumed that Antamina would generate investment. Some NGOs viewed a road through the park as no worse than a bypass around it. Given that over more than four decades, environmental justice groups in the Northern Hemisphere had challenged the placement of polluting industries in areas home to socially and economically vulnerable people (e.g., ethnic minorities), it was expected that TMI would find allies in environmental networks in the global North. The International Union for Conservation of Nature (IUCN) and the U.S.-based Conservation International—the latter with experience in the rainforests of Peru, Bolivia, and Ecuador—both responded to overtures from TMI. The visit by a UNESCO official to the site was also helpful. According to an Antamina executive, "A negative finding from UNESCO would have ruined our financing" (Schmidt 1999:72). With Antamina's support, TMI set up a meeting in Washington, D.C., with Rothschild N.A., the financial group that was backing Antamina and represented major investment banks from the USA, Canada, Japan, and Germany. According to Pratt (2001:40), TMI declared at this meeting that as a field-based conservation and development organization—as opposed to an advocacy group—it would not lead a campaign against the mining company. It also warned, however, that if Antamina constructed a road through the park and other groups protested, TMI would support them to a certain extent.

A decision by Antamina to traverse the protected area would have caused UNESCO to list the park as endangered and probably trigger a sovereignty debate. Hamilton (1998a) refers to conflicts between international and national levels of authority in the United States following the adding of Yellowstone National Park to UNESCO's List of World Heritage in Danger: "When World Heritage sites are involved, fortunately there is some international leverage that can be used with the respective governments, and there is a threat of putting the site on the World Heritage in Danger List. This has to be done nowadays with great sensitivity, due to touchy sovereignty issues. . . . Bills are still being introduced in Congress and in State legislatures to 'restore U.S. sovereignty' from UNESCO and other international take over!" Adding Huascarán National Park to the UNESCO list would have attracted the interest of other environmental groups and led to protests in countries such as Canada, the United States, Germany, and Japan, where the financial institutions were headquartered (Pratt 2001:40). Protests could have delayed the operations, triggering contract penalties, increasing personnel costs, and spooking investors. The Jabiluka uranium mine in Australia's World Heritage–listed Kakadu National Park faced international pressure for six years before the project was finally cancelled in 1998 (Katona 2002). It is not difficult to imagine that social conflict at the start of the Antamina project would have rendered it unviable given similar examples in Peru: termination of the Tambogrande mining project in 2003 followed local protests, which attracted international media attention and compromised the company's inability to obtain sufficient finance. Shareholders and Antamina's financiers were aware of this possibility (Botts et al. 2001).

In May 1998, INRENA, a decentralized agency of the Ministry of Agriculture, evaluated the southern route around the park, which would avoid crossing the protected area, and concluded that it would not have significant environmental impacts (Botts et al. 2001). NGOs, UNESCO, and creditors were consulted about temporarily using the central route while the southern highway was being constructed. UNESCO tried to level the playing field between private business and the government by requesting the nonbinding opinion by INRENA about the options for the route. This proposal was accepted, and since INRENA had formal state responsibility for protecting Peru's natural richness and biodiversity, it increased the participation of environmental institutions in the project. Due to some then-recent controversial decisions, the organization was under pressure from environmentalists.[14] Promining interests also pressed INRENA, fearing that the agency would place additional limits on certain investment projects in order to protect ecosystems. INRENA had twenty days to deliver its findings but ultimately sought more time to evaluate the alternatives. The request for INRENA's input illustrates both the importance of environmental concerns being considered in the early stages of a mining project—and, more specifically, at the time when the company is looking for investors—and the relevant role that a state environmental institution, even a subordinate one such as INRENA, can play.

The change in project ownership two years after winning the concession, together with new personnel employed in the environmental division, led Antamina to reevaluate the ore transport options. New company partners Noranda and Teck Corporation, both Canadian, favored the construction of a pipeline, while Rio Algom supported the construction of a highway (Zavaleta 1998b). Environmental managers from the three companies visited the sites and examined the EIA report with attention to socioenvironmental conditions. Antamina replaced the EIA contractor Klohn Crippen—SVS S.A. Ingenieros Consultores with another Canadian firm: Knight Piésold. For the first time, the identity of the team's environment professionals was revealed in the environmental impact statement. This was a gesture of a more open approach. In October 1998, MEM approved the EIA and the additional points, after INRENA approved the temporary use of the central route. Ultimately, in January of the following year, addendum 3 was presented to MEM and the public (K&H 1999a, 1999b).

Anthropologist James Ferguson (1994) empirically demonstrates the strategy of presenting oneself as an objective and apolitical expert as a discursive weapon to obtain authority and protect against criticism. Until the final addendum, following Antamina's replacement of the consultancy firm, the environmental impact statement did not carry the names of its individual authors (K&H 1999b). This relative anonymity contributed to a rhetoric of professional objectivity—a constructed distance through which a project is understood to have been prepared not by people with subjective views, biases, or networks, but by a purportedly objective institution. That the environmental impact statement is not prepared directly by the mining company protects that organization from criticism, allowing a convenient strategic distance, with blame for errors in the assessment always able to be shifted to another party.

Six months after the presentation of addendum 3, in June 1999, the president of Antamina traveled to Paris with the director of INRENA to present UNESCO with the southern route plan (around the park) and the temporary use of the central route. This mission demonstrated the power of the mining company and the political and economic importance of the socioenvironmental discussion. UNESCO approved the plan subject to three conditions: monitoring of the affected area, reporting on the state of the park, and establishing a working group to support park management. Antamina improved the existing central route using bulldozers but without altering the width of the road. Watering twice a day temporarily reduced dust, although it returned a few hours later. The quantity of vehicles on the route greatly exceeded the estimates, causing traffic congestion but not leading to a decrease in the number of visitors (GTH and INRENA 2000). Antamina finally built the pipeline around the park. While the choice of a pipeline led to higher than anticipated up-front costs, it was probably more cost-effective in the long term for the company, which may well have underestimated the costs associated with the road transport option.

Multiactor Supervision

TMI presented itself as an organization attempting to make mining extraction compatible with conservation. As TMI's Andean program director stated, "The position of values that we wanted to demonstrate was that development of this type, with extractive resources in an area near the environment of a national park, can adapt to the special conditions which that area presents." The organization sought consistency with its work with local communities in the park without leaning too far toward the "strictly naturalist" or purely conservationist. He acknowledged TMI members recognized the "world of comfort" based on metals (e.g., goods such as watches, or trips by airplanes or motor vehicles) and this prevented them taking "an absolute position." He emphasized that the concept of development implies "creating capacities to enter the debate and create opportunities for debate," with trust being essential to ensuring a discussion of development options. He concluded that such exchange can run into difficulty when monolithic "class structure" discourses intervene based on "distance" and the "absence of democracy."

The Huascarán Working Group was formed in response to the UNESCO request to support INRENA in monitoring Antamina's temporary plan to traverse the park via the central route—while the southern route around the park would be under construction—and to prevent potential conflicts by facilitating fluid communication between all parties. This would become an exemplary mechanism that, by using as a point of departure the acknowledgment by both sides that they each distrusted the other, led to the development of a system of reciprocal vigilance that in turn helped to overcome the trust issues. The group brought together TMI, INRENA, UNESCO, and Antamina. It included three U.S. NGOs (CARE, TMI, and Conservation International), two Peruvian NGOs (Pronaturaleza and SPDA), government agencies (INRENA and MEM), and a national university located in Ancash Department. This collective coordinated with another mine in the park (Mitsui), which along with TMI and Antamina funded joint activities. Barrick Mining Company joined later.

The group's principal assumption was that "understanding objectives, priorities, and mutual concerns is the basis for achieving good negotiations," where the "lack of communication between Antamina and the Park has created misunderstandings." Inconsistencies in the park's boundaries displayed on the respective maps held by MEM and INRENA illustrated the poor clarity of government information, regulations, and policies regarding mining in protected areas (Botts et al. 2001; GTH and INRENA 2000). The group supervised the temporary use of the central route and became a communications network aiming to make mining activity compatible with sustainable development. It offered to support park administration by organizing information on potential impacts (GTH and INRENA 2000). A UNESCO representative mission praised the group as a "pilot experience for park authorities, who can use the learning gained . . . for other problems of equal complexity with tourism operators and energy companies that place strong development pressures on the Park" (GTH 2000:2).

Huarmey Against the Pipeline

An analysis of the ore transportation mechanism decision-making process would be incomplete without an examination of events that followed selection of the pipeline, including repeated blockages of the Pan-American Highway—the most important along the coast—by residents of Huarmey. Nationally broadcast coverage of these events highlighted the fears held about potential pollution of the ocean. The media obscured that these protests were also fueled by development dreams. Many people favored the truck transport option because of the business opportunities they envisioned with paved roads that would improve commercialization of their agricultural products. Others expected to work as drivers for Antamina or offer services for associated needs such as housing, food, or repairs. Indeed, the expectations raised by the highway option are key to understanding the response of Huarmey residents to the choice of the pipeline. Farmers assumed that the road would pass by their land and improve their market access:

> Councilperson: The irrigators happily stated that we will have a paved road, so we, the farmers, wanted Antamina to come.
>
> Author: And you didn't see any flaws to the highway?
>
> Former President of a Committee of Irrigators: Not at all, because a highway was necessary for us. They had planned a certain number of vehicles that were going to transport their mineral, but they would allow vehicles to transport food staples for the population.
>
> A: The road was going to pass right by the fields?
>
> C: Yes, by the fields.

I repeatedly found this script during my fieldwork. The hope was that Antamina would create a "development pole" in Huarmey, with restaurants and accommodation for truckers. This offer was not, however, included in the EIA report, which only mentioned an "equipped camp to house and feed the Antamina staff" (KS 1998b:22).

Antamina had raised expectations about development throughout its entire area of influence, and Huarmey was not immune. The then minister for Energy and Mines, Amado Yataco, had referred to the importance of the mine in the "reactivation of Ancash [the whole department], based on the construction of a superhighway" (*El Comercio* 1998:E01). The media fed this (see chapter 2), as the following editorial from *El Comercio* (1999:A23) shows: "The 500 million dollars invested to date has alleviated the isolation that sunk the Callejón de Conchucos into poverty. And extracting the mineral, from this point to the port for shipment in Huarmey bodes well for the emergence of a new economic corridor in Ancash, with effects in the generation of employment and services, as well as improvements in transportation infrastructure."

Besides hope, however, Antamina also stimulated nightmares, particularly among Huarmey's fishermen. The most repeated public concern at a meeting on

January 16, 1999, was the contamination of marine waters and the effect of that on fishing (K&H 1999a:8-12). Eight months later (August 19), while the modification still remained undecided, the mayor of Huaraz (the capital of Ancash), Waldo Ríos, led a forty-eight-hour strike in protest against Antamina and Barrick (Pierina mine) claiming that the mining operations were causing "serious damage to the economy and tranquility of the city and the region" (Incháustegui 1999:A15). The protestors blocked roads, and Ríos painted slogans such as "Waldo, *luchador social*" (social fighter) on several Ancash mountains.[15] Augusto Baertl, Antamina CEO and president of the SNMPE, oblivious to the underlying causes, regarded the protests as "a phenomenon of social destabilization promoted by people with political purposes, which are unimportant since the work of Antamina and Pierina continues" (Mendoza 1999:B03).

On March 3, 2000, a twenty-four-hour regional strike protested against the environmental impacts of the proposed pipeline. The residents were worried that sewage would pollute the port of Huarmey. Antamina asserted that a reforestation project would absorb any residual waste (see chapter 5). Huarmey's mayor, Juan Pacífico, demanded "revision of the Antamina EIA, which was done with no consultation, behind the backs of the people" (*Crónica Viva* 2001). A roundtable was established to facilitate dialogue, and the municipality absorbed an environmental monitoring committee previously established by some community members.[16] Baertl announced with satisfaction, "We have had a constructive meeting with municipal authorities, and the concerns they had have already been resolved" (*El Comercio* 2001a:B03).

Fifteen months after the regional strike, on June 12, 2001, when the Ancash Regional Administration Transition Council and Huarmey's Provincial Municipality organized a debate on the environmental impact of Antamina, another violent demonstration took place in Huarmey's main square. The Pan-American Highway was again blocked the following week, by a group known as the Frente de Defensa de los Intereses de Huarmey (Front for the Defense of the Interests of Huarmey). While the population continued to maintain that the pipeline would lead to pollution in Huarmey, Energy and Mines minister Herrera invoked the specter of foreign investment being threatened by the protests. Antamina's corporate relations vice president claimed that "the blockade is just an excuse to draw the government's attention to the problems of Huarmey" (*El Comercio* 2001b:A10; GTH and INRENA 2000). The highway blockade was halted after forty-eight hours, following undertakings to hold a *mesa de concertación* (agreement roundtable) promoted by MEM, the National Environmental

Council, and the Catholic Church. The table was subsequently postponed in favor of a multisector technical committee to address the environmental concerns of Antamina's operation (see chapter 5).

Throughout this period, the media coverage ignored an important factor: local expectations associated with the construction of the highway. An Antamina employee told me the pipeline plan "wasn't as widely circulated as had been the highway plan." He also pointed out that the company had never, in fact, planned a new road through the Huarmey Valley, an idea that in his view had been disseminated by Front for the Defense of the Interests of Huarmey based on a newspaper article. Instead, Antamina had planned to use an existing paved road in Huarmey and to build new sections at specific points. But according to Martín, of the Front for the Defense of the Interests of Huarmey, the belief that there would be a new paved road became so strongly held that many residents believed it to be World Bank compensation "in exchange" for the purported environmental degradation that Antamina would cause, including to "the foundations of the houses in Huarmey."

On May 9 and 10, 2002, the Pan-American Highway was once again blocked in a protest led by the Front for the Defense of the Interests of Huarmey. Residents demanded the construction of the highway promised in writing by the government using a $110 million contract fine against Antamina (see chapter 5). The government tried to retreat from the promise by interpreting it to mean only the repair of existing roads. An agreement to stop the blockage was reached, but only after use of tear gas. Two years later, further strikes occurred demanding a highway from Huarmey to Aija and Recuay. Paving of this road began in 2005, but to date remains incomplete.

Pipeline Leaks

On July 25, 2012, twelve years after its construction, a tube at a valve station of the ore pipeline ruptured and caused a leakage of copper and zinc ore that affected the small town of Santa Rosa (population approximately two thousand) in the district of Cajacay, showing how the allegedly infallible pipeline and emergency systems failed (see map 4). A design flaw led to a loss in pressure, which was compounded by a malfunction in the automatic monitoring system and which in turn led to failure in notification of the fault. A guard noticed smoke, discovered the leak—left undetected by the "Advisor" system—and, with the help of local residents, closed a valve and stopped the flow. Of the forty-five-ton leakage, three tons escaped the station's containment systems and reached nearby soil. Fortunately, the residents constructed an improvised channel to divert the ore into an abandoned alpaca and llama dip in order to avert the serious risk of the ore reaching water sources. The locals had neither protection against chemical hazards nor emergency response training.

The government subsequently discovered environmental damage to "natural soil, eucalyptus and pine trees, which had to be felled" (OEFA 2013:13). A year after the event, the concentrations of arsenic and copper in the soil still exceeded the referential values. Antamina estimated that the area directly impacted was less than one hectare and promised to replace the trees. It noted that Ministry of Health evaluations confirmed "no persons with health problems associated to the incident" (*Diario Gestión* 2013). The OEFA (Organismo de Evaluación y Fiscalización Ambiental, or Evaluation and Environmental Supervision Office) (2013) fined Antamina approximately $76,000 for the environmental damage and its failure to provide complete information in reporting of the incident using government emergency formats. The penalty amounted to a small speeding ticket for such a large corporation.

Three months later the Cajacay peasant community mounted a demonstration against Antamina. This led to a roundtable meeting chaired by the National Dialogue and Sustainability Office, a then newly created body located in the Presidency of the Council of Ministers (MINAM 2015). Two months later a provincial Development Dialogue Roundtable was established. It consisted of three working groups: health, agriculture, and environment. The latter subsequently presented the community with a final report on the environmental aspects (water, air, and soil), a risk management plan, and a district health intervention plan. Five years after the incident, the Cajacay case remained listed as an "active" conflict in the national inventory of the Peruvian ombudsman. The ombudsman noted that the community "demands that Antamina assume its responsibility for the mineral spill" (DP 2017:30). The episode illustrates how a purportedly flawless technology failed and was unexpectedly saved thanks to traditional reciprocal collective networks. It also illustrates the limits to the rhetorics of EIA along with inflated corporate sociotechnologies of disaster containment, all based on a twofold strategy: reserving information and—once again—portraying nature impacts as limited, controllable, and compartmentalized. Finally, the incident further exhibits how direct actions and roundtables have become consolidated as participatory dynamics for disputes between corporations and vulnerable citizens in Andean contexts.

Enacting Strategies

Empowerment and Shame

The knowledge and capacities of the environmentalists enabled them to generate anxiety within the mining company due to their potential to damage the company's reputation at a vulnerable moment, when the corporation was searching for investment funding. A "politics of shame" strategy created a political equilibrium, based on the possibility that the park would be placed on the UNESCO list of endangered World Heritage sites, a scenario that would have drawn attention from international media and probably driven activists to the doorstep of the headquarters of the mining company. This would have detracted from the project's legitimacy, scaring investors and raising costs because of delays and associated contractual penalties. This situation momentarily redefined the relationship between Antamina and the NGOs and promoted conversations aimed at reaching mutual understanding.

The EIA and the broadened scope of the public hearings allowed groups without significant representation capacity to be considered as stakeholders and exert some influence on certain decision-making processes. If, as we saw in chapter 2, during the San Marcos displacement process, international investors ceded power to residents when they appealed to the World Bank, then in this case, TMI's intervention altered the perception of financiers about the project's costs and benefits. Subsequently, national agents helped the people of Huarmey gain government attention. TMI was unsuccessful in its attempts to find allies among NGOs in Ancash, but then found a receptive audience among its peers in the Northern Hemisphere, who then contributed both experience and social networks. In each case, the strategy was to search for stronger allies—financial actors in the case of TMI or the state in the case of Huarmey—in order to level asymmetries at the negotiating table. As TMI's Andean program director told me, "To make these debates more egalitarian, one must close existing breaches in communication, information and capacities." Pratt (2001:42) acknowledges that the communication became more efficient when directed to those at the highest levels of the mining company: "[TMI] succeeded in 'leveling the playing field' with the corporation by engaging the attention and support of the financial institutions funding Antamina. Without the support of Antamina's backers, TMI probably would not have succeeded in getting Antamina to take its expertise seriously." Environmentalists' voices were heard because these international institutions were visible to the investors. The contacts, prestige, and negotiation abilities of the conservation advocates, exemplified by the TMI director's former role as a World Bank official, was critical to the organization's ability to act.

These social actors capitalized on the mining company's fear that the project would grind to a halt, assembling an effective and direct "weapon of the weak" (Scott 1985), similar to strategies deployed by social and environmental movements. The closest prior Peruvian referent to such a tactic would be long-standing union mobilizations. The environmentalists' claims became a resource that strengthened their position in a negotiation by connecting with more powerful allies, directly or through the national media. The call for a network of environmental institutions and the "politics of shame" strategy worked efficiently, first for TMI, which was able to foresee the threat, and then for the Huarmey residents, who seized on the national press to denounce the company. The risk of a confrontation in the media with international stakeholders, coupled with the prevailing sensitivity to environmental issues, would have had unpredictable costs for the mining project. The threat of public disgrace proved to be a potent deterrent that influenced the mining corporation's behavior.

Rhetorical Greening Battles

The investors sought to minimize the risks through preventive measures that can be conceptualized as long-term investments that internalize initial costs in order to minimize hazards. The change in ore transport option indicates how groups with certain capabilities can use alliances to modify a large-scale mining design and process on the basis of socioenvironmental issues. The environmental institutions, led by TMI, used two strategies in the initial stage. First, they adopted a holistic view of impacts that transcended consideration merely of what might happen a few meters from the road. Second, TMI directly contacted shareholders and suggested they consider other risks—not previously raised—that could jeopardize the project. As such, they translated environmental concerns into terms that the company would understand as promoting its reputation and its long-term financial interests, both working as insurance for the investment. They incorporated additional international standards as risks and costs that the EIA had not considered, probably because the consultants were unfamiliar with the way problems were framed locally, or simply because these risks were inconvenient for the mining company. "TMI was able to offer a broader perspective and more objective advice than the consulting firm hired to carry out Antamina's EIA," stated TMI's director (Pratt 2001:41). She argued that financial investors need "independent information" about environmental regulations obtained from "reliable third-parties" and greater internal capacity for financial scenario analysis. The environmental impact statement contains limited information due to the reliance on secondhand data and a lack of incentive to identify all risks, particularly those in the medium and long term. The consultants come from the private sector and are selected and employed by the mining company, whose objective is rapid approval.

Large mining projects requiring complex financial solutions are most vulnerable at the capital-seeking stage. The mayor of Huallanca put it this way: "The larger the project, the weaker it is," especially prior to the initiation of operations. At the time Antamina submitted the environmental impact statement, the company was facing financial challenges: the funding was not guaranteed and the company was looking for capital from various lending agencies (e.g., U.S. Eximbank and the Canadian Export Development Corporation). Several of these had expressed concern about Huascarán National Park. For a large mine like Antamina, the socioenvironmental ramifications of the project were a source of concern because the company depended on international financers aware that such variables could hinder the project. These firms were aware of the risks associated with investing substantial sums of money in remote locations historically marked by violence. Socioenvironmental concerns in Tambogrande had prevented the Manhattan Company from securing the initial funding. Anthropologist Anna Tsing (2000) analyzes the activities of mining companies during the search for financing and considers them akin to conjuring acts that aim to persuade potential investors that the project will be profitable. Aware of the speculative nature of multinational mining capital, especially at the preliminary financial stage, companies apply rhetorical strategies—occasionally exaggerated or illusory—to prove the feasibility of the project. The Bre-X Busang mine in Indonesia (Tsing's case study) is an extreme example in which the supposed wealth of the mine was invented in order to obtain the financial support. Antamina's EIA contained a rhetoric that sought to guarantee targeted and controlled change, including coverage of all pipeline disaster scenarios.

This proved unrealistic, as accidents such as the leak in Cajacay District were to demonstrate.

Scoping Participation

The importance of defining the scoping process is one of the most significant lessons that Antamina, TMI, and the Huascarán National Park authority all underscored. Following approval of the EIA, Antamina acknowledged the critical role of international actors in its decision-making processes (Botts et al. 2001). International NGOs were better able to exert pressure given their financial and human resources capacities and their greater access to information. The elegant, first-world mineral duct engineering solution satisfied the conservationists after a technocracy argued it could control ecological damage, claiming a win-win solution. Yet they had to face a more typical developing-world scenario. The protests in coastal Huarmey illustrate how the restricted participation of some social actors led to a complicated consequence: expectations in Huarmey were left unsatisfied as a result of the change in transport option.

As we have seen with displacements (see chapter 2), a lack of clarity led to confusion. The complex and technical EIA jargon was beyond the comprehension of local people, especially for those for whom Spanish was not their first language. The contrast between the environmental expertise of TMI and that of the municipality of San Marcos is a clear example of the difference. It took the municipality more than two years after the land purchasing process to discover and use different negotiation resources, such as protest letters sent to the World Bank (see chapter 2). By contrast, TMI's technical knowledge and its connections accelerated the organization's efforts and allowed it more influence in the EIA decision-making process.

To better understand the importance of participation in designing operations, it is useful to introduce into the discussion, as general models reflecting larger social phenomena, the clash of two mining cultures. On the one hand, we have the historic approach by mining companies in Peru that remained widespread in the Andes until the 1980s, hardly open to civil society and accustomed to negotiating solely with the state. This antiquated model justifies environmental costs in terms of national economic growth. Like the government, the companies rely on a development rhetoric that claims that mining generates social benefits via the national and subnational redistribution of tax revenue and the creation of scarce but highly paid employment in areas where poverty rates are high. This old model degraded the environment of neighboring communities while at the same time increasing consumption of local products and the use of certain services, promoting improvements to education and health services and the construction of roads. The rise of Shining Path violence proved to be a turning point for this model, generating widespread distrust and creating distance between groups. Fears sparked by the history of armed violence in the Andes probably led to decreased openness from businesses.

On the other hand is a mining culture more aligned with the approach of international investors, portrayed as more "domesticated," with more clearly defined notions of guilt and a clearer understanding of the potential risks and conflicts stemming from legal attacks and battles over the cost of environmental degradation. These claims were made in the context of a more institutionally organized civil society, such as Canada, which had not witnessed Shining Path–style violence, a basic cause for suspicion from an entrepreneur's perspective. Antamina's then CEO, together with the initial Community Relations staff in San Marcos, had previously worked at the Milpo mine in Cerro de Pasco, one of the world's most heavily polluted areas (Glave and Kuramoto 2002). Antamina's vice president of environment, health, and safety, Steven Botts, summed up the clash between Peruvian and international mining cultures by revealing the difficulty he had convincing company staff of the need for public participation: "We need to do consultations, we need the input, but that can be scary to Peruvians within the company. 'Why risk it?' is their response. [Just] 'do it through the old boy network, where nobody is going to oppose a two billion dollar project.' They haven't had a lot of experience in this sort of iterative process" (Schmidt 1999:68).

Botts started work as an Antamina director in 1997 and within two years had reached vice president level. He embodied a more international corporate mining culture. He told me how he recognized his responsibility for the overall management of environment systems, and the health and safety of Antamina, including permits, compliance, and loss. He was also responsible for relations between shareholders and communities, as well as with NGOs and the Peruvian government. Prior to joining Antamina, he had been the director of environmental affairs in Echo Bay Mines, managing the environmental corporate program. This included the audit program, due diligence activities, and permits for project operations in Canada and the USA, as well as activities at sites in Brazil, Canada, Mexico, the Philippines, and Russia. He had also worked for Amax Gold Company, Sonora Mining Company, the U.S.-based Newmont

Gold Corporation, and the Canadian Barrick Goldstrike Mine. Environmental groups heavily criticized Echo Bay Mines for the buildup and lixiviation of cyanide in extracting gold from the mines near the Blackfoot River in Nevada, USA. The operations were previously handled by Phelps Dodge Corporation and Canyon Resources Corporation. The former sold its shares to Echo Bay Mines following criticism from environmentalists (Speart 1995:58).

It seems reasonable that the members of the Antamina consortium would initially follow Peruvian approaches for building social relationships with residents in the belief that local experience would be the most informed and trustworthy reference. For some observers, Antamina represented a turning point for civil society in its demand for greater participation in the decision-making processes for extractive projects. Special mechanisms proved necessary in order to promote better interpretation in socially complex contexts under political and economic vulnerability. The presence of an ideally neutral and multidisciplinary scientific mediating body for the parties would arguably improve the process of cultural translation.

Public hearings for an EIA should aim to bring together the stakeholders involved in a project to provide feedback. Here, however, the environmental impact statement was presented as a final document to be explained, as opposed to a work in progress. Ideally, the EIA would evolve from local and multiple scientific concerns and entail the presentation of alternatives about which affected citizens and other relevant interested groups would comment prior to its finalization. Antamina was only legally obliged to hold a public hearing when the project moved from the exploration to exploitation stage. This was problematic because during the exploratory stage, machinery, discharge, and waste were already present and affecting the environment and neighboring populations. This condition has slightly improved due to new mining company obligations following the issue of a concession contained in the 2008 regulation on citizen participation in mining.[17] This rule requires the provision of information to local residents on issues such as the scope of the concession rights, the environmental obligations, and the norms regulating the activity, including the rights and obligations of the populations involved.

The government is highly visible when closing the mining concession contract, but its presence—not necessarily neutral, given its interest in collecting revenue via foreign exchange and taxes—becomes vital as a provider of resources for meditating the relationship between the company and the neighboring populations. More recently there have been advances in state presence at mining sites and in negotiations. However, these only relate to the period following the granting of a concession. Unlike a hydrocarbon concession, the sale of a mining concession does not require a prior consultation with the affected communities. And the final approval still remains in the hands of the state, meaning that the consultations are not processes of consent, as demanded by several Indigenous organizations in Peru. In terms of the deliberative politics model—considering that participants should have the ability to question or modify the ground rules for a decision and to set the agenda—the prior consultation process and participatory process for the EIAs remain mostly informative. In order to most effectively prevent conflict, the ideal scenario would be to require consent of the local population affected by a mining concession. Citizen participation in socioenvironmental mining issues should be timely and informed. Other than a few recent advances, these features are still weakly developed in Peru. The approval process for the EIAs is the most visible case in point.

Conclusion

Anthropologist Tim Ingold (2003:332) emphasizes that environmental perceptions constitute social learning based in "the practical business of dwelling in the world." Cultural experiential knowledge holds the base of political interactions about nature. In this chapter I have examined citizen participation claims in the design of the mining project. The exploration has shown the way in which the perceptions of nature held by different groups are mediated and marked by the political and economic interests of those groups. It also illustrates how social networks and access to information become fundamental to decision-making processes from the different positions within a social structure of knowledge and power. In the debate over ore transport options for Antamina, the concepts of boundary, value, and risk were socially constructed and argued for as elements that reflected the prioritized interests of groups. These definitions can be opposed, even among so-called technical experts in similar disciplines claiming to have natural science on their side. The approval by World Bank experts of the road option in the face of the evaluations by environmentalists—embodied by TMI—exemplifies such divergence. Sovereignty discussions within the EIA negotiations indicate how the limits and the categories used to draw these boundaries become flexible depending on the necessities of each stakeholder.

TMI advocated conservation values that transcended the physical limits of the proposed road, and criticized the compartmentalized preferences of the EIA by highlighting the impact on ecosystems. But TMI did not raise concerns about the risks of the port or other potential accidents that could occur along the route of the pipeline to the coast. Antamina was firmly focused on the physical boundaries of the road and the operations area, despite the fact that it also intended to use and impact the nearby natural protected area.

This case also embodies the state's weakness in the face of the need for rapid economic growth and foreign exchange. That INRENA and MEM had conflicting maps of the protected areas is evidence of a government apparatus lacking the necessary resources for environmental conservation. It was virtually absent, unable even to protect fauna and road users, given Peru's dismal accident statistics and the risks posed by vehicles to other ecosystems (e.g., exhaust emissions that affect glaciers). The environmentalists' perspectives primarily influenced the modifications to the design. The differing interpretations of what was a legally viable and environmentally desirable transportation solution proved to be problematic, especially since Antamina's plan to cross the park had not encountered resistance from the Peruvian government, the media, or the World Bank. The EIA served as the ultimate tool to formalize the project's viability. A centralized public administration in which a rural environmental conservation focus is practically absent, but an eagerness for the tax revenues generated by mining is evident, has only a modest incentive to engage in environmental protection.

The process examined shows how pressure to safeguard financial investments and maintain the pace of construction were key elements that influenced the company to redesign its infrastructure in response to environmental considerations. Antamina's position and its motivations can be traced to the lessons learned by their investors, who had experience with regulations and conflicts in other countries with higher regulatory safeguards and stronger institutions. Furthermore, the company was guided by the literature of corporate stakeholder consultation (e.g., World Bank guidelines) and the requirements of its financiers. The latter slightly exceeded the Peruvian legal requirements in place at the time. These factors probably encouraged citizen awareness about public participation in this type of project. "Understanding who the affected people are," and understanding the different positions of the groups and their motivations, was a cultural learning process, a key exchange in the negotiation, as recognized in a document jointly prepared by Antamina, TMI, and the Huascarán National

Park authorities (Botts et al. 2001:16). For the TMI Andean program director, the lessons were clear. The debates arise among groups in a decision-making process under "power structures in development," as he detailed to me, where each supports its arguments according to its own interests and perceptions: "Evidently, those from Huarmey have been affected. If it is a perception or how real it was [is another discussion] . . . perhaps much of the Chavín population would have preferred a highway to travel faster across Pastoruri."

Furthermore, as this chapter has shown, this conflict, particularly its resolution, offers insights into alliances and dialogues that are unanticipated within the context of orthodox models of monolithic social power structures, where class interests would not permit much dialogue. Intuition might suggest that conversations and alliances are not possible between a large profit-oriented extractive corporation and a nonprofit organization concerned with conservation and local development. Yet in this case, the unexpected result was that environmental institutions were able to a conduct practical dialogue with a mining company on sensitive issues. The alliance of international NGOs formed a negotiation counterweight that was rooted in their experiences and established social networks. In TMI's case, these network advantages facilitated direct access to dialogue with the investors. The TMI director illustrates this point well. Having worked in the World Bank and private organizations, she was familiar with the inner dynamics—and probably the human face—of these groups.

This chapter has evidenced how reputation threats, information, and networks, when deployed at strategic moments, can broaden the spectrum of participation and temporarily even out asymmetries between different groups with vastly dissimilar access to financial resources. We shall pursue these repercussions in the next chapter, in which I will explore the evolution of development myths around mining by examining the contests for participating in the benefits and the subsequent use of resources transferred as a consequence of the extractive activities.

CHAPTER 4

From Roads to Coliseums

The Long and Winding Road of Development Myths

Between mountains, between hills,
between the countryside of the ravines,
curve by curve, the car travels by the river.
. . . .
It is hope and also progress,
this road we have today,
Along which new life comes,
with the nectar of love.

—MAURILIO MEJÍA, "THE ROAD FROM AIJA TO HUARMEY," 2002

ANTAMINA WAS FORMALLY OPENED BY PERUVIAN PRESIDENT ALEJANDRO TOLEDO ON NOVEMber 10, 2001. A smiling mining company CEO, Augusto Baertl, proclaimed "mission accomplished" and offered to increase national mining production by 30 percent. After unveiling the commemorative plaque, the head of state—echoing the CEO's offer—gave a speech in which he highlighted the impact of the project on the national economy and his pride that the country was able to attract foreign investment of such magnitude. He assured Antamina's partners that the government was committed to "contribute to legal stability" and to respect "the rules of the game" (Rosales 2001). They could rest easy. While aimed at Peruvian citizens in general, his discourse contained the oft-repeated mantra of investor security, and in so doing sought to calm fears of expropriation that dated back to the military government of the 1970s. At the end of the ceremony, the president found himself surrounded by mine workers. But instead of responding to requests to speak with them directly, he slipped away, claiming that his aircraft awaited and the powerful Andean winds would soon make takeoff impossible (Rosales 2001). But perhaps he simply did not know what to say or how to reach out to the people directly as citizens. The opening ritual contained no mention of the neighboring communities, who were absent and unrepresented on the day. They claimed to be excluded from the mine.

The opening ceremony can be regarded as a metaphor for development conflicts where local residents demand more participation in accordance with their own set of expectations. An Antamina official told me that it was common for members of the public attending environmental impact statement presentations to stand up and invoke "that famous comment by Raimondi, that 'Peru is a beggar sitting on a bench of gold.'" Local residents did not feel invited to the party. Corporate social responsibility was the mining company's response to local demands. Adjacent populations challenge mining practices that evoke the perception of neo-enclaves. An operations area complete with modern office facilities and comfortable rooms in a remote corner of the Andes contrasts sharply with the impoverished conditions in which neighboring populations live. It is a place of forbidden passage. In this extraterritorial space, it would be worth asking to what extent the neighboring communities would ever feel completely satisfied with what the mine could offer. Local relationships between earlier mining companies and the people of San Marcos were more peaceful because of the employment and opportunities for local trade. Chapter 2 shows how the expectations of development in San Marcos were based on people's memories of the employment and trading opportunities that the earlier mines brought with them, on the promises of wealth that Antamina itself publicized, and on the job offers that some of its staff had somewhat recklessly made in the beginning. It is also not surprising that expectations grow in proportion to the size of each project.

Figures 9, 10, and 11 could summarize the central theme of this chapter. Another photograph would complete the picture: a Peruvian Army artillery helicopter launching tear gas mortars in Huarmey when residents blocked the Pan-American Highway on May 10, 2002. The irritating effects of the chemicals lasted for hours. The next day, a two-meter-high pile of empty tear gas canisters lay in the central plaza. The scene exemplified the local drama of social development when a state apparatus is probably too close to a mining company. In what follows, I examine and contrast definitions of development. To this end, by following the trail of the funds, I trace decisions on gifts, compensations, negotiation agreements, and other fiscal transfers produced by Antamina's activity in San Marcos, Huarmey, and Huallanca. The central assumption is that the local understanding of what constitutes a path to development is revealed by the way in which a collective (e.g., peasant community or municipality) uses

FIGURE 9 A bullring in Huallanca. 2002. Author's photo.

FIGURE 10 A newly paved street in Huallanca. 2002. Author's photo.

FIGURE 11 Electrification in the community of Ango Raju de Carhuayoc. 2002. Author's photo.

financial resources to promote that development. I also contrast local demand for projects to improve the well-being of the communities with Antamina's "corporate social responsibility" programs that adopted symbols conjuring up development ideals.

The chapter has two divisions, reflecting how mining has landed in the Peruvian Andes under the soundtrack of rhetorical development myths. The first part—covering the long-term national scale—provides the framework for the examination of the regional scale of the Antamina arrival. I begin by unpacking the evolution since colonial times of the rhetorical promises of mining for development. The overview contributes to understanding expectations and rhetorics deployed in contemporary battles for mining benefits. In the second segment, starting with the section titled "Primal Impacts," I discuss the entrance repercussions of Antamina while I unveil the mining rhetorics and practices emplaced through sociotechnological regimes of social responsibility. Finally, I unpack the local priorities for the use of resources, revealing negotiations under reciprocity requests and patterns of expectations of well-being improvement. As we shall see, while most mining myths for development aim to justify the extractive activities, they also create conditions for social and political actions for participating in well-being improvement.

Mining Hopes: From Colonialism to Development

Gold is most excellent; gold is treasure,
and he who possesses it does all he wishes to in this world,
and succeeds in helping souls into paradise.

—CHRISTOPHER COLUMBUS, "LETTER OF COLUMBUS ON THE FOURTH VOYAGE," JULY 7, 1503

We have to put an end to the idea that Peru is big. . . .
Peru is small and it belongs to all of us.

—ASHANINKA LEADER, *CARETAS*, 2004[1]

Mining was already ancient in the Andes when Peru entered the global economy in the sixteenth century as a colonial center of mining production in the New World. Pre-Hispanic Andean people were less interested in the use of minerals for war or transport than were their European conquerors (Lechtman 1984). Vestiges of metal objects used to make projectiles for Andean hunters up to five hundred years before the Spanish Conquest have been found. Pre-Inca groups made tools and weapons, as well as ceremonial and ornamental pieces, developing a sophisticated metallurgy (Cárdenas 1999:20). The most important property of a metal for many of these people was its color, over and above its solidity or resistance (Hernández 1999:63).

More focused on plundering and on melting the metals of the Aztecs and Incas, mining formed only a partial element in the plans of the first conquistadors. The Spanish colonial regime was the first in the region to rely on a discourse of development to validate mining exploitation, a model whose only beneficiary was the system itself. A more significant element for the Spanish empire was the taxes agreed on by Francisco Pizarro and Queen Isabel in 1529. The official policy of Quinto Real, or Royal Fifth, reserved for the Crown 20 percent of all precious metals as well as other commodities "extracted by mining, acquired by the monarch's subjects as war loot, or found as treasure" (Hein and Cecot 2017:7). From the early 1600s the fifth was lowered to *diezmo* (one-tenth) in some places, a 10 percent tax on mining extraction, and sometimes one-twentieth, in order to stimulate production (Macleod 1997:246). In 1736 the Crown halved this principal mining tax as a general policy, seeking to stimulate the output (Brown 2012:27). These policies were foundational for the colony and marked the inhuman conditions of Indigenous labor in the mines

(Gálvez 1999). The Indigenous population suffered brutal conditions of forced labor, which contributed to the drastic population decline in Ibero-America from more than sixty million on the eve of the conquest to less than ten million at the height of the seventeenth century (Dore 2000:6).

After the first phase of the colonial conquest decimated the Caribbean Indigenous population in the effort to extract precious metals, the discovery of silver in Potosí, in Alto Perú (now Bolivia), made the colonial economy redraw its social and spatial organization, giving way to processes of urban planning and the reorganization of rural production to supply the mines. This process meant more pastures for the mules that transported minerals, trees harvested to build tunnels, and dams for the mills (Dore 2000). Colonial Peru revolved around mining, particularly of gold, silver, and mercury. The latter was essential to extract the silver. New towns formed around the mining sites, bringing with them other economic activities. Groups of immigrants were attracted by the economic bonanza: Native peoples, working in conditions of slavery in the mines; Creoles, linked to the use of animals to transport the minerals; and the Spanish authorities and traders, seduced by the increase of money in the region.

Potosí, where Cerro Rico (the largest mine in colonial Peru) was located, illustrates the dynamism driven by extractive activity. At various points between 1555 and 1705, it reached a population more than twice the size of Lima (Aldana 1999). By the early seventeenth century, Potosí was one of the largest cities in the Western Hemisphere (Dore 2000). At the start of the colonial era in Potosí, the Indigenous people supplied food and basic products. They were producers, traders, and consumers in an expansive market, linking remote regions in Andean commercial networks (Assadourian 1982; Larson 1995). The colonial mining sector was dominant and determined the importance of other regional production. Mining produced and reproduced a mining agrarian structure, maintaining a "strong articulation with the peasant subsistence production" through a "subsidy from the peasant economy to the mining production" (Assadourian et al. 1980:34–36). This was mainly due to *mita*—or "turn" in Quechua, referring to obligatory shift work, a term subsequently appropriated by the colonialists to designate drafted mine labor—the dependence on round-trip journeys, and, finally, the production in the plots of the *mitayo* and the communal land (Assadourian et al. 1980; Mayer 2002:337).

Figure 12 shows the villa of Conchucos in the long natural corridor of the Callejón de Conchucos, where Antamina is located. The Conchucos silver mine was discovered in 1644 (Aldana 1999). The mines established trading circuits

FIGURE 12 *La villa de Conchocos, minas de plata* (The town of Conchucos, silver mines), by Felipe Guaman Poma de Ayala ([1615/1616] 2004). Courtesy of The Royal Library, Copenhagen.

linking diverse populations. The policy of *reducciones* and *encomiendas* transfigured the spatial distribution of the pre-Hispanic settlements. *Reducción* comes from the Spanish verb *reducir*, which means "to reduce, subdue, persuade or reorder" (Mumford 2012:1). The Reducción General de Indios (General Resettlement of Indians) in 1569 ordered the Native peoples of the central Andes to move to new towns or *reducciones* designed under a Spanish model, and "congregated dispersed populations into nucleated villages" (Mayer 2002:338; Mumford 2012:1). An *encomienda* designated "a group of Indians given by royal grant to a Spaniard" overlord, constituting a central institution of the early colony (Mayer 2002:335; Mumford 2012:28). The pre-Hispanic Andean model of the "vertical archipelago," proposed by the anthropologist John Murra (1975:80, 59), meant "vertical control of a maximum of ecological tiers." This pattern of settlement and organization and simultaneous control by a single ethnic group of various geographically dispersed tiers was transformed into a series of concentrated villages. Here the Indigenous people better served the Spanish crown by being more easily recruited for the mining *mita* and for the collection of taxes. The colonial authorities appropriated the name of the Inca *mita* and the rotating and obligatory work in the mines the concept entailed. They expanded the system in spatial and temporal coverage while adding cruel forced labor and punishments.

Mining underwent transformations throughout the colonial period and through to independence. The Nuevas Ordenanzas de Minería (New Mining Ordinances), implemented in Mexico in 1783 and with small alternations transferred shortly thereafter to the Andes, "provided the legal underpinnings of the Spanish American nations' approach to mining until the late 1800s" (Brown 2012:91). The ordinances established that the Crown was the owner of the mines, which could be assigned to private subjects in exchange for a share of the extracted minerals.

Once independent in 1821, as part of the myth of national development, Peru experienced a guano and nitrate extractive boom and passed laws to protect mining activity. That year the government exempted mining equipment from taxes. Extractive activity was again perceived as the sector that would boost the economy, reflecting the growing demand for metals from Northern Hemisphere nations (Dager 1999:281). Railway construction was one of the consequences. The railroad connected Lima to the central mining region of La Oroya in 1893 and reached Huancayo in 1908 to supply food to the capital (Wilson 2004). Formed by private investors, the National Mining Society of Peru wrote Peru's first mining code in 1900. Individual owners were able to buy mines in perpetuity with the sole condition that they paid taxes. Mining equipment remained tax exempt.

With the turn of the century came bankruptcy, and the national railways passed into British hands with the formation of the Peruvian Corporation, which transported minerals for export. At the same time, the U.S. company La

Cerro—then named Cerro de Pasco Mining Company—constructed the railroad from La Oroya to Cerro de Pasco, or "the Royal City of Mines," as dubbed by the Spanish. By the middle of the century, the state had almost abandoned the construction of highways in the Andes, and U.S. mining companies were building their own. By constructing these road networks between the towns and the mining sites, these companies rewarded certain localities that were providing the mining labor (Wilson 2004).

Company ownership provides a framework for tracing the most important moments in Peruvian mining during the twentieth century. By the early years, the government had already sold most of the large mines. Between 1910 and 1950 there was an aggressive denationalization of Peruvian mining (Thorp and Bertram 1978). Great Britain was the largest buyer for a time, but was superseded by the United States, particularly in the copper sector. Both countries needed copper for their industrialization and for electricity and communication devices (Rizo-Patrón 1999). By 1901 La Cerro had acquired approximately 80 percent of the mines in the central Andes. This company constructed infrastructure that promoted economic growth across the region. Foreign investors began to work in other areas (e.g., the northern Andes). From the 1930s, Peruvian capital began to return to the mining sector, attracted by rising prices for silver, gold, lead, and zinc. Foreign-owned projects remained focused on copper, which fell in price. Pressure on the government led it to create the Banco Minero, to provide low-cost loans, and the Peruvian Institute of Mines, to advise the industry.

For the Peruvian historian—and member of a mining family—Heraclio Bonilla (1974:47), the mining hubs must be considered development poles in spite of the abuses that occurred during colonial and republican periods. Studies, such as the detailed account of the Muquiyauyo peasant community by the anthropologist Richard Adams (1959), suggest that the vitality of Peru's central highlands during the twentieth century was financed in no small part by remissions from miners to their native villages. Mining work contributed to differentiation among peasants. Although large-scale mining promoted local trade, the penetration patterns were heterogeneous, reflecting the complexity of Andean ecology. The transformations evidenced the complex Andean ecosystem, as manifested in heterogeneous penetration patterns that exacerbated regional socioeconomic differences. The social change in the Peruvian central highlands—dominated by La Cerro—promoted the development of transportation networks and provided opportunities for local entrepreneurs to raise cattle or grow sugarcane, although the transformation reproduced or exacerbated socioeconomic differences (Mallon 1983).

From the early to mid-twentieth century, the peasants of the central Andes—the most densely populated and economically differentiated upper Andean region—experienced the effects of an economy that was powerfully impacted by La Cerro. The company generated numerous small accumulation processes, the product of exchanges with peasants, contributing to differentiated development (Long and Roberts 1984). The process meant the qualification, proletarianization, and unionization of *castellanizados* (Castilianized peasants). A sector of more affluent peasants came to lead communal and district institutions (Laite 1980; Long and Roberts 1984). Peasant mobilizations during the 1960s in the Peruvian central and southern highlands revealed the role of the mining centers in raising consciousness. Many "invasions" of the haciendas were carried out by peasants who had spent time in mining centers. With the central Andes dominated by La Cerro—and its large-scale mining that included mineral processing, livestock operations, road networks, hydroelectric plants, mining camps, dams, and refineries—the economic opportunities it created moved the model away from the traditional enclave, especially considering that the wages of the workers were spent in the area (Long and Roberts 1984; Mallon 1983).

La Cerro contributed to the evolution of a regional economy in the central Andes with unequal sectors that were at times in conflict, such as the agriculture with capital, peasant entrepreneurs, and smallholders dependent on communal resources. The impact accentuated differentiations and confrontations and changed the socioeconomic composition; for example, many industrial workers also belonged to the estates of the richest peasants (Laite 1984; Long and Roberts 1984:23). Bonilla (1974:24–25) argues that in the twentieth century, La Cerro opened the way for the emergence of an "enclave capitalism" that was dependent on external demands for accumulation and internally fragmented into sectors and social groups. This process had significant and differentiated impacts on regional economies.[2] The predominantly foreign capital limited the consolidation of industrial clusters around mining, especially given the mining suppliers located away from the mining regions or outside the country (Kuramoto 2000).

La Cerro generated dynamic commercial relations with other mines due to the mining processing service that it provided at the La Oroya smelter. That did not occur for other mining companies with weak ties unable to generate productive chains (Kuramoto 2000:21), such as Southern Peru Copper Corporation (or La Southern) and Marcona in the south. Each had massive capital, was large in scale, and generated vast profits and significant rates of repatriation in the face of national industries unable to supply their needs, all while tending toward importation (Thorp and Bertram 1978). In 1965, La Southern spent 9.5 percent of its sales on local labor, 10.3 percent in taxes, and 5.3 percent on purchases of local materials and services. The value retained in Peru was only 20.9 percent. By comparison, in 1959–1968 La Cerro's retained value in Peru was 76 percent: 21 percent of its gross income (sales plus other income) was used to pay local labor, 14 percent went in taxes, 30 percent was used to purchase minerals and pay freight, and 12 percent was used to acquire local supplies and services (Kuramoto 2000:23).

Between the 1950s and 1970s, the mining code encouraged foreign capital (e.g., tax regulatory benefits and deductions), marking a domain of international capital in mining, especially copper. For example, favorable conditions allowed the Toquepala project to recover its investment in just five years. Industries supplying the mines grew, especially in the central Andes. La Cerro controlled about 100 of the 220 mining projects in the country. Additionally, there were industries for the mineral products. This expansive process reflected the growing urbanization of the nation, which generated greater demand for metallic products, such as copper cables for electrification and telephony. Most of these companies set up in Lima. The mining institutions also continued to expand, and in 1969 MEM was created (Glave and Kuramoto 2002; Kuramoto 2000).

During the 1970s, the nationalization of mining under the regime of General Velasco (1968–1975) meant improvements in housing, health, and services for workers and families living in mining areas. Some mines implied a certain contribution to neighboring populations, which eventually, and often with limitations, were able to benefit from modest infrastructure such as hospitals or schools. However, it was common that the children of foreign employees were in classrooms separate from the children of the local workers. Employment in mining grew. The proportion of skilled office employees also rose to 17 percent during the Velasco government, whereas between 1945 and 1967, it had hovered around 8 percent (Dore 1988:148, 151; Thorp and Bertram 1978).

The nationalization plan reproduced the old export growth model (Thorp and Bertram 1978). The novelty was the nationalization of companies in different sectors under a modernization rhetoric. This fueled expectations: "On radio and television, in official speeches and newspapers, the names of the mines that were key to Peru's development and that promised to make all Peruvians rich were repeated like an incantation" (Dore 1988:174–175). The use of an anti-imperialist discourse unaffiliated with communism characterized the symbolism of the Peruvian Revolution. According to historian Elizabeth Dore, "Eventually all of the nationalized companies were compensated, in some cases beyond the expectations of their directors. . . . In general the companies were satisfied with their indemnification" (Dore 1988:165). The reforms facilitated foreign private investment, attracting large capital for the construction of colossal infrastructure, especially in mining, oil, and agricultural irrigation (Dore 1988:165–166).

From the late 1960s to the mid-1970s, Peruvian mining entered a crisis marked by declining productivity and rising wages. Only a few projects—such as Tintaya and Cerro Verde—were exploited during the Velasco regime. Although the government contracted many loans to develop mining projects, implementation proved too costly. Several estimates exaggerated the potential of the deposits, and these were coupled with overly optimistic price projections (Dore 1988). Barely a single project was completed. The government was trapped with large interest debts and lacked the exports to finance them.

Following the nationalization under the Agrarian Reform of the lands managed by La Cerro's Livestock Division, the company wound the division up and ended the subsidy for the consumption of its workers and their families. The cost of living for La Cerro employees rose rapidly, and this contributed to strikes in 1970 and 1971. Between 1957 and 1972, mining stoppages went from 0.6 to 25 percent of the national total (Guerra 1999:383). From 1966 to 1974, mining stoppages grew by an average of 32 percent per year (Dore 1988:170–172). The longest strikes occurred at La Cerro and were associated with demands for its nationalization. Following calls to consider the national good and other forms of pressure, the workers were ultimately forced to give up their wage struggles.

Other than construction, private investment between 1969 and 1972 continued the downward trend in its contribution to gross national product (GNP) that had been evident since the 1950s (Thorp and Bertram 1978). In 1974 the state expropriated La Cerro's holdings and created Centromin. Despite the private sector's lack of interest in these mines, the state argued that they were critical for the development of capitalism in Peru. Dore (1988:171) details how, although the government accompanied the purchase with a strong anti-imperialist rhetoric of nationalization "for internal consumption, to bolster government's popular support," the process did not in fact represent a threat to the larger interests of U.S. capital, since the government negotiated agreements and mining ventures in southern Peru. The Velasco government expropriated companies such as La Cerro and Marcona, which it considered crucial for national development but judged to have made insufficient operational investment (Dore 1988:174). La Southern decided that it was prepared to invest, and as a consequence, the government favored it.[3]

In mid-1975 General Velasco was replaced by the cautious Morales Bermúdez, who abandoned the so-called Velasco revolution and reclaimed the political and economic support of the private sector while social property was reduced (Thorp and Bertram 1978). The military period since 1968 had discredited the ideals of autonomy, nationalism, and reform by failing to deliver changes that met national expectations. These unfulfilled hopes created favorable preconditions for the subsequent privatization.

Although the return to the presidency of Fernando Belaúnde in 1980 saw private investors encouraged to participate in state companies, they chose not to do so because of the meager profitability these offered. Taxes on profits and exports decreased, and state policy to participate in refining and commercialization almost disappeared. During the period 1979–1984, national participation in mining capital fell to 13 percent, and in 1976 international capital grew from 55 percent to 62 percent. On their return, foreign firms adopted a cautious approach and were strengthened by transformations achieved during the military period. U.S. companies did not participate in outdated mines or machinery, investing instead in production with greater profitability (Dore 1988). The macroeconomic crisis of the 1980s negatively affected mining, reduced investments, and generated overexploited mines (Kuramoto 2000). There were also dramatic cases of environmental pollution. Mining was considered the most polluting activity, particularly affecting Andean productive activities (Glave and Kuramoto 2002:529). Mining environmental degradation had deepened since the 1950s due to the open pit method, which improved working conditions but increased the degradation of soil and left it covered in toxic waste. This generated enormous damage through the removal of mountains and the destruction of valleys and farmland. "Often these residues were recklessly discarded, initiating a chain of soil, water and air contamination that altered the ecosystems of large areas" (Dore 2000:16).

From the 1980s to the early 1990s, Shining Path sabotaged and attacked mines (e.g., destroyed electric power utilities and murdered mining officers) in its search for explosives and money (CVR 2003). The strikes it organized also affected considerable mining areas due to the closure of several mining units that left their local workers unemployed. According to the Truth and Reconciliation Commission (CVR 2003), the internal conflict led to almost seventy thousand deaths, the highest recorded in any single struggle since Peru's independence. It was also a demonstration of the vulnerability of the Indigenous and rural population, which was overrepresented among the victims. Since the 1990s, local mining conflicts have led to more debates that weigh local costs against national benefits, contrasting local expectations and demands in the new globalized context of increased environmental awareness. The turn of the century saw Peruvian mining companies largely under the ownership of traditional mining groups, such as the Benavides (Buenaventura), Hochschild, and Baertl (Milpo) groups. These have sought to professionalize their management. Some have established alliances with foreign companies (e.g., Buenaventura and Newmont in Yanacocha) or started operations abroad, such as Milpo, through its Iván Zar mine in Chile (Glave and Kuramoto 2002).

Mining Expansion Under Neoliberalization

Investment in basic metals such as copper rose during the 1990s. These required long-term capital. The increase responded to rises in metal prices, the privatizations of state-owned companies, and the facilities established by government policies to attract foreign investment. Copper, gold, and silver all saw large price rises in the 1990s (Torres 2014). Simultaneously, opposition to and legal action against mining activities in the USA and Canada reached an unprecedented peak. In the *Engineering and Mining Journal*, Joe Porter (1994:66) states, "There are areas in the USA where mining is nearly extinct because of public criticism and increasing regulation, forcing mining companies to pursue new frontiers in Latin America and elsewhere." A show of force had been witnessed in the court dispute between communities and the mining giant BHP over the Ok Tedi mine project in Papua New Guinea in the 1990s.[4] While at the start of the 1990s, 12 percent of the world's mining capital was located in Latin America, by the end of the decade this had risen to 30 percent. No other region held more at that time. Global investment in exploration grew 90 percent. In Latin America it quadrupled from 1990 to 1997. In Peru it increased twenty times (World Bank 2005b:20). These transformations in Latin America were encouraged by international commitments. The Washington Consensus was the most representative. This economic manifesto identified the state as a barrier to prosperity, calling for the dismantling of trade barriers, the eradication of budget deficits, the privatization of public companies, and an openness to foreign investment (Bouillon 2003; Davis 2005). Privatizations were tied to loan arrangements with the IMF and the World Bank (CVR 2003:84; Dore 2000:21).

To recover from government bankruptcy in the 1980s, the Fujimori regime sought financial resources by privatizing state enterprises.[5] Macroeconomic stabilization, legislative changes, and the peace process all contributed to the return of foreign investment. As much as $9.8 billion entered Peru between 1992 and 2004 due to privatization and the arrival of capital (World Bank 2005b:23). The Lima Stock Exchange was the world's most profitable by 2005–2006, and the most lucrative shares belonged to mining companies, seven of which grew between 126 and 513 percent (Campodónico 2006a).[6]

Peru is an illustration of the global trend toward expansion of the mining frontier. Up until the 1990s, mining took place in 105 countries, whereas by the middle of the decade it was present in 151 (de Echave 2001:21). The large mining projects of the 1990s began their operations on the foundations of privatized state enterprises. They did not aggressively pursue exploration. Junior Canadian companies purchased mining claims and struck exploration alliances with Peruvian concession holders. The number of concession requests processed by the state more than doubled between 1991 and 2000, from 31,508 to 72,379 (Glave and Kuramoto 2002:532). According to Peru's Geological, Mining, and Metallurgical Institute, in 1991 there were only 2.2 million hectares under mining concession rights. Subsequently, the country has experienced two notable periods of expansion: 1993–1999 (from 2.3 to 15.6 million hectares) and 2002–2013 (from 7.4 to 26.8 million hectares). The decrease in 1999–2002 reflected prices for metals and a lower financial support (CooperAcción 2016:5).[7] The peak recorded in 2013 represented 21 percent of the national territory, before a reduction over the subsequent three years to 14 percent (18.9 million hectares). The expansion of these concessions found most departments with significate percentages of their territory under this arrangement (e.g., 44 percent of Ancash and 52 percent of Moquegua), compromising surface land dedicated to other purposes (CooperAcción 2016:6). Over the period 1992–1998, 56 percent of peasant communities (3,200 in total) were located near to exploration activity and 5 percent (300 in total) to mining operations (Aste 2000:92). According to the 1994 National Agrarian Census, some 40 percent of the country's agricultural land was managed by peasant communities, a proportion that remained virtually unchanged in the 2012 census

(Castillo 2013). The 2012 census also showed peasant and native communities to be in control of 60.5 percent of the agricultural area. This land consists primarily of natural pastures in the Andes and forests in the Amazon. The advance of the mining frontier poses risks to the health of the environment and to vulnerable rural livelihoods that depend on it to reproduce the household economy. The situation is especially delicate for agropastoralists in the highlands, where mining is concentrated and competes for the water supply. The precarious connection between the nation and its smallholder farmers exacerbates the problem.

Peru was contributing 6.1 percent of global copper in the middle of the first decade of the twenty-first century (World Bank 2005b:168). More recently, the U.S. Geological Survey ranked Peru's 2016 copper production as the world's second largest—behind Chile but ahead of China. Antamina represented the most significant mining investment during the late twentieth and early twenty-first centuries, before major expansion of mining ventures in the southern Andes (e.g., Cerro Verde and Las Bambas; see figure 13). Antamina was at one time recognized as the third largest mine on the planet, with one of world's largest copper reserves. It has represented the country's largest copper extraction project. It was also the world's first combined copper and zinc extraction project and the country's largest ever mine investment (CMA 2005a, 2007).

The mining expansion of the 1990s was criticized for its failure to reduce poverty in the Andes, where most of the projects are located. In a provincial level study, economists Escobal and Ponce (2008) found that between 1998 and 2005, the reduction of poverty in the Andes in certain regions stagnated or even reversed. Peru's poverty map (Díaz 2006:22) showed the highlands to exhibit the highest level of infant malnutrition (42 percent), the highest female illiteracy rate (23 percent), and the highest percentage of population without sewerage (35 percent). One-third of the Andean population lacked safe drinking water facilities and 42 percent was without electricity. Official estimates in 2016 showed the country's poor to remain concentrated in the highlands (48 percent), followed by the coast (34 percent) and the Amazon (16.9 percent). Furthermore, 70 percent of those in extreme poverty lived in the Andes (INEI 2017:63). A panorama of vulnerability was juxtaposed with the extractive bonanza.

Official 2016 figures claimed that roughly one-fifth of the country's population lived in poverty, while chronic infant malnutrition still affected 14 percent of Peruvians, an improvement from the figure of 23 percent registered five years earlier (INEI 2017:42).[8] According to official estimates, the average national

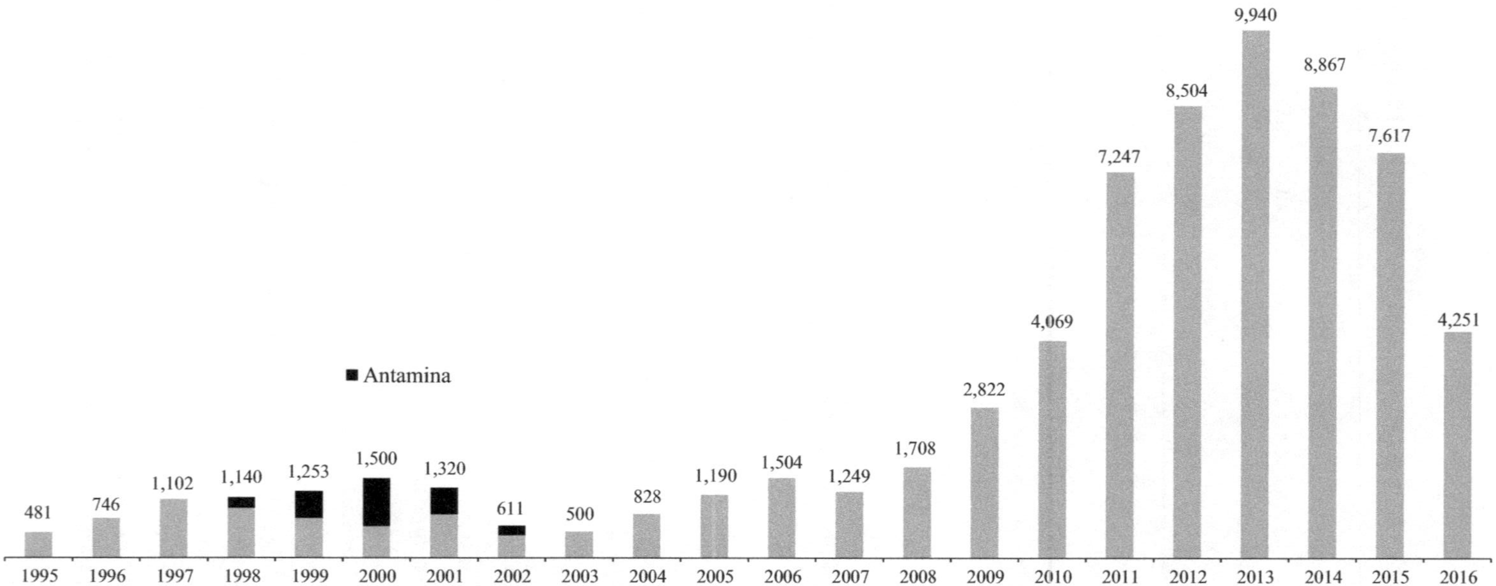

FIGURE 13 The evolution of mining investment in Peru (1995–2016) and Antamina (1998–2002). Prepared by the author based on Boza (2006:33), Peru's Central Reserve Bank (BCRP), and MEM (2007, 2017).

Annual mining investment includes preparation, exploration, equipment, infrastructure, and exploitation (MEM 2017). MEM recorded the investment in Antamina (1998–2002) as $2.27 billion, a figure that probably included a contractual penalty.

anemia rate for children (less than three years old) in 2007 was 56.8 percent and by 2018 had reached 46.6 percent, the third highest prevalence in Latin America. The incidence in the Andes of 54.2 percent was above that of both the Amazon (48.8 percent) and the coast (42 percent) (*El Comercio* 2018). Those considered to live slightly above the poverty line still find themselves in a precarious situation. Poverty estimates in recent years have been criticized for being one-dimensional, and their credibility has been called into question. The poverty line is approximately one hundred dollars per month. It covers INEI's *canasta básica* (basic food basket) but ignores living conditions and expenses such as education and health. A more realistic, multidimensional, and sociological approach would include such items.[9] According to the former head of the INEI, Farid Matuk, the estimated reduction in poverty as measured by the government is "false because it duplicates the real reduction of poverty" by equating a decrease of 15 percent in malnutrition with a decline of 28 percent in the poverty rate for the period 2006–2016. He concedes there has been a decrease, but argues it to be smaller, accusing the APRA (Alianza Popular Revolucionaria Americana, or American Popular Revolutionary Alliance) government (2006–2011) of "adulteration" of the official figures to report a "fabulous" 14 point reduction in poverty at the national level (Zambrano 2017:10–11).

The distribution of benefits that came after the privatizations of the 1990s was associated with an evident divergence between Lima and the regions. Per capita GDP of Lima was 1.73 times that of the rest of the country in 1995–1996, and 1.69 times in 2003 (PNUD 2005:68). The high economic growth experienced in the departments with the largest mining investments (just six received 80 percent of the canon during 1996–2003) did not necessarily lead to a recognizable reduction in poverty. In 2004, three years after the Antamina operations began in Ancash, the department had 55 percent of its population living below the poverty line (ranked fourteenth out of twenty-four departments) (World Bank 2005a). By 2016, twenty-three years after Yanacocha—the largest gold mine in Latin America and one of the most profitable in the world—commenced operations in Cajamarca, it remained the country's poorest department, a distinction held jointly with Huancavelica. In that same year, fifteen years after Antamina began, Ancash was among the eleven poorest of Peru's twenty-four departments (INEI 2017:47, 48).

Given the difference in income for those areas producing minerals and hydrocarbons by comparison with those where there is no extraction, canon transfers have meant the creation of great inequalities at the subnational level. Just five departments (Ancash, Cajamarca, Tacna, Moquegua, and Arequipa) concentrated more than 60 percent of the canon in 2013 (Dargent et al. 2017). More recent research has begun to examine these unequal district-level impacts.[10]

Prior to the 1990s, mining companies had assumed that their contribution to the nation was limited to certain inputs to the local economy (jobs, basic infrastructure, and improvement of local markets) and fiscal transfers through taxes and concession payments (World Bank 2005b). But pressure to take their socio-environmental responsibilities more seriously increased. Mining is criticized for the scarce direct employment (3 percent) it generates. The discussion about development and mining since the 1990s has national and local dimensions. The latter includes the subnational divisions (i.e., departments, provinces, and districts). At the national level, the indicators highlighted are macrostatistics such as GDP, exports, employment, and taxes. Debates on mining profits reveal the power of the mining sector. A 2003 change to the canon transfers saw its calculation increase from 20 to 50 percent of the income tax paid. New contributions from mining were approved, such as the introduction of mining royalties in 2004, imposed on production rather than profits of large and medium-sized companies, as a national compensation to exploit a nonrenewable resource. These payments meant a range between 1 and 3 percent of the renting value of extracted minerals and were a deductible cost of the calculated income tax (Dargent et al. 2017). Also approved in 2005 was a windfall tax on price extraordinary profits (*sobreganancias*). Advocates had pointed to the enormous rise in metals prices that Mexico, Bolivia, and Ghana were also taxing in this way. The canon, royalties, and annual subsurface fees (*derecho de vigencia*) transfers allow the participation of subnational governments in the economic rent collected by the state, on behalf of the nation, who owns the resources (de la Cruz 2011).

Eleven mining companies—including Antamina—appealed to the Tribunal Constitucional (Constitutional Court) over the royalty payments. The court ruled that the royalty was *contraprestación* (financial compensation) rather than a tax and was therefore excluded from the protections provided by the contract. This allowed the government to apply the levy to companies with Fujimori-era *contratos de estabilidad jurídica* (legal stability contracts). The government, however, chose not to demand royalties from this protected group. The royalties were primarily applied to the medium-sized mining sector, belonging mostly to Peruvian entrepreneurs. Within the large-scale mining sector, only Southern Peru Copper Corporation was affected because its tax stability agreement had ended.[11] The state also chose not to collect the windfall profits tax, accepting instead a voluntary and temporary economic contribution. This contribution, known as the Programa Minero de Solidaridad con el Pueblo (Solidarity with the People Mining Program), was the transformation of a presidential election promise made by the candidate Alan García (second term, 2006–2011). It lasted with his term. Instead of the additional contribution promised, the government negotiated a single one-off donation known as the *óbolo minero* or *aporte voluntario* (voluntary donation from miners), consisting of 3.75 percent of net profits after the payment of income tax and before the distribution of dividends.[12] According to the government, this alternative aimed to avoid legal action that might have scared off investors. Paradoxically, during the 1993–2002 period, of the 257 legal stability agreements in existence, almost half were modified at the request of the companies (Campodónico 2005; SUNAT 2002, 11).

Export and Employment

The state auctioned large mines to foreign investors who arrived in the 1990s, such as BHP-Billiton and Anglo-American. New technologies increased mining extraction, and Peru became one of the largest producers of zinc, gold, lead, copper, silver, molybdenum, and tin in Latin America and the world. By the middle of the first decade of the twenty-first century, Antamina was the largest mining exporter (19 percent), leading in the extraction of copper (38 percent) and ranked third for zinc (14 percent) (BCP 2006). A decade later it would be surpassed by the Sociedad Minero Verde, reflecting the expansion of the Cerro Verde mine in southern Peru.

Peruvian minerals were exported primarily to industrialized countries during the 1990s. Iron and copper prices rebounded because of urban growth and industrialization in China. By 2016, China—the main destination—represented 34 percent of the value of the total of minerals exported, followed by Switzerland (12 percent) and the United States (10 percent). Some 52 percent of Antamina's sales were going to Asia by the middle of the first decade of the twenty-first century. A decade later this figure had risen to 80 percent. China was overwhelmingly the principle buyer (BCP 2006; CMA 2016; Wolfe 2006).

In the period from 1950 to 2016, although mining accounted for about half of exports, it only represented 5 to less than 10 percent of GNP until the new millennium, when it crossed the 10 percent barrier, reaching 20 percent by the middle of the first decade to decrease afterward toward 15 percent (Cano and Otárola 2017:59).[13] Although mining generates the majority of foreign exchange through exports, it has not represented an important source of direct employment. Since the 1990s, large-scale mining has demanded more sophisticated technology and less local unskilled labor. The large-scale mining sector drastically reduced the number of personnel it directly employed. Official figures show that large-scale mines employed 58 percent of miners (29,373 out of 50,684). By the end of the decade, the figure was 39 percent (23,413 out of 59,813), followed by medium-sized (51 percent) and small-scale mining (10 percent). Meanwhile, the production of most metals grew by more than 50 percent, and in some cases by more than 2,000 percent. Between 1997 and 2003, the hydrocarbon and mining sectors grew at 7.62 percent but only contributed 0.66 percent of the jobs. This placed it last on a list headed by the agriculture sector, with 33.63 percent (World Bank 2005a:38).

Labor deregulation weakened unions and allowed mining companies to contract private services for tasks previously undertaken internally (Glave and Kuramoto 2002). Between 2007 and 2016, the mining sector, from artisanal through to large-scale operations, employed on average just 163,000 workers. Contractors added an average 93,000 workers (MEM 2017). An estimate sponsored by the mining industry argued that every mining job generates another 6.25 jobs in the rest of the economy (IPE 2017). It did not indicate if this referred to temporary or permanent positions. Mining companies point out that they are among the few industries that operate above 3,500 meters. However, much of the work for contractors is under temporary contracts.

The increase and decentralization of large-scale mining has generated a limited relationship between new mines and the national producers of mining inputs and equipment. National industries have been unable to fully satisfy the demand for advanced technological equipment. In addition, many projects purchase products from certain suppliers in compliance with conditions set by their investors (Kuramoto 2000). It is common for investors to favor certain agents in their networks of reciprocity.

With rare exceptions, despite growth in mining that saw the primary sector increase its share of total exports from 30 to 45 percent during the 1990s, economic inequality in Latin America increased (Bouillon et al. 2004:14; Pulgar-Vidal and Aurazo 2003:24). Virtually all sources agree that at the beginning of the decade, Latin America was "by far the most unequal region in the world" (Hoffman and Centeno 2003:365). In Peru, while the production of almost all metals grew more than 50 percent and some more than 2,000 percent, economic differences also increased (Glave and Kuramoto 2002). In this decade, inequality increased from 0.46 to 0.49, as measured by the Gini coefficient (Bouillon et al. 2004:14).[14] Illustrating the country's socioeconomic divisions during the 1990s, the Cuánto Institute and UNICEF reported that the poorest 50 percent of the population received 20 percent of the income, whereas the richest 20 percent received 50 percent of the income (Sheahan 1999:118). According to official estimates, this situation has been changing gradually during the current century.

Primal Impacts

Beyond the displacement of people (see chapter 2), one of Antamina's first impacts was the cutting of access to a road necessary to reach grazing land (see chapter 1). Although occasionally the road could be used with a permit obtained in San Marcos or Huaraz, the loss of direct access undermined local livelihoods by adding extra time in herding transportation costs. Complaints about access had not characterized earlier mines in San Marcos, such as Contonga.

Temporary foreign workers arrived in San Marcos during the construction phase. New restaurants opened and several residents rented out rooms. Bars and discotheques were opened but then closed shortly after due to complaints of fights and noise. While some would later recall nostalgically a period of great economic activity, others would claim that there was little interaction between the workers from Antamina and the surrounding area. They said that, other than on occasions when some workers left the mine during their rest periods, the workers did not buy goods in the town of San Marcos and did not share activities. The miners used the Antamina highway, which bypassed the town on its way to Huaraz and Lima. Lucas, a former Ango Raju president, recalled the great expectations that accompanied the opening of Antamina:

> Many of us thought there would be work, income. However, Antamina has not consumed a single product from the area. There was a small mine [Contonga with Sociedad Minera Gran Bretaña] from 1980 to 1991. I think it provided more income to people because we sold all kinds of products: meat, milk, cheese, even crafts, without an agreement or anything. . . . You would go with your merchandise and do business with honey, cheese, potatoes, oca [*Oxalis tuberosa*], everything we have in the area. Additionally, the people who worked there

> consumed and it was advantageous because—knowing there was a market—we had to produce. Everyone was a winner. [We imagined] that when Antamina came it would need produce. Because they told us that at the beginning there would be more than four thousand workers. Unfortunately it was not like that at all, because of their technology. When they started they were like five hundred workers, but it didn't last long, like a fair. (grammar modified)

The environmental impact statement indicated that the construction of the pipeline was going to require 962 short-term employees for "skilled operators of heavy machinery and inexperienced workers" and that "the construction [was] likely to generate considerable local employment, demand for goods and services, local contracts, and significant short-term profits in the local economy" (K&H 1999b:13–14). However, the document did not explain how many employees were needed in each category or how local expectations would be met.

As profit is only generated once a mine comes into operation; canon transfers often begin between eight and fifteen years after commencement of the exploration phase (CAD 2005b). In 2006, about ten years after Antamina won the concession, at a ceremony in which Peru's president, Alejandro Toledo, was present, Antamina handed over its first income tax (480 million soles, or $148 million), which the government added to the fiscal canon transfer to the Ancash regional government. The $148 million was close to half of the total national mining canon for 2005 (CAD 2005a:2). Canon distribution meant $12.4 million allocated to San Marcos, an unprecedented sum in the locality. To grasp the significance of the change in local resources ($120,000 to $12 million), it helps to realize that the mining canon received by San Marcos the year before (2005) was already the largest in Huari Province and represented more than half of the total canon transferred ($212,000) from all sources in the province, including hydroelectricity, fishing, and forestry (CAD 2005b:24) (see figure 14).

Corporate Contribution

The company's preference for imports rather than national procurement seems evident from the fact that in 2000 it reported only 39 percent of investment for the latter (i.e., $274 million of a total of $690 million). The company's imports consisted of "capital goods, mining equipment, and technology." With 31 percent of total acquisitions for operations, the USA headed the list (70 percent,

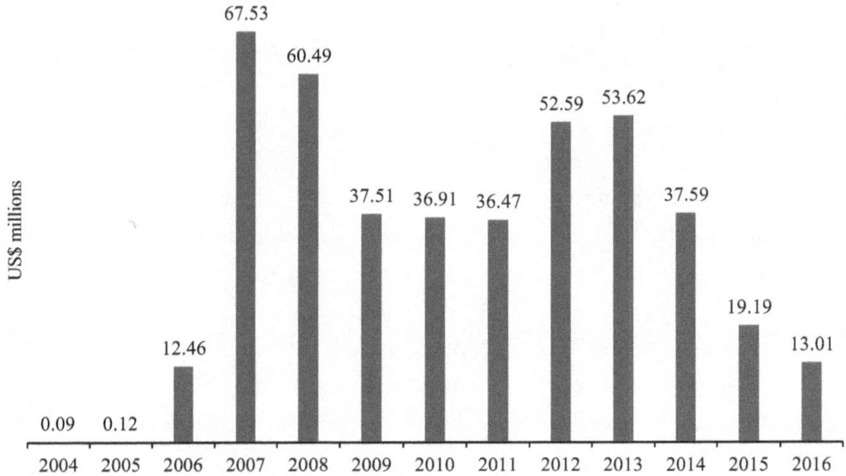

FIGURE 14 Canon transfers to San Marcos Municipality, 2004–2016. Prepared by author based on Peru's Central Reserve Bank (BCRP), SBS, and Ministry of Economy and Finance.

$155 million), followed by Peru (21 percent, $45 million), Japan (3 percent), Canada (2 percent), Chile (0.42 percent), and nine other nations (0.67 percent) (CMA 2001b:52–53). This distribution reproduced a pattern where investors did not select suppliers from the country where the resource was located (Kuramoto 2000). Antamina justified the distribution of its purchasing on the basis of provisions in the "finance granted that committed procurement of various items to the countries of origin of the financial entities." It added that the "[Peruvian] supplier industry was unprepared to meet the demand of a world-class mining project like Antamina," and that national firms had not developed sufficiently to be able to sustain a megaproject since the Cuajone experience of the 1970s (CMA 2001b:52–53). In 2014 Antamina reported imports of $18 million. The USA continued heading the list (44 percent), followed by Chile (27 percent) and Canada (10 percent). Of the 1,322 suppliers, 141 were from Ancash, with a trade value of $27 million (2.8 percent of the $957 million total) (CMA 2015:47).

Antamina's workforce during the construction phase peaked at approximately 10,000. Unsurprisingly, due to the dependence on high technology, the number dropped to 1,156 for the start of operations. Lima was the principal source of workers (40 percent), followed by Ancash (31 percent). Foreigners constituted 7 percent (CMA 2001b:7, 26). Of the 6,346 contractors employed in 2000, only 18 percent (1,184) were from Ancash and only 5.3 percent (337) were from Huari, the province where the ore deposit was located. Indeed, a greater number (377, or 5.9 percent) came from Bolognesi. And even the very distant province of Huarmey provided 31 workers (CMA 2001b:27).[15] At the 1993 census, San Marcos had a population of 11,647, of which 3,516 comprised the economically active population. Even had all the subcontractors from the province of Huari also been residents of San Marcos in that year, together they would have constituted less than 10 percent of its working-age population.

Many residents of San Marcos stated that the contractors preferred to employ workers who were foreign, Chileans in particular (CMA 2001b:27). Lazarus, the former president of Ango Raju community, related to me the "discontent" created by the fact that only a dozen heads of household in a community of approximately two hundred households had "stable" employment at Antamina. The company's vice president of corporate affairs acknowledged in a televised interview that Antamina's initial preference was for contracted, foreign, medium-skilled labor, even though this was more expensive. He argued that the company felt that these workers had more experience in Andean megaprojects. Reciprocity debts probably also influenced the labor hiring policy.

In 2006, five years after starting operations, Antamina's establishment consisted of 3,587 direct jobs (1,457 employees and 2,130 "partners and contractors"). According to Antamina, this meant a multiplier effect between 1.7 and 2.5, adding between 6,000 and 8,900 indirect workers (Wolfe 2006:22). This estimate is less than the average for Peru of 4 and considerably below that of the USA of 15 (Glave and Kuramoto 2002). By 2014, Antamina claimed to have 2,825 employees (811 direct employees and 2,014 "operators") and another 4,869 "strategic partners" from within its area of influence. Of the direct employees, 34 percent were reported to be natives of Ancash (CMA 2015:38).

In 2000, months prior to starting operations, Antamina contributed $4,269,311 in income tax (mainly through the dependent employee category), representing between 0.4 and 0.6 percent of the projected sales (CMA 2001b:50). Within two years, national mining production had grown by 13 percent, due mainly to the commencement of operations at Antamina (Mendoza and de Echave 2016:18). Peru's GNP rose by 1.2 percent during Antamina's first year. In 2005 Peru produced 6.1 percent of world copper and had increased its production by more than 52 percent since the start of production at Antamina (Wolfe 2006). That same year, thanks to the increase in the price of copper, Antamina exported

$1.8 billion, more than double its most optimistic initial projection of annual exports ($700–900 million). The estimate had almost tripled ($2.42 billion) a decade later (CMA 2001b:50; 2006b; 2015). Antamina was the largest mining exporter in Peru during the period 2010–2014.

Third category income tax was paid three years in advance thanks to unexpectedly high prices for mineral commodities that generated earlier profits (CMA 2006b:1). The $296 million paid in tax in 2006 was equivalent to 16 percent of Antamina exports for the previous year, when it realized a net profit of $815 million (Campodónico 2006a). The canon for Ancash amounted to $148 million. In 2014, and with much higher copper prices, Antamina paid $390 million in taxes, approximately 16 percent of its net income (i.e., $2.43 billion, consisting of net sales plus income from financing investments and asset sales) (CMA 2015:17).

Also in 2014, CODELCO (Corporación Nacional del Cobre, or National Copper Corporation), a Chilean state-owned mining company, produced approximately 10 percent of the world's mined copper. No other country extracted more. Chile was considered a model of promarket development in Latin America because of its economic growth and neoliberal reforms (CODELCO 2015). Copper has come to represent more than 50 percent of Chilean exports and CODELCO has produced more than 20 percent of that, amounting to 3 percent of GDP (CODELCO 2015; MMSD América del Sur 2002). In the forty-four years following its nationalization in 1971, CODELCO contributed more than $115 billion to the treasury. In 2004 it employed 16,778 workers, a figure that had reached 19,078 a decade later (CODELCO 2006:13; 2015). It is worth asking to what extent a state model such as CODELCO is appropriate when a nation is exploiting a resource that represents national patrimony by virtue of being a nonrenewable resource. This discussion has been abandoned in Peru because of experiences of inefficiency and corruption attributed to state-owned enterprises.[16]

Responsibility, Reciprocity, and Paternalism

While Antamina was receiving social responsibility awards between 1999 and 2002, many were complaining about its socioenvironmental impacts, as detailed in this book. This raises the question of how social responsibility is defined and evaluated. The "corporate social responsibility" paradigm arose in industrialized countries during the 1960s in the search for a purpose beyond mere profit in order to secure investments and legitimize business activity. Economist William Frederick noted that until 1970, corporate social responsibility involved examining the obligations associated with working for social well-being. Milton Friedman proclaimed that concepts of social responsibility that go beyond maximizing profit for shareholders undermine the foundations of a free society. A more ethical approach supposes acting responsibly with stakeholders and seeking to improve the quality of life of workers, their families, the local community, and society in general (Moir 2001:18). The approach presumes the voluntary attitude of a company to harmonize its particular goals with those of a more collective nature (Portocarrero et al. 2000). It entails the idea of a company that defines its goals, chooses its path, and assumes the consequences—that is, one that recognizes its responsibility.[17]

The application of these ideals is complicated by the fact that the commitments are voluntary and are defined by the company itself and, particularly in the case of Peru, the way in which old models of paternalism and patronage are evoked. Foreign companies, and those with large amounts of capital—in particular mining and oil enterprises whose projects are in general risky and have to respond to the requirements of investors—were the first in Peru to use social responsibility rhetoric (Benavides and Gastelumendi 2001:55; Caravedo 2003:11). The precedent in mining manifested in the form of the "friendly" or environmentally "clean" technologies that arrived in the 1980s, two decades after they had become commonplace elsewhere. The Antamina vice president of corporate affairs acknowledged that economic "globalization caused socioenvironmental standards to globalize," and that this promoted "greater sensitivity" to the issue. He also noted that the "greater competition for risk capital" and the "more active role" of NGOs had promoted better practices and higher standards (Cantuarias 2004:1).

Social responsibility has been optional, and ways to monitor compliance have not been defined. The codes of conduct for Antamina and SNMPE, the peak mining guild in Peru (CMA 2006a), each invoke—only in general terms—the need to manage the relationship with local communities carefully. The *compromiso previo* (prior commitment) guidelines promulgated in 2003 and the Antamina *código de conducta* (code of conduct) made apparent steps forward because they included subcontractors and temporary workers.[18] The extensions provided by the state for environment remediation at Doe Run's La Oroya smelter, in the face of evidence of significant deterioration in infant health, exemplified the limited effectiveness of self-regulation when applied to these voluntary principles. SNMPE applied its code of conduct in this case, but on a confidential basis only (Pulgar-Vidal 2006). The organization's *Pronunciamiento* (statement) on February 16, 2006, contained merely general criticism, together with exhortations that were neither time bound nor specific. SNMPE avoided sanctioning Doe Run Peru. It would be a further three years before the company's membership of the organization was suspended and a further year before it was expelled.

Why should a private company involve itself in local development in a country like Peru? Although several of Antamina's reports state the company's aim to "avoid paternalism in every way possible" (CMA 2001b:20; 2003b; 2004), none contain a definition of the concept. Antamina personnel reported that the company received requests for gifts and buildings. A member of the Community Relations team told a radio station in San Marcos of the dilemma they confronted, the "fear of doing too much, because if we did a lot. . . . [It] would be paternalistic," yet by waiting "too long to do things, we then had conflicts." This generated internal debates about financing local development projects, reflected in the following quote from an Antamina publication: "It is not easy for all officials and workers to support initiatives allocating resources to projects that have nothing to do with production, or that do not translate into well-being for their families" (CMA 2001b:18–19). The social responsibility paradigm gained acceptance because it made sense for the mining business even if some remained skeptical. An Antamina staff member pointed out to me that the project's neighbors would be its best "guardians" since they would never attack the source of their development projects. The vice president of corporate affairs claimed that social responsibility "is a good investment in the long term, since it facilitates harmonious relations with the surroundings and prevents situations of conflict, saving expenses implicit in the crises" (Cantuarias 2004:2).

Evolving Corporate Responsibility

In practice, development for the company implied the application of a set of remodeled projects using a trial and error process. This approach reflected changes in its discourse and variations in the perception of mining employees themselves, as well as power struggles and criticism internal to the company. By the end of 1998, more than two years after obtaining the concession, Antamina established the Community Development Office in San Marcos. It was initially dedicated to solving problems associated with land acquisition. The following year, after incorporating more personnel, the office began to work on social issues. The demand for development projects was evident from the first encounters with the residents. The abundance of proposals was evidence of the enormous expectations. The company was unprepared for the avalanche. Several Antamina employees told me that the consultation processes were new to them. Antamina Community Relations documents made no reference to similar experiences elsewhere in Peru—for example, oil extraction projects in the Amazon and the Yanacocha mine in Cajamarca.

Antamina's initial so-called development projects in San Marcos—implemented between 2000 and 2003—focused on forestry and on experimental agriculture and livestock stations (see table 6). Among the largest and most heavily criticized projects were these two investigational stations, neither of which had been requested by San Marcos. The Shahuanga Granja Demostrativa de Crianza Bovina (Bovine Breeding Demonstration Farm) project sought to "improve the standard of living and income of the herders in the area of influence of the mine through the genetic improvement of sheep" (CMA 2003b:59). Investment in the Cochao Fundo Agrícola Modelo (Model Agricultural Estate) was three times greater than the Shahuanga project, and came to represent 22 percent of the total ($5,665,128) invested on development projects in San Marcos. Antamina claimed that it included seventeen hectares of nurseries, fish farms, apiaries, and a marketing company for San Marcos and Chavín de Huántar, together with "profitable products and an assured market" (CMA 2001b:44).

Both experimental centers operated through agreements with NGOs (e.g., CARE in Cochao) and the National University Santiago Antúnez de Mayolo. After 2003, both stations were operated by private entities supervised by the Ancash Association (Asociación Ancash 2004:4), created the previous year with Antamina funding. This organization, originally led by an anthropologist and formally chaired by Antamina's general manager, channeled funds from the mining company. Initially it claimed to fund forty projects arising from local initiatives. It subsequently included tourism projects, including traditional cultural displays. In practice, the experimental stations resembled 1960s Green Revolution projects, which had been criticized for their vertical approach but were relatively successful in combating famines and conflicts resulting from the population explosion in countries such as India. In San Marcos these experimental modules addressed food security only from a short-term production perspective, failed to directly include residents in the design, and did not tackle inequalities in the search of better conditions for regional markets. It is therefore unsurprising that the Shahuanga project closed in 2005 following an external "participatory evaluation" (CMA 2006f:64). Simultaneously, the first of several attempts to transform the Cochao project began through a "Pilot Center for Organic Andean Agriculture" (IDMA 2004:19). A "center for the production of guinea pigs" was tried about five years later (CMA 2010).

In Huarmey, as in San Marcos, Antamina's sociotechnological responsibility apparatus initially prioritized infrastructure, education, and agropastoral activities that it considered to represent local development (see table 7). Since Huarmey lacked expensive agropastoral projects—such as Shahuanga and Cochao in San Marcos—infrastructure clearly headed the priorities.

Criticism of the experimental centers focused on unfulfilled promises of reciprocity. Antamina was considered to have used the funds allocated to the projects on high salaries for personnel employed in the Office of Community Development. The Community Development Plan contained in the environmental impact statement had offered $6.4 million—a figure beyond regional parameters—for the first three years in four districts of the province of Huari. Huaraz and the El Pinar housing complex for Antamina workers were also included, although both were outside Antamina's immediate area of influence. The environmental impact statement indicated that Antamina would allocate $1.1 million to technical assistance salaries and more than $2 million to the social development of infrastructure, including El Pinar. These two line items had the effect of halving the finance proposed in the environmental statement.

Rivalry among families also had an influence over the initial selection of projects by the Community Development Office in San Marcos (see also chapter 1). The associated tensions slowed the process of achieving consensus on proposals. Additionally, in the interests of passing internal evaluations, the company chose projects that were easy to measure. A mining corporation requires immediate results and thus favors short-term monitoring metrics. In this case, indicators such as plant and animal size and quality met the criteria and led to projects much simpler in scope than, for example, activities that might have relied on, or even aimed to rebuild, social networks in a community where complex and long-standing hostilities existed. The experimental stations were also criticized for the unclear temporal or spatial scale of the benefits they aimed to deliver to rural people who were impoverished and highly vulnerable.

TABLE 6 Funds for community development programs and community relations in San Marcos District, 2000–2003

	2000	2001	2002	2003	TOTAL BY SUBTYPE	PERCENT OF THE TOTAL
Agropastoral						
Agriculture and grazing: Cochao**	N/A	$916,000	$250,000	$92,477	$1,258,477	
Grazing: Shahuanga**	$125,535	$78,000	$76,000	$179,000	$458,535	
Agroforestry program***				$241,220	$241,220	
Production				$33,702	$33,702	
Subtotal	$125,535	$994,000	$326,000	$546,399	$1,991,934	35
Infrastructure						
Infrastructure in the Ayash Basin***	$100,000	$170,000	$243,627		$513,627	
Compensation for contamination protests		$433,503			$433,503	
Infrastructure in San Marcos and Chavín***		$152,800	$71,455	$15,575	$239,830	
Road maintenance	$40,000	$58,600	$116,333		$214,933	
Multiuse coliseum		$85,714	$45,714		$131,428	
Schools			$57,460		$57,460	
Local Huaripampa employment			$36,717		$36,717	
Sports		$100	N/A	$34,200	$34,300	
Subtotal					$1,661,798	29
Resettlement assistance	$90,000	$60,500	$188,274	$466,912	$805,686	14
Education						
Production courses	$54,753	$30,400	$116,774	$5,000	$206,927	
Student scholarships	$66,000	$23,000	$62,300	$23,000	$174,300	

Teacher training***	$129,667	$31,400	$1,850	$300	$163,217	
Reactivation of the San Marcos Technology Institute		$30,400	$51,545	$12,000	$93,945	
Kindergarten and radio programs**			$30,000	$17,000	$47,000	
Education				$20,185	$20,185	
Courses		N/A	N/A	$13,000	$13,000	
Subtotal	$250,420	$115,200	$262,469	$90,485	$718,574	13
Health*						
Health***	$93,000	$233,800	$1,935	$14,380	$343,115	
Alcohol and drug prevention			$30,000		$30,000	
Subtotal					$373,115	7
Social						
Microenterprises	$10,000	$27,300	$45,928		$83,228	
Tourism**	$4,500			$14,293	$18,793	
Andes Gold Corridor	$4,000	$4,000	$4,000		$12,000	
Subtotal	$18,500	$31,300	$49,928	$14,293	$114,021	2
TOTAL					$5,665,128	100

Source: Prepared by the author based on CMA (2001b, 2002, 2003b, 2004). N/A: Not available.

*Antamina, CARE, and CLAS implemented the Programa Comunidad Saludable (Community Health Program) in 2001. CARE withdrew in 2002.

**In 2003 these projects were operated by private entities supervised by the Ancash Association with funds from Antamina.

***Since 2003 this includes some funds managed by the Ancash Association.

TABLE 7 Funds for community development in Huarmey (Valle de Fortaleza and Huarmey District), 2001–2003

	2001	2002	2003	TOTAL BY SUBTYPE	PERCENT OF THE TOTAL
Infrastructure	$378,390	$98,165	$89,060	$565,615	28.19
Education	$135,240	$140,031	$234,602	$509,873	25.41
Agropastoral	$125,356	$208,677	$29,497	$363,530	18.12
Fishing	$8,595	$58,801	$193,721	$261,117	13.01
Social	$92,700	$20,219	$73,269	$186,188	9.28
Health	$8,950	$39,750	$71,415	$120,115	5.99
Total	$749,231	$565,643	$691,564	$2,006,438	100.00

Source: Prepared by the author based on CMA (2001b, 2002, 2003b, 2004).

Antamina settled on a discourse summarized in the simple objective "create entrepreneurs." The rhetorical policy was active, placing advertisements in newspapers and immense billboards at strategic locations to announce projects. Placing photographs in official documents as iconic representations of successful community relations was among the company's preferred discursive tools. It is difficult to imagine how the residents of San Marcos—inserted into an incipient mercantile system—could have become the type of competitive market-oriented entrepreneurs that the mining company envisaged. Such a change would have entailed another level of financial investment, training, and testing. It also would have put at risk delicate agricultural livelihoods in the effort to service the demands of new markets, in particular that of meeting large regular supply quotas. A potato variety expected to be attractive for the markets of Lima was rejected by the people of San Marcos because of its flavor. From a sustainability perspective, when designing a project aimed at external markets, it is worth asking to what extent internal factors and markets should also be considered.

Antamina argued that the experimental projects were part of a larger plan to overcome what it viewed as an obsolete local development model that failed to prioritize markets. Mining representatives claimed that this model was mostly promoted by NGOs. The mining company claimed that the paternalistic *asistencialismo* (welfare-based model) primarily benefited the NGOs themselves, without ensuring project effectiveness or sustainability. They claimed that the NGOs had failed to provide a long-term presence in rural areas. It was certainly true that in some cases NGO representatives had only visited projects occasionally, particularly during the armed violence of the 1980s. The lack of paved roads, together with a focus by some NGOs purely on the indicators necessary to secure future funding, also may have played a part on the modest results of some projects.

Yet Antamina itself would also engage certain NGOs (e.g., CARE for the Cochao project) in reaction to criticism it received on many fronts. This may have been an attempt by a profit-oriented business to relax its initial rhetorical criticism of NGOs. It also may have been a corporate strategy to share responsibility and deflect blame should conflict arise. The NGOs became aware of the complicated sociopolitical landscape in San Marcos and several withdrew from the area. CARE left in 2003, citing the need to minimize damage to its institutional reputation. It would later return to San Marcos and in 2010 be subcontracted by Antamina to support a project in genetically improved guinea pig breeding at the Cochao farm. After 2003, Antamina took control of the development projects in San Marcos, reduced staff levels, and directly hired several NGO personnel who were working in the area. Antamina justified this change on the basis of the fall of copper prices in the 2000–2001 period, although these recovered the following year and then experienced a dramatic climb over the following five years.

In 2005, four years after Antamina began operations, road blockades against both it and Barrick's Pierina mine in Huaraz confirmed the demands for infrastructure. The demonstrations were led by the mayor of Huaraz and had multiple motivations: environmental impacts, a demand to contribute through *obras* (works) such as road construction, and royalty payments. At that stage, Antamina claimed that its contract gave it protection against royalty payments. Barrick's exoneration by the government from $141 million in taxes also played an important role (Rosales 2005). Three months later, about seventy members of the community of Huaripampa used violent means to enter a sector of the Antamina mine to demand a new road to link the localities of Ayash and San Marcos.

In the period 2007–2011, Antamina contributed 773.1 million soles ($236 million) for the "voluntary, extraordinary and temporary contribution" for aforementioned Solidarity with the People Mining Program to the Ancash Department and more locally. This fund was mainly financed by seven companies that, like Antamina, had tax stability contracts that—they alleged—made them exempt from mining royalties. Mendoza and de Echave (2016:88) estimate that Antamina, Cerro Verde, Yanacocha, and Milpo provided $515 million as mining grants under this program while avoiding the payment of $631 million in taxes after invoking the profits reinvestment tax benefit between 2001 and 2011. Therefore, in addition to unpaid royalties, citizens in mining areas missed out on approximately $316 million in mining canon. These voluntary contributions proved to be more convenient for the companies than for the state or nation. The agreement between the state and Antamina for the local and regional Antamina Mining Fund under this program represented more than 90 percent of the program for the department, and a little more than a third of the total provided by all mining companies. By 2011, at both regional and local levels, infrastructure was certainly the greatest priority for the funding (more than 35 and 40 percent, respectively). At the departmental level, education and nutrition came next, almost 20 percent each. Education projects (more than 15 percent) and projects to stimulate productive activities (15 percent) were the next priorities at the local level (GPC 2012:5).

From 2013, Antamina announced it would begin implementing a new strategy of social investment under a *multiactor* (multi-stakeholder) model involving coordination with national and subnational actors (e.g., regional governments and municipalities), including international cooperation for executing development projects for local development. Antamina changed the name of its Relaciones Comunitarias (Community Relations) team to Gestión Social (Social Management), arguing that the former was associated with a bilateral company-community relationship. Later that year, Huaripampa delivered a petition to Antamina containing a long list of requests for "prioritized projects." These included the construction of a soccer stadium with grandstands, ten buses for public transport, ten tipper trucks, ten trailers (all Volvo), 10 percent of the mine's profits, and the hiring "on payroll" of two hundred young people from the community (Espinosa and Aybar 2016:annex 6). Two years later Antamina declared that of its "development projects" for the area of influence, less than 20 percent were for infrastructure development, and prioritized the "preparation of development and other planning documents" and projects for "economic development" (CMA 2016:55–56). The pattern that sees emphasis placed on infrastructure works may have continued in the development discourse but it has not led to changes in the urban landscape of San Marcos, which, ironically, to date still lacks a good potable water system, with no more than two hours of connection available to just a small number of fortunate users.

The World Bank (2005a:169–170) has reported a considerable number of mining companies that supported projects in neighboring locations under the following categories: road rehabilitation (93 percent), local activities (70 percent), sports activities (66 percent), electricity supply (63 percent), and donation of books (60 percent). This assistance tends "to be punctual economic compensations based on informal agreements and do not contribute to development frameworks whereby communities are empowered through a process of capacity building and understanding of their own priorities. This fairly typical approach . . . does not help in developing a more integral relationship among the stakeholders." It would be easy to criticize the distribution pattern for almost disregarding other important aspects, such as education. However, it is worth remembering that the majority of Peruvian roads are unpaved: 87 percent in 2001, 85 percent in 2004, and 70 percent in 2015, according to the Ministry of Transport. Most of the unpaved roads are located in rural areas. Likewise, there is a supposed advantage in physical infrastructure projects, which are presumably easier to measure, with the benefits usually considered more visible by comparison with—for example—education programs, especially in the short term. Equally, corruption scandals associated with infrastructure tenders in recent decades—the Odebrecht Company being the most publicized—show the vulnerability of an audit culture facing institutionalized practices of bribery and fraud when large budgets are in play.

Development, Work, and Trucks

Huaripampa applied most of the money obtained from the land it sold to public *obras*, or infrastructure. Ango Raju bought two trucks and materials for electrification. Within a few years, the financial situation in each community was inversely proportional to the amount received for the sale of the land. As seen in chapter 2, Huaripampa, the largest and oldest peasant community in the district, sold 2,337 hectares, or 43 percent of its land, for approximately $1 million, while neighboring Ango Raju disposed of approximately half the amount of land (1,129 hectares). Through its superior management of the negotiation process, Ango Raju obtained a written commitment that Antamina would hire the vehicles the community intended to purchase with the proceeds of the sale. Rather than rely on the general and voluntary nature of corporate responsibility promises, Ango Raju translated the concept into a measurable commitment through a signed document. Since both communities sold their land at a convenient time for the company, in each case the arrangement probably contained an element of reciprocity for Antamina.

FIGURE 15 Huaripampa main square. 2002. Author's photo.

The investment decisions also reveal how the respective communities conceived of development and are indicators of the kind of change they thought would lead to improved living conditions. Huaripampa spent most of its income on poles and the service to install electricity. It also rebuilt its main square, this time illuminated with new light poles to replicate the plazas of San Marcos and Huaraz (see figure 15). Electricity would constitute a daily symbol of modernity.

Ango Raju allocated most of its money to the purchase of two trucks and also obtained electrification equipment through an arrangement with the government, under which the community paid for the installation. It drew on its own *faenas* (reciprocity-based labor activities) for installation of the poles (Mayer 2002:124). In 2000, two years after the land sale process, the community purchased two additional trucks and a van to transport communal officials. Each community had electricity connections installed to homes. Some in Huaripampa later protested against payment of the monthly electrical bill because they had mistakenly believed that electricity would be free of charge, like the water in the irrigation channels, even though the latter were under communal control and maintenance depended on reciprocal rotating labor provided by all community members. By 2003, five years after the sale of land, of the nearly $1 million received, Huaripampa had just $10,000 remaining, plus a bullring, an extension to its school with underutilized computers, and a small health post that only opened its doors when a doctor paid by Antamina was present. A dozen community board members had been accused of embezzling collective money. Inexperience in business accounting had allowed several builders to inflate prices.

Different development strategies underpinned the respective decision-making processes. The people of Ango Raju initially considered simply distributing the funds obtained from the land sale to each family. They subsequently decided that investing instead in vehicles that they would lease to Antamina would generate direct sustainable income in the future in a way that regular distribution of the funds—or infrastructure, for that matter—would not. The profits from the leased trucks were distributed on a monthly basis in the amount of $100 per family. In the collective sphere, they expected public works or infrastructure. The ideal expectation of development at domains of the household and for the individual was to hold a job. Vehicles that could be rented to Antamina represented a job that would be of communal benefit. Salaried work was conceived locally as the most sustainable means to improve individual and family well-being. Infrastructure works, being a public good, were regarded as beneficial for everyone. The offer of a job was an individual accolade, whereas a health post was a resource that anybody could access.

As an illustration of how negotiations that embrace reciprocity probably include sequels, we appreciate how in 2009, a decade after the sale of land, Antamina paid $1.7 million to Ango Raju, arguing that this was to support projects for "sustainable development and to reinvigorate the communal enterprise" that managed the trucks (CMA 2009). The payment was the result of a negotiation arising from resettlement of families from the Neguip estate (see chapter 2), land that had recently become necessary for the company's operations. The communal board decided to distribute the money among the 170 members of the community on the basis of enduring expectations that the communal enterprise would generate redistributable profits.

Infrastructure, Coliseums, and Reciprocity

It was puzzling to find significant segments of populations lacking certain basic services prioritizing the construction of *coliseos multiuso* (multipurpose coliseums) used primarily for bullfighting. Huaripampa used part of the money obtained from selling land to Antamina for this purpose. Huallanca also chose a bullring coliseum as compensation from Antamina for damage to the town's infrastructure (i.e., house walls and the main square). The municipality of San Marcos similarly used funding from Antamina to partly finance a $300,000 "multipurpose coliseum" (CMA 2004:84). This logic may be comparable with preferences in more urbanized and Western societies, where improved entertainment facilities are perceived as a condition for an enhanced quality of life. From the Roman coliseums to the multimillion dollar stadiums in the USA built with public funds, these monuments to entertainment have been central to the mood and the economy of many social sectors.

Antamina's arrival in Huallanca was notable in the history of modern large-scale mining in Peru. It was a relatively nonviolent process, with the exception of some complaints about damage to houses and the main square—and the massive influx of temporary workers. When the mining operations began, the mayor demanded service and reciprocity from Antamina: "Huallanca has experienced the greatest negative social impact but its people have been the ones who helped the most, protested the least, and strove to overcome their problems without upsetting Antamina . . . its reconstruction is three years overdue. Don't be stingy with the people that saved you large sums by allowing you to bring forward the construction schedule" (CMA 2001b:68).

San Marcos and Huallanca had common expectations, and these were based on the recollection of the experience from earlier mines. The people of Huallanca valued the relationship with Santa Luisa's Huanzalá mine, a neighboring mine associated with employment, infrastructure, and services in areas such as health and education (see chapter 1). Huallanca's remoteness from Antamina's mine site probably led to lower expectations, which minimized the number of complaints by comparison with San Marcos, where the experience was one of unfulfilled expectations and promises of reciprocity. It was clear from the moment that the first enormous mining trucks began entering Huallanca's narrow streets that the mine would affect this small town of about seven thousand people (CMA 2006f). Huallanca's bridge sounded as if it were about to collapse when the convoy of heavy vehicles made its daily passage through the town. The townsfolk stared in astonishment at the constant passing parade of the "monstrous fleet"—in the words of one of the residents—and some reported damage to their homes. The town of Huallanca was unprepared for the twelve-month occupation by approximately 1,200 Antamina workers beginning in 1999. Some workers slept in the church before the municipality encouraged residents to rent rooms in their houses to cover the urgent lodging demand. The urban landscape was disrupted by the presence of more than fifty vehicles parked in the tiny streets. Prostitution and street fights became a part of the nightlife. The most visible impact was the accumulation of garbage, which was subsequently managed by a collection vehicle and a disposal site.

Mayor Luis Barrenechea came from a well-off cattle family and was born and raised in Huallanca. After finishing high school, he left for Lima, where he studied mechanical engineering. Augusto Baertl and Luis Barrenechea met at university. Baertl came from a very wealthy mining family and would later become the CEO of Antamina. He graduated as a mining engineer in 1965 and started working at La Cerro's San Cristóbal mine. Two years later he moved to Milpo, a mine owned by his family. From 1997 to 2003, Baertl was president and CEO of Antamina (CMA 2003a). He subsequently worked as a consultant and a board member for different firms, most of which were exploration companies. Baertl hired his former classmate Barrenechea as a consultant to advise on relations with Huallanca residents prior to Antamina's decision to use the town as a transit point for the passage of construction materials to the mine site. Barrenechea had a livestock business in Huallanca and visited regularly. Thirty-five years after leaving the town, and following a long career in the private sector in Lima, he was nominated, while still a consultant to Antamina, for the position of mayor, and was elected in 1998. His term coincided with the mining company's most intense contact with the town.

When Antamina realized that its gigantic trucks would negatively affect Huallanca's infrastructure, it proposed the construction of a new road that would bypass the town. Barrenechea then suggested an alternative: the vehicles could come through the town, which implied the destruction of the historic main square and other damages, with the company paying collective compensation for the likely destruction of the historic main square and restoring the damaged streets. The arrangement saved Antamina $2 million in road construction costs. The proposition was politically risky for the authorities, given that further damage to the square would be painful for the residents. As the mayor emphasized, it did not matter how beautiful it was, the important issue was that the historic square "was yours."

The compensation, which was in addition to the restoration of the square, signified a major *obra pública* (infrastructure project) that implied the exchange of a gift (see figure 16). In his famous essay *The Gift*, Marcel Mauss (1990 [1950]) maintains that the exchange of a gift (*le don* in French) carries with it the personality of the giver and constitutes an obligation of reciprocity that

FIGURE 16 Huallanca main square following refurbishment with Antamina compensation funds. 2002. Author's photo.

promotes solidarity. Anthropology recognizes that the exchange of gifts ideally takes places among equals; otherwise, it resembles charity, as in the case of gifts to individuals considered to have lower status, or, in the converse, the delivery of tribute (Kaplan 1998). Seeking to encapsulate the idea of mutual benefit with a "strategic alliance," the mayor told me, "We give them leather, so that later they give us the belt."

Once Antamina had accepted the proposal to direct its vehicles through the town, the Huallanca municipal government convened a public meeting to discuss what additional compensation the town would request. Following a prolonged debate, the mayor's proposal was accepted. In addition to restoration of the square, the construction of a bullring valued at approximately $180,000 was agreed on. This was a very large sum for this small Andean town. I asked the mayor why the citizens of Huallanca had not followed the general pattern of requesting infrastructure often regarded as more directly useful or productive, such as medical facilities or schools, in the style of their peers in Huaripampa. In his office, surrounded by bullfighting symbols, he explained:

> In a traditional conception of development, Chimbote [one of the largest Peruvian fishing ports] was impressively rich. The people there made a lot of money.

> However, there was no cultural development . . . no identity. And that is as important as economic development. That's why we recognize ourselves as *pueblo ganadero* [a livestock town] and organize activities [e.g., folk dances]. Also, any time someone comes to ask for money, we give them the bullring to collect funds. . . . [And] a coliseum like this would have never been financed by the government. . . . We are finishing the paving of the roads to Huallanca, because we want tourism to be the axis of development.

The model envisaged attracting different types of travelers to pay an entrance fee to watch bullfights and traditional dances at the multipurpose stadium. The residents of Huallanca themselves would view for free from the adjoining slopes (see figure 17).

The anthropological use of the concept of identity can be somewhat ambiguous. It could be used to cover properties of unique individuality and to refer to general shared qualities. In the second sense, the mechanism assumes a classification of features consciously accepted by the individual through evaluative or emotional characteristics, from which the individual could derive self-esteem, with a sense of complicity or belonging (Byron 2002:292). The mayor amplified the observation by stressing that a lack of self-esteem among the population was what stood in the way of development. Valuing local identity, in order to increase self-respect, as the basis for improved material conditions in town seems irrefutable. This idea suggests social development beginning as an individual task.

The region had particular pride in its cattle-raising heritage, and its favorite ritual was bullfighting, a tradition in the Andes that originated with the Spanish Conquest. Several of the municipality's offices were decorated with artistic representations of bull heads, and a colorful painting with bullfighting scenes entirely covered the largest wall of the mayor's office. Contrary to the old Spanish ritual and its moment of ecstasy when the bullfighter plunges the sword into the wounded animal, in Huallanca the bull was not sacrificed. People in Huallanca told me that the reason was that cattle were essential to their agricultural work, and this established a bond of gratitude and friendship.

According to the mayor, the municipality of Huallanca received approximately $7 million from Antamina in 2002, funds that were allocated for public works such as bridges, garbage collection, and the paving of roads. The amount was equivalent to about seventy years of the normal municipal budget. The town implemented a waste collection system using a vehicle obtained from

FIGURE 17 (a, above) Bullfighting in the Huallanca coliseum, and (b, right) audience. 2002. Author's photo.

Antamina, an unusual approach in an Andean town of its size, and contrary to the widespread practice of simply dumping rubbish in the river. A local university designed the landfill site. The perceived successful relationship between Antamina and Huallanca contributed to the selection of Mayor Barrenechea as coordinator of the group of mayors in the so-called Golden Corridor of the Andes. This brought together twenty towns across five provinces in the departments of Ancash and Huánuco. The name was later changed to the Corridor for Sustainable Development of Gold of the Andes. Evoking the riches contained in the colonial myth of El Dorado, the image of a golden corridor sought to mobilize municipal governments to work together and reconcile extractive activities with social development. The villages would ideally work in partnership with the mining companies in tourism and productive projects that would leverage the boom in mining. According to Barrenechea, this conciliatory approach was inspired by "the Inca trilogy" as a negotiation pattern based on "affection, knowledge and development," prioritizing integrated work and symbols of friendship with conquered peoples.[19]

To what extent could the request of a bullring by citizens neighboring a mine legitimize social asymmetries between a corporation and its impoverished neighbors? As in the acceptance of a gift, the reception of a "great work"

FIGURE 17 *(continued)*

implies a certain recognition of a differentiated order from a subaltern viewpoint or condition. The concept of "generalized reciprocity," formulated by Sahlins (1972), helps to understand this asymmetric exchange, which lacks a precise measurable return beyond legitimizing an unequal relationship and investing in a peaceful interaction. The act supposes a minimum redistribution that is rather symbolic when seen against the formidable profits of a mining operation. Many Andean rites revolve around this ethic. Occasionally, the organization of an Andean *fiesta* (a feast for the whole village) is sponsored by a *cargo*—literally, "burden," derived from a civil religious hierarchical position—selected among the least impoverished members of the community who activate their social networks and reciprocity chains to raise funds and share the costs of the rite (Mayer 2002:122, 335). This call to reciprocity legitimizes social structures. The Andean festivities would thus constitute organizational instruments for the reaffirmation, reconstruction, or reordering of relationships and social networks. Laite and Long (1987:28, 50–51) studied the *cortamonte* (tree cutting ceremony) in the central Andes, including the mining town of La Oroya, finding that the expansion of capital and migration from the early twentieth century increased economic differentiation and led to political conflicts. In La Oroya, the rite was organized around the most affluent groups as a prestigious event. It consolidated economic alliances, which had political repercussions. The gifts provided by the more affluent become a way to build prestige and consolidate economic alliances to legitimize a political status through Andean rituals and festivities sponsored by well-off families.

On one occasion I became the casual witness of a senior Antamina executive instructing subordinates to conceal their friendship with a resident who lived near the mine site so as to protect that individual's relationship with other community members. Local authorities were trapped in a double bind, similar to that encountered in the aftermath of the Bhopal (India) socioenvironmental disaster, as related in the ethnography of Kim Fortun (2001). The concept arose in Gregory Bateson's work about the reception of contradictory messages. In the communities neighboring the mine, the local authorities risked being labelled as having *vendidas* (sold out) if they were perceived as too friendly with the company. Many in San Marcos and Huarmey did indeed accuse the mayor of Huallanca of having sold out to Antamina.

To what extent was Antamina's arrival in Huallanca a success on a collective level? Like the experience of the Huascarán National Park negotiation (see chapter 3), the education level of key players played an important role. In addition to his high level of education, the mayor of Huallanca maintained personal relationships with Antamina senior executives and had professional experience in large companies. This might, to some extent, explain how important arrangements were reached without signed documents. The mayor explained that these agreements were "*gestiones de palabra*," which translates as "gentlemen's agreements" to build "friendship based on mutual respect."

The experience of reciprocity with the arrival of the mining company differed between San Marcos and Huallanca. The residents of San Marcos perceived Antamina to have fallen short of a complete corresponding reciprocity. Antamina occasionally resorted to the argument that much of what was claimed by the community—such as employment offers—lacked formal status through a legal document. By contrast, in Huallanca—as in Ango Raju and Huaripampa—the residents participated in the decision to assign the collective compensation to infrastructure work. Because Huallanca—in contrast to Ango Raju and Huaripampa—had sold no land as part of its negotiation with the company, the bullring resembled a gift, even though their walls were damaged and the main square was destroyed. The work on the main square went beyond repair and took the form of a complete and modern restoration. This work of public infrastructure, referred to locally as a *gran obra* (literally, a "great work"), can be interpreted as a gift. The gift from the "big man" was granted on time (Sahlins 1963). The term *big man* as a sociological type derives from the ethnographic work of Marshall Sahlins (1963) in Melanesia and Polynesia. The typology characterized the astuteness of the leader who obtained his political influence through asymmetric exchanges—especially in the form of gifts—that indebted his relatives and neighbors. This kind of acquired influence stood in contrast to authority achieved through inheritance. The circle of reciprocity was closed within its expected parameters in Huallanca. The perception of incomplete reciprocity in San Marcos in contrast with its symbolic completion in Huallanca has explanatory power for understanding the high level of protest—measured both in number and in intensity—in the former by comparison with the latter.

Blockages, Penalties, and Public Development

As chapter 3 showed, the paralysis of the Pan-American Highway at least six times between 2000 and 2004 reflected the fear of contamination of the port city of Huarmey and included claims of incomplete reciprocity. The residents of Huarmey had expectations of development through employment opportunities and the great "gift" of paved roads that would connect them to markets, enable trading at better prices, and reduce transport costs. We should recall that the design modification that replaced a new paved route with a pipeline triggered conflicts and led to the Pan-American Highway blockages. The obstructions in 2001 were directed against Antamina. Those that occurred in May 2002 sought completion of a reciprocity perceived to have been unfulfilled by the state, which had promised to pave new roads using funds from a fine levied on Antamina but which had instead merely repaired existing roads using only some of the funds. The residents considered this breach offensive. In each case, the government sent military forces to control the demonstrations, including helicopter gunships that fired tear gas at protestors.

Roads were viewed as a fundamental ingredient for collective development during the time of the Incas. During the colonial era, they facilitated the conqueror's tax collection, mineral transport, and the movement of human resources. During the republican era, mining gave a major boost to road and railway construction. The ancient development dream had a new expression when Antamina found itself facing a shortfall of $372 million to deliver its investment commitments by the five-year limit stated in the concession transfer agreement, and opted instead to pay a contractual penalty of $111.5 million, equivalent to 30 percent of the difference between the "committed investment" and the "executed investment" at the start of commercial operations (Corvetto 1996:5.1). The government announced it would use the money to pave roads in Huarmey. However, the people of Huarmey were subsequently surprised to learn that this would only cover the repair of existing and unpaved roads. In 2005, following several strikes and roadblocks, the government finally began to build a highway, which at present remains unfinished.

Antamina's official version of events sought to emphasize the benefits for the region and avoided the term *penalidad* (penalty). It employed rhetoric such as the following: "The fact that Antamina has opted for the optional obligation of cancelling this *pago complementario* [supplementary payment] has ensured that it is not the Company that decides how to invest the balance originally expected, and that it instead provides a transfer of resources for regional development" (CMA 2003b:17). The agreement made no mention of a "supplementary payment." It referred to a penalty, which, if ignored, could have led to the government canceling the concession for breach of contract and even to a subsequent lawsuit. The strategy of avoiding mention of a penalty and replacing it with the term *supplementary payment* generated much local criticism. Many claimed that the company was failing to acknowledge its responsibilities and was simply giving the appearance of generosity when in fact it was merely fulfilling a contractual obligation. Nearly five years after payment of the fine, Antamina's website timidly referred to the amount as "a payment modality foreseen in the contract ('penalty')" (CMA 2006d).

Thanks to pressure exerted by local authorities and members of Congress from Ancash, together with support from Antamina, the 2002 Public Budget Law included a provision specifying that the penalty funds would be invested in improving and paving roads, as well as electrification, health, and education in the mine's area of influence. The struggle for these complementary resources relied on arguments about sovereignty and territoriality. The government created FIDA (Fondo de Inversiones para el Desarrollo de Ancash, or Ancash Development Investment Fund) to channel the penalty funds. It consisted of mayors from Antamina's area of influence and representatives of the state. The first debate was about who would be a member, which in turn would impact which population would receive benefits. The members were to be determined spatially. Chimbote, one of Peru's largest ports and demographically the country's fifth largest city, successfully demanded inclusion in the area of influence. Its mayor argued that the mine pipeline could affect the city and impact a larger population than in Huarmey. The mayor of the latter countered that authorities in Chimbote had failed to support earlier protests over the pipeline and had only spoken up after the penalty funding became available. Due to its closer proximity to the pipeline and the higher associated risks, Huarmey obtained greater rights to the funding.

The FIDA fund distribution illustrates a hierarchy pattern for development, shared by the national and local governments and the mining companies, that placed infrastructure at the top, especially roads. Under the priorities established for the fund, 57 percent was allocated to paving roads and only 5 percent for education (see figure 18). Antamina then announced "a new stage in the sustainable development of Ancash" (CMA 2005a). A cycle of opening ceremony rites was launched as mining propaganda and was accompanied by politicians. By 2016 a balance of $15 million remained in the fund. Congress approved its use for a competitive investment program to be known as the FONIPREL (Fondo de Promoción a la Inversión Pública Regional y Local, or Fund for the Promotion of Regional and Local Public Investment). This would cofinance public projects

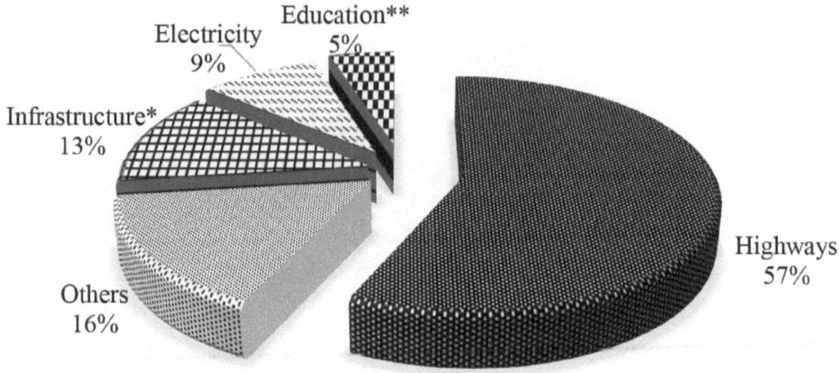

FIGURE 18 Distribution of FIDA funds by project type, 2004.
*Infrastructure: focused on health in San Marcos, a dock in Huarmey, and a water and sewage system in Chimbote.
**Education: two universities in Huaraz.
Prepared by the author based on CMA (2001b, 2002, 2003b, 2004, 2005b).

and preinvestment studies for services and basic infrastructure judged to have the greatest impact on reducing poverty.

Three moments (2005, 2011, and 2016) in the expenditure allocation of municipal funding reveal priorities for development and political impacts of the large injection of funding in San Marcos. The highest priority project in 2005—four years after the start of the mining operations and financed with canon transfers in the municipality of San Marcos—was the "construction of a main square" (22 percent, \$43,369). The provincial municipality of Huari assigned its highest priority to coliseum construction (18 percent, \$23,662). In Huarmey, the provincial government deemed pedestrian paths to be the most important (78 percent, \$158,921). As Huallanca already had a stadium, the district council prioritized the construction of "houses and centers of culture" (44 percent, \$64,981) (CAD 2005b:29–37). With only one exception, the budgets of the district municipalities in the eight principal mining departments gave the highest priority to "urban development," allocating in each case more than one-quarter of the total allocation (Boza 2006:98–100). Up until the middle of the first decade of the twenty-first century, by law the canon could only be used to build infrastructure, in order to avoid funding running expenses and salaries.

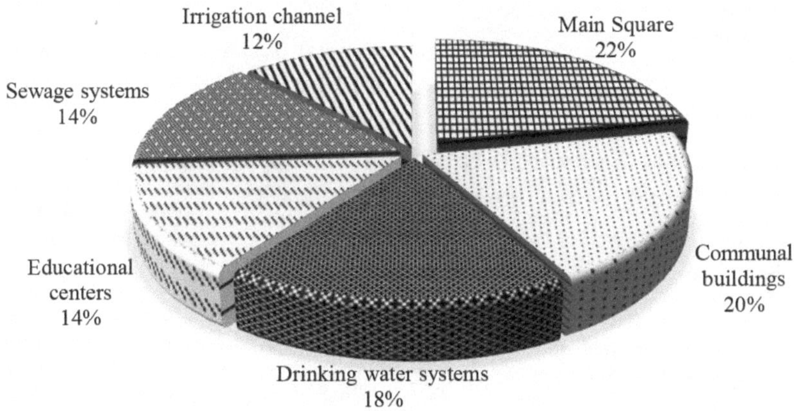

FIGURE 19 Distribution of canon funds to projects in San Marcos District, 2005. Prepared by author based on CAD (2005b:36).

Canon transfers to the district of San Marcos began to increase markedly from 2006, when Antamina handed over its first income tax in a public ceremony, a decade after the start of the Antamina concession (see figure 14). In 2011, the "survey of perceptions" of the most important local problem, an inspection formulated by the MIM (Mejorando la Inversión Municipal, or Improving Municipal Investment) interinstitutional initiative, reported that the people of San Marcos prioritized their development challenges as follows: access to safe drinking water and sewerage (21 percent), education (19 percent), environmental contamination (17 percent), and transport (12 percent) (MIM 2012:27).[20] That same year, however, the municipality allocated 49 percent of its budget on a "planning, management and contingency reserve"—essentially administrative costs and maintenance of public infrastructure. It disbursed only 6 percent on sanitation, 4 percent on education, and 9 percent on environmental issues (MIM 2012:27). This allocation reflected a populist municipal strategy that distributed canon income to working-age residents through temporary employment via the Pilot Plan for Maintenance of Public Infrastructure. This program paid a wage for maintenance of basic infrastructure, such as wall repair and street or road cleaning, that was about four times higher than that paid to agricultural workers. Apparently, these temporary occupations promoted by the municipality of San Marcos were perceived locally as an indirect redistribution of and participation in the profits from mining.

According to the Ministry of Economy and Finance (MEF 2017), by 2016, fifteen years after the start of the mine's operations, the municipality of San Marcos was spending most of its funds on "budget allocations that do not result in products" (62 percent, or $28 million), followed by activities and projects for agricultural water resources (14 percent) and the National Rural Sanitation Program (7 percent). The aforementioned budget line for activities "that do not result in products" prioritized funds for "without product" activities and projects (40 percent, $3.4 million), followed by the expansion and implementation of an educational complex in Carhuayoc (11 percent) and the construction of three sports complexes (9 percent). The municipality assigned 89 percent ($3.1 million) of the "without product" item to temporary work in the maintenance of infrastructure, public lighting, parks, and gardens. The practice of using funds for temporary or casual employment constitutes a generalized and redistributive reciprocity that is functional for clientelistic mechanisms, particularly during municipal elections where local residents claim direct benefits from mining extraction. Local struggles for access to fiscal transfers for mining would also explain the level of political fragmentation in San Marcos, reflected in the increase in mayoral candidates. In 2014 there were seventeen candidates, and the victorious candidate obtained only 18 percent of the votes cast.

Conclusion

By uncovering historical governmental myths of mining for development, I lay the foundations and terms of the dilemmas of mining hubs as development poles versus neo-enclaves, which lie at the core of the supply and demand proposals regarding mining benefits. The large-scale discussion—in terms of time and space—and critique of mining contributes to framing the case for the negotiations of benefits and the allocation of state transfers based on the arrival of Antamina. To track interpretations of development, it was necessary to consider the myths created around improved living conditions and how the ideals of different groups (local communities, the mining companies, the government, and others) interacted with local expectations, as well as with the mining regimes established as a response. The evidence presented demonstrates how, in practice, the concept of development could be controversial and changes from one social group to another, functioning in turn as an engine of collective behavior. A mining company can be requested by locals to finance expensive investments that are normally the responsibility of the state, such as road infrastructure or electrification. Brant Hinze, CEO of the Yanacocha gold mine, reflected on this complicated balance, recognizing that "it is our responsibility to return to communities some of the wealth," and warned, "If you're not careful you become the government. We should not become it" (*Economist* 2005b). For local residents, the arrival of Antamina represented an opportunity, with the company scorning what it considered to be antiquated and paternalistic development models, fearful of replacing the state yet simultaneously involving itself in a range of projects so diverse that at times it was difficult to know where the line was drawn. This lack of definition benefits the mining company because it is able to apply voluntary parameters at its own convenience. To what extent should companies accept requests for development projects that could be limitless and changeable? Lessons learned from development demands at sites such as the Tintaya copper mine highlight the convenience of having a permanent local negotiation strategy. With this a company can better enter into forms of reciprocity to service the social demands of impoverished communities subject to the kind of environmental risks that accompany minerals extraction.

The development imagined with the arrival of Antamina had two central dimensions. For the individual it meant getting a job at the mine. At the collective level the goal was the *gran obra*, particularly an item of infrastructure as a public good. A great work supposes a big gift under a personalized business relationship involving reciprocity. This is in tune with traditional Andean transactions and some long-term commercial activities in more urban contexts. These interactions probably represent an insurance strategy over a prolonged period of time. This type of business reciprocity can explain how a group of expensive foreign workers came to be preferred by Antamina over more affordable local options. This was coherent behavior for some contractors who sought reciprocity in the form of future contracts. Reciprocity was also evident in the demands by investors that Antamina procure quotas from their home markets. Antamina assimilated these symbols, and a year after starting operations supported the construction of a "multipurpose stadium" in San Marcos.

The discourse of social responsibility in mining served as Antamina's entry point for community development. It did not imply reciprocity because the commitment was presented as good neighborliness or citizenship. Antamina's internal debate in the design of its first sponsored development projects reveals central aspects of the role of corporate social responsibility and its effects. The company discussed who would be the first beneficiaries and whether to invest in the most vulnerable or instead concentrate on a local middle class that would hire the more vulnerable and thus create a trickledown effect. Antamina approached this debate by diversifying the projects. In San Marcos, the absence of a rapid local consensus about which projects would be preferred created a problem for the company in terms of selecting projects that would also be functional for the company. In this context, the mining development apparatus began by applying resources under a rhetoric of targeted activities and experimental plant and animal centers. Although Antamina criticized development projects of the 1960s, it, too, made similar mistakes by failing to clearly identify project benefits and engage local participation. Antamina's initial approach applied an "anti-politics machine" model (Ferguson 1994) through its purportedly technical apolitical development apparatus. Over time, because of failures and protests, the company reoriented its approach toward more inclusive and supposedly participatory models, such as employing dialogue or development roundtables to discuss its plans.

While the choice of a bullring could legitimize social asymmetries, the decision challenges an order that prioritizes utilitarian and productive alternatives. The preference for an entertainment venue would—the local authorities assured—contribute to improved self-esteem through an investment that would reinforce collective identity while promoting infrastructure that would allow local fund-seeking activities, including tourism. The fact that Huaripampa, San Marcos, and Huallanca are all home to coliseums as a result of the arrival of Antamina could give rise to a critique probably rooted in ethnocentrism. While the Antamina project was still getting started, the U.S. city of Hartford, Connecticut, decided to build a gigantic stadium using government funds. Should entertainment be the monopoly preserve of only the most urban and financially privileged places? It is a valid discussion, especially where the artistic contribution and issues of identity and self-esteem are valued over and above the income that enters the local economy through tourism or entrance fees. The issue could be explored comparatively, examining costs—beyond questions of taste—together with proposals for long-term social change that consider the rights of communities to set their own priorities in a consensual manner that involves ongoing learning and regular evaluation of development options.

The complex impact of the funds transferred over the last decade is a subject that requires greater attention. The predilection for modernity infrastructure services suggests a symbolic connection to ideals of progress more related to urban areas, all consistent with rural-to-urban migration trends. The more than

$400 million transferred to San Marcos for the mining canon (see figure 14) appears to local communities as a mirage when they also see how even the fortunate families with a water connection can only enjoy the service for a couple of hours each day.[21] Corruption has increased in mineral-rich departments such as Ancash, Cajamarca, Pasco, and Cusco, where several governors have been accused and sentenced for corruption in the exercise of their functions. Several government authorities from the Ancash regional government and the San Marcos District government—areas that have benefited the most from the mining canon over the last decade—have been involved in embezzlement scandals.[22] The aftermath of this corruption, together with the impact of lost revenues and opportunities, merits more systematic exploration.

In this chapter I have provided an overview of development myths produced by the state and the Antamina mining project to legitimize the extractive activities, and examined how, in practice, ideals of development were contested, negotiated, and materialized by different subnational groups involved in contentious cultural and political dynamics for accessing and managing mining benefits. Complaints and negotiations for mining benefits rarely occur in a vacuum, frequently appearing closely or intertwined with contamination claims, as we will appreciate in the next chapter, where I consider distinct scenarios of participation in socioenvironmental protests.

CHAPTER 5

"Dear Engineer, Could You Explain to My Donkey That This Cloudy Water with a Bad Smell Is Clean?"

The Politics of Pollution and Environmental Risk

HUMOR WAS ONE OF THE STRATEGIES USED DURING THE CONFLICTS OVER POLLUTION IN ANTAMina. The title of the chapter is a quote from a San Marcos peasant, overheard during a public presentation by Antamina. It reflects a clash of cultures over the environmental risks presented by the mining project. This section examines the political culture associated with environmental degradation complaints and their causes and strategies. Culturally, a conflict arises when different perceptions lead to a dispute in which one party feels it has a justified complaint. The Antamina protests took different forms, from mere humorous asides at public meetings to more aggressive modalities such as marches, lawsuits, and road blockages. The first part of the chapter describes the social mobilizations that took place in San Marcos and Huarmey and examines local concerns about the environmental impact of mining.[1] A comparison of the protests that occurred in Huarmey with the environmental degradation negotiation tactics used in San Marcos helps us understand the environmental conflict there. As San Marcos was where the mine was located, it was the first district to register socioenvironmental impacts through population displacement and discharges into its air, soil, and water sources. In Huarmey the effects were felt in areas bordering the port, as detailed in the subsequent section. The two cases highlight social networks and strategies, which in turn reveal causalities in the confrontations. They demonstrate cultural disagreements and power struggles for control of the environment and for control of the ethics that define legitimacy. The second part examines the behavioral logics that were chosen as tactics. It addresses the clash of cultures in the face of nature and environmental risks and the power strategies in the conflicts that arose over disagreements. Starting at the "Risk, Pollution, and Conflict" section, I introduce basic conceptual tools for the discussion of environmental risk perception for mobilizations. Subsequently, I present a debate on how to limit environmental degradation, including structural debates on regulations and historical fears from mining in Peru. The evidence contributes to understanding the distrust in the claims about contamination and the demands for participation in the demarcation of contamination.

Water, Air, Ethics, and Aesthetics in San Marcos

A former Antamina employee recalled that when he arrived in Huarmey and San Marcos in 1997, "there was no negative reaction [to Antamina], but [there were] expectations of benefits." Mateo, a senior Community Relations executive of Antamina, was struck that despite the fact that the earlier Contonga mine had caused contamination in San Marcos, there had been just a single complaint, which had been registered by the mayor. Mateo was aware that the large scale of Antamina had the potential to generate a directly proportional level of fear in the district. He also recognized that in the collective memory of San Marcos, the Gran Bretaña company was associated with employment in mule transport and the purchase of local products:

> The people have seen mining here before. They have seen Contonga and they are all a disgrace, in environmental terms. For them—and it is very deep-seated here—there has been mining for fifty years and all the mining companies have contaminated. Antamina has now come and in that regard is responsible. It is more complicated when the mining company is bigger, because being bigger, it would contaminate more . . . what happened was that they changed their scheme . . . the neighboring inhabitants were hired by the Contonga mine and they changed their economic activity.

On balance, Contonga's environmental impact did not greatly affect the residents in an economic sense, since, just as La Cerro had done in La Oroya in the early twentieth century, Contonga significantly hired local people. La Cerro had indeed undertaken significant hiring of individuals unable to continue their grazing practices because of the contamination caused by the mine. The experience had not, however, been free of protests (Flores Galindo 1993 [1974]).

The operations area in San Marcos is located at the source of the Ayash and Carash Ravines (see map 2), into which Antamina discharged water from the mine. The concentrator plant has a daily treatment capacity of seventy metric tons of ore and produces thirty metric tons on average (CMA 2003b:13). The tailings from this plant are stored in a deposit in the springs of the Ayash Ravine at a height of 135 meters. During the operational life of the mine, currently estimated at thirty years (up from the initial estimate of twenty-four), it will produce more than five hundred million tons of tailings and form sediment behind the dam and a lagoon to be used as a primary source for the supply of water for the concentrator plant (AUDITEC 2000:16). The mineralized body is located at the bottom of the Antamina Lake, which was drained in 2000 under a special state permit. The company built a small dam in the Antamina Ravine to capture the majority of the solid waste. A 2.6-kilometer tunnel transports the ore to the primary crusher.

At the start of operations, Antamina discharged from the open pit into the Carash River and poured from the tailings pond into the Ayash River. These practices generated the biggest protests at that time. The mobilizations over contamination in San Marcos began with the exploration and construction phases and were focused on water quality impacts. Antamina reported eighty complaints in 2000, almost half of which were due to contamination, with most of those related to water conditions (CMA 2002:41). These protests, initially considered by Antamina to be mere "perceptions" about "aesthetic" characteristics—smell, color, and taste—generated a cultural and political discussion about which of these parameters should apply. At that time, water color was the only one of the three that was measurable in a laboratory. The company considered smell and taste to be subjective and therefore unsuitable for measurement. The debate raises ethical questions, such as who is qualified to intervene in discussions and decisions about environmental risk and how these individuals or groups should approach these tasks. Below, I present three scenarios related to affected air and water in the Canrash Lagoon and in the Carash and Ayash Ravines, each of which the local residents regarded as having been caused by the mine.[2]

Landslides, Spills, and Trout in the Canrash Lagoon

An episode in the Canrash Lagoon in 1999 was one of the first environmental impacts to draw a response from the community. Antamina had begun work on its new road between the operations site and Conococha, and rainfall had caused sediments to reach the lagoon. Testimonies reported that "the hill was weak," and in the rainy season sediment would be released and begin to "stain" the Canrash Lagoon. That is to say, waste from the slopes caused a reddish coloration and turbidity in the waters. Turbidity indicates the cloudiness or haziness (lack of transparency degree) of a liquid, based mostly on the presence of suspended particles.

The San Marcos Environmental Committee and other local residents protested and were able to put a stop to the roadworks. Created in 1999, this group was one of the first civil associations formed in response to the presence of Antamina. Together with the Asociación de Delegados de Medio Ambiente de La Oroya (Association of Environmental Delegates of La Oroya) instituted that same year, it was among the oldest of its type. La Oroya smelting complex probably represents the largest mining contamination museum in the country (Kuramoto et al. 2002). The San Marcos committee was established following a proposal by participants at a public multisectoral meeting convened by the municipality. Its legal status changed three years later, and it was renamed the Asociación Civil Comisión Pro-Conservación del Medio Ambiente de San Marcos (Civil Association Commission for the Conservation of the Environment of San Marcos). The company itself claimed that "on the initiative of Antamina an Environmental Committee was created" in San Marcos, and another in Huarmey in 2000 (CMA 2001a:22). It is probable that Antamina preferred to deal with individuals other than the traditional local leaders because it considered the latter more expert at negotiation and more difficult to persuade. Subsequently, the Asociación de Protección del Medio Ambiente de la Cuenca Ayash (Association for the Protection of the Environment of the Ayash Basin) was created, together with two environmental committees in the basin, one in the Ayash Huaripampa sector (Huaripampa community) and the other in the Santa Cruz de Pichiú community (CMA 2006f).

Many trout died in the Canrash Lagoon as a consequence of the initial mining operations. This 1999 disaster was the most alarming environmental event.

It also affected the Mosna River basin. Sediments in the lake encourage trout migration. Antamina admitted that the construction of the access road to the mine "had inadvertently altered the hydrology of the lake outlet." The water level dropped more than was usual at that time of year. The company agreed to build a hydraulic outlet structure that would restore the hydrology. Antamina reported that it had used biodegradable flocculating and coagulating products to reduce the water's turbidity and reddish tone (CMA 2001c:9). Once the construction of the highway concluded, the protests diminished and the state issued Antamina with a fine.

Two years later, a spill of coagulant and flocculant material from two tankers loaded with toxic materials occurred ninety-seven kilometers along the access road to the operations. Rainbow trout died up to a kilometer and a half downstream from the entry point of the spill into the Canrash Lagoon. Residents approached Antamina with dead trout as evidence, and the San Marcos Environmental Committee lodged a protest. Antamina acknowledged that nearly one thousand fish had died, but maintained that the tanks had been "vandalized." The company said the flocculant and coagulant "could not be retained by the secondary containment system and entered the stream that drains into the lagoon" (CMA 2002:54). DIGESA (Dirección General de Salud Ambiental del Ministerio de Salud, or the General Directorate of Environmental Health) investigated Antamina for negligence for having left the chemicals near the river. Antamina then promised to cover the loss by introducing four thousand trout into the lagoon. It also asserted that it redesigned its stations and used new materials to control erosion, including containment walls to stabilize the land. It employed forty-five local residents as unskilled labor on a temporary basis as part of the process, a strategy that can be interpreted as a mechanism to silence protests from potential litigants (CMA 2001d:8–9).

Antamina offered to remedy the problem by pumping water from the lagoon into the Canrash Ravine to increase the flow and dissolve the spilled flocculants. Antamina and the Directorate of Environmental Health undertook parallel sampling in the presence of both neighbors and the San Marcos Environmental Committee. It was one of the first instances in which the mining company had recognized the need to build confidence and avoid conflicts through greater local participation in environmental monitoring. The company claimed to have improved the infrastructure of the flocculant system by building a weep berm annexed for the control of sediments at the ninety-seven-kilometer point. Antamina later reported the abundant presence of trout at the exit of the

Canrash Lagoon (240 individuals in a section of 150 meters) and considered this to be evidence of the "good quality of the water" (CMA 2003b:42).

The company acknowledged that thirteen of the twenty-one "environmental and safety incidents" in the first year of operations had been "spillages," mostly particularly of fuel (CMA 2002:52–55). The following year Antamina proudly claimed that it had been the subject of just a single complaint, although in an area with high illiteracy and little access to legal advice, it only counted "formal complaints received in writing" (CMA 2003b:51). Four years later, EcoMetrix (2005:2.4), under contract to Antamina, indicated that one of the measures employed by the company to minimize the "turbidity column" in the Canrash Lagoon had been to divert most of the runoff from the road and the hillside around the lagoon to carry it to the overflow stream (Caracho Ravine). The water coming from the road continued to be treated with chemical flocculants to reduce its turbidity.[3]

Drainage and Turbidity in the Carash River

The emptying of the Antamina Lake during the construction phase produced a constant turbidity in the Carash River. Due to the displacement of sediments from the open pit and the placement of this in the water, the latter "became like chocolate," to use the words of a former Antamina official. The changes were striking, although locals noticed some seasonal variation, especially during the rainy period when sediments move from the river and landslides occur. Following Antamina's arrival, the change in the Carash Ravine was greater than usual. At the beginning of the operations, and contrary to reports by the locals, AUDITEC (Empresa de Auditoría e Inspectoría Sociedad Anónima Cerrada, or Auditing and Inspection Company Limited Company), a company on contract to MEM, reported that the drainage of the Antamina Lake complied with water quality norms: "No significant impacts of the drainage downstream of the Antamina Ravine have been detected outside those predicted, and change to the Mosna River receiving body is imperceptible" (CMA 2001c:annex 9, p. 2). The audit company summarized the concerns of the mayor of San Marcos and the environmental committee as follows: lack of knowledge about the environmental implications of mining, distrust of the explanations provided by Antamina, absence of the state, abnormal water quality signs in the Ayash Ravine; and concern about the impact on aquatic life and animals.

Although its report does not discuss these issues in detail, it does acknowledge the need "to improve communications, have a greater presence in the field, and for there to be comprehensible and timely environmental technical explanations from internal [Antamina] environmental managers to the communities" (CMA 2001c:annex 9, p. 3). The following year, the San Marcos Environmental Committee reported that earthworks from the open pit had caused changes to the Carash River due to sediment discharge. The two knowledge systems—the mining company's experts and the information provided by local residents—and their indicators were not communicating with each other. The focus was limited to passing mining technical information to the local residents. The communication referred to by the auditing company seemed asymmetric and unilateral. The assumption was that a knowledge vacuum existed among the population and needed to be filled. Under this simplified logic, the mere act of transmitting the message would almost automatically resolve any conflict in perceptions.

Tailings in the Ayash River

In the words of an environmental NGO representative in Ancash, the first discharge of the tailings dam into the Ayash River was a "vomit." In quantity, density, and the variety of compounds, it was greater than those that followed. It also generated protests in Ayash, located downstream from the dam. The giant tailings dam, the world's highest of its kind (4,015 meters), collects sixty-five thousand tons of waste per day. Over thirty years it would store more than "550 million tons of sterile material" (CMA 2003b:14). This dam periodically dumps tailings effluent into the Ayash River, which leads to complaints. José, of the San Marcos Environmental Committee, highlighted the "somewhat strong smell" and the turbidity of the water, as well as "leakage" below the dam. According to Antamina, "It is only discharged actively during the rainy season" (EcoMetrix 2005:3.5). The problem was particularly serious, given that outside the rainy season (November–April) and in the absence of water in springs and *acequias* (irrigation ditches), the populations of Ayash, Huaripampa, and Santa Cruz de Pichiú relied on the river. In a typical example of the complaints that arose, Lazarus, of the Ango Raju board, recalled that people came out in rashes and pimples when they bathed or washed their clothes, and the water also killed animals and caused trout to disappear.

One year after mineral extraction began, the San Marcos Environmental Committee stated at a public meeting with Antamina officials, "The discharge of the tailings dam into the river of the Ayash basin has altered the natural state of the water, with changes in its smell, taste, and color, the presence of foam and unusual volumes, and this is cause of protest by the communities of the basin." A farmer from Ayash Huaripampa insisted that some "little fish" from the Ayash River were "disappearing." In Santa Cruz de Pichiú, located close to the site of operations, the head of the small medical post told me that clothes washed in the ravine that flowed from Ayash caused "skin problems" and that animals who drank the same water suffered "hair loss." A former Antamina employee recalled, "There were complaints about tailings, acids, dead cows and trout, sheep with hair loss, etcetera. It was a disaster for the locals." In the Santa Cruz de Pichiú community, I could see foam. The intense smell of the water reminded me of a chlorinated pool. CAO (2006:annex A, p. 16) noted that "the number of taxa and invertebrate abundance and diversity decreased" in the period 2002–2004 in "both near to and far-field locations," concluding, "These decreases in population measures indicate that the benthic community may have been impacted."

According to the Water Law, category three waters such as the Ayash River were suitable for irrigating edible vegetables and for consumption by animals (CMA 2001c:3). Environmental lawyer Doris Balvín told me that since not all water sources were classified, the law was inapplicable and served merely as a reference for health security. She pointed out that the water needed to be category one (fit for human consumption), since people were drinking it. A MEM environmental audit acknowledged the existence of leaks (AUDITEC 2000:34). Antamina maintained that the dam's permeability was "controlled" and that the "turbidity of the Ayash River reflects the presence of suspended solids that are dispersed in it," causing a "reduction in its transparency" (CMA 2001d:5; 2001c:5). Having admitted fault and atoned, Antamina's expectation was that local residents would began to trust that the impact on nature would remain controlled.

A resident of Ayash Huaripampa told me her perception of the mining impacts on the water: "In the Ayash River there were some small fish and now they are disappearing. In Chocopampa they have found one thirty-five centimeters long and another one of ten centimeters. Yes there are fish, but not here, they have gone and I do not know what happened. There were six of us in the house. Before we cooked and the boys caught the fish, the trout, by hand.

Not anymore. This is doing us harm. The townspeople complain. We want to know what is happening to these species because we need them for our food." A year after Antamina began operations, the Santa Cruz de Pichiú community lodged a claim over a dead horse that was presumed to have drunk from the Ayash River. At a protest meeting, an Antamina staff member paid compensation, an act that was taken to be an admission of guilt. Three months after the incident, at the third Public Meeting on Environmental Issues in San Marcos, an Antamina official claimed that an autopsy had shown the cause of death to be "suffocation" due to pneumonia (CMA 2003b). Having already received its compensation, the community was left skeptical.

The San Marcos Environmental Committee inspected Ayash after the first discharge and suggested a fish farm be installed to serve as a bioindicator of water quality. It also suggested a model land plot to track the effects of dust caused by mine explosions. The committee claimed that its demands had, for the first time, brought the state to the region in order to provide explanations about the impact on the Canrash and Carash Rivers (see chapter 2). In 2001 DIGESA declared valid an appeal by Antamina to allow it to continue discharging into the Ayash Ravine (see figure 20), having been previously questioned by the same institution.[4] The company could continue to dump cyanide and other industrial effluents from the waters of the tailings dam. Antamina reported complaints and a letter from MEM (CMA 2002:53). In the middle of that year, Ayash requested that Antamina attend its communal assembly. It embarked on a peaceful march to the base of the tailings dam and once there named a commission to meet with Antamina, who it denounced for having caused "environmental contamination" and the foam on the Ayash River. Later, at an assembly in Ayash and with the support of Antamina, they collectively agreed to the construction of a school, an expansion of its drinking water distribution, and the building of a fish farm as a bioindicator of water quality. The company undertook to monitor water discharge from the tailings dam and began to acknowledge complaints. It admitted that the concentration of several metals in the water exceeded Canadian parameters (CMA 2001d).

Antamina acknowledged that the level of trout in the basin was the lowest recorded since 1999: "The cause of this decrease may be related to several factors, including mining operations and/or environmental conditions" (CMA 2001d:27). It claimed that more evaluations were needed to determine if there was direct influence from the mine on the fish communities. Four years

FIGURE 20 Antamina tailings discharge in Ayash. 2002. Author's photo.

later, EcoMetrix (2005:3.5, 3.6) indicated that for 2003 "there were substantial increases in sulfur, molybdenum, total dissolved solids, hardness and conductivity" in the water of Ayash, reflecting "the filtration of the tailings reservoir." Antamina maintained that it had executed filtration control measures, and apparently two years later none of the metals, with the exception of molybdenum, exceeded the limits for state classes two or four, or the internal guidelines for aquatic life. The consulting firm established that molybdenum "continues to show a clear trend related to the mine, as the concentrations decrease with increasing distance from the mine." EcoMetrix (2005:3.18) concluded in an environmental evaluation for the period 1998–2005, "Except for metal levels in the tissue of worms and higher levels of some metals [copper, cadmium, and zinc] in fish liver, data for water quality, benthic invertebrates and fish all suggested that the Antamina operation did not have a significant effect on the environmental conditions of the Ayash Ravine from 1999. Although some levels of metals in invertebrates and fish liver appeared to indicate a trend related to the mine, there had been no negative effects on the health of benthic invertebrate and fish communities to date." Further downplaying the change, EcoMetrix (2005:3.18) added that some of the metals found in fish tissue could be due to "natural variability."

Blasting, Roads, and Territoriality

Near the mining operations area, I observed houses with walls that were cracked, presumably as a result of mining explosions.[5] Residents of the Mosna sector claimed that dust from these blasts was damaging their crops. Antamina initially argued that these residents were located too far from the operations area. However, it then recognized the problem some months after the initial operations and visited the area of Pincullo, which claimed its pasture was covered with particles. Another dust cloud incident occurred in the hamlet of Juprog the year following the commencement of operations (CMA 2003b:51). The problem seemed to diminish during the rainy season because the precipitation effectively washed the dust produced by the crusher. Antamina then maintained that these latter areas were beyond the "zone of influence" and too far away to be affected. The technical rhetoric was at odds with local indicators. It was frequently claimed that when a "bomb" burst, the toads would flee and dust would cover the potato flowers. An Ayash resident told me that the animals *enflaquecían* (became weaker and thinner) because of the dust and that her family's maca plants had "gone bad." She claimed that her relative—an Antamina worker—had told her that "the mining company has caused something." In common with its approach to the debate over Huascarán National Park (see chapter 3), the mining company's choice of a focused impact rhetoric sought to distance it from ecosystem dynamics and interactions. As Antamina staff member Mateo told me, "We operate within the permissible limits, and we do not generate major environmental impacts in areas outside from the mine. Evidently, you generate an impact when you make a hole, but it is inside your property, in the mine, or in Ayash. You discharge, and anyway there have been changes in the conditions of odor, water, etc."

Other conflicts arose around territoriality. These centered on restrictions placed by Antamina on transport routes, particularly those used by farmers and herders to reach water sources. As mentioned in chapter 1, access to the San Marcos–Antamina–Llata road, built over several years using communal labor, was cut by Antamina in 1997. Thereafter locals could only utilize it through a permit issued in Huaraz by Antamina. Access to a spring was also cut. Farmers from Pincullo complained that their rights to a water source used on a daily basis had been lost, however, Antamina regarded the site as being under its ownership (CMA 2001d:16).

Environmental Committees, Monitoring, and Negotiations

Shortly after Antamina's operations began, the company organized the First Participatory Workshop on Environment. It invited state institutions, NGOs, communities, and the San Marcos Environmental Committee, among others. The aim was to "gain the trust of local people in relation to water quality in the Ayash river" and to show an openness to environmental monitoring (CMA 2001c:13). The event included a presentation of the "monitoring plan," the sampling system, and the "chain of custody." Five months later, the first water quality "joint monitoring" mission was carried out. The samples were transferred to three laboratories in Lima using a chain of custody formed by representatives of the various interested groups. The process was comparable to the Huascarán Working Group model and aimed to build trust based on shared control and mutual supervision (see chapter 3). The independent samples cost approximately five hundred dollars for each analysis. Just six laboratories in Lima were certified to perform the task.

Once Antamina had been inaugurated, the U.S. firm Pincock, Allen & Holt performed quarterly environmental inspections that were additional to its audits of the financiers of the project (CMA 2001e). Antamina delivered quarterly reports to the San Marcos environmental committee. MEM argued that Antamina could cause changes in the environment and that the area had to be monitored to assess potential impacts (AUDITEC 2000). Their studies indicated that the substances monitored in the water and air were, on average, below the maximum permissible limits (MPL). The Ministry of Health's DIGESA carried out quarterly analyses, MEM issued a semiannual report, and the mining company monitored its operations on a daily basis. Government evaluations were based on averages; however, these obscure the peak readings that are crucial to understanding impacts on socioecosystems. The Local Communities of Health Administration program in San Marcos reported an increase in acute respiratory infections, especially among infants, and severe diarrheal and stomach illnesses in the period 1998–2000 (CLAS San Marcos 2001). According to a doctor, the cause of stomach ailments was due to the rural pattern of cohabitation with animals, especially considering the excreta close to the houses. These diseases had decreased from 1997 to 1998, just prior to the start of the mine's construction. The coincidence met with an evasive response from a district-level health sector representative, who told me that it was impossible for him to question Antamina as it would have led to problems with the Ministry of Health, which was supportive of the mine's presence.

The joint monitoring consisted of the company, state entities, community representatives, and the environmental committee. Ayash also participated through the Association for the Protection of the Environment of the Ayash Basin. The initial samplings showed values within the MPL. The San Marcos Environmental Committee inspected the sedimentation tunnel outlet and reported "foam in the Ushpajanca Gorge." Antamina offered to reduce the drainage from dam into the Ayash River. It hired some of the claimants as laborers. MEM DGAAM (Dirección General de Asuntos Ambientales Mineros, or General Direction of Environmental Issues in Mining) took water samples and Antamina collected countersamples.

Eight months after the opening of Antamina, the Canadian company Beak presented the baseline study of soils and crops to the San Marcos Environmental Committee. They reported four cases in which Canadian MPL had been exceeded: the presence, "probably of natural origin," of high concentrations of zinc and molybdenum in the Ayash Basin, near the tailings dam; phototoxicity and excess molybdenum in livestock protection (pastures) in some plots of the Carash Basin; excess lead on a plot in San Marcos; and higher concentrations of cyanide in Juprog, although not "in excess" of what was "established" (CMA 2001d:14). Peruvian regulatory guidelines for the metals content of soil were absent at the time and would remain so until 2013. The Ayash Basin showed high concentrations of zinc and molybdenum near the tailings dam. Antamina concluded that this "probably" had "natural origin" and on this basis sought to evade liability (CMA 2001d:14).

Downplaying the sampling techniques became a rhetorical defense against unfavorable results. Faced with the high concentrations of zinc and molybdenum, Antamina maintained that there was no evidence "that these observations are related to the project. In fact, they may reflect the fact that these sampling stations are a short distance from areas that present a high natural content." Antamina emphasized that samples used for the EIA prior to the mine's construction had revealed "naturally high levels of a series of metals [e.g., zinc and arsenic] . . . in the superficial soils very close to the current location of the mine" (CMA 2001c:9). Antamina acknowledged that it had not fully complied with the maximum permitted levels and admitted "slight changes in the benthic community [invertebrates of the watercourse bed] of the Ayash system," recognizing that "these suggested effects related to the mine" because of the reduction of aquatic insects and other indicators. It asserted that the trout had not undergone significant change (CMA 2003b:45; 2004:46). Antamina admitted that the Carash Gorge received effluent from the operations and some rock dumping, leading to excess copper and zinc. It offered remediation works. The company promised to install drinking fountains for each affected family in Ayash. One year later, Antamina used communal labor to build the potable water infrastructure ($262,576) in Ayash (Huaripampa and Pichiú; see figure 21) (CMA 2003b:61). Six months later the company installed part of a fish farm in Ayash ($52,000), also using local labor.

The juxtaposition of the local indicators and those of the mining company represented a struggle of authority, confidence, and power. Antamina sought to resolve the initial environmental claims in San Marcos by joint monitoring and the installation of infrastructure (e.g., drinking fountains), while skepticism remained. As Levi, a member of the San Marcos Environmental Committee, told me, "The Ayash River has changed color and has a different smell. But the samples show that the water quality has not decreased, it has not deteriorated. But how do I explain this to the animals? How do I tell the donkey that the water is the same quality as before, that he can drink it and nothing will happen? Because animals do not want to drink that water and that's important. . . . If the animals do not want it, that's an incredible bioindicator."

Huarmey: From the Welcome Road to the Dirty Mining Pipeline

The unfortunate chain of events that culminated in tear gas bombs dropped from a state helicopter in Huarmey (see chapter 4) led me to ask how the politics and relations between the billionaire mining company and this impoverished coastal town were conducted in the context of a centralized state in dire need of taxes and foreign currency (see figure 22).

"An environmental impact statement that is not very credible: The original environmental impact statement has changed in several aspects, especially in relation to the transportation of concentrates from the mine to the sea and in the dumping of wastewater into the sea. The changes made have raised doubts about the preventive nature of the document" (CONAM 2001:33). This quote summarizes the findings of the Multisectorial Technical Commission formed to mediate the conflicts in Huarmey, which had led to several protests. The arrival of Antamina created great expectations of a new road from the mine to

FIGURE 21 (a, above) Town and ravine of Ayash, and (b, right) drinking trough. 2002. Author's photos.

FIGURE 21 *(continued)*

FIGURE 22 Port of Huarmey and fishing boats. 2002. Author's photo.

the port. The decision to use a pipeline, promoted by environmentalists as a way of protecting Huascarán National Park (see chapter 3) was a disappointment for an important sector of the population of Huarmey who had imagined the benefits associated with new roads, including trade and the selling of services. The uneasiness was exacerbated by fears about the mining pipeline, which was initially allowed to discharge wastewater toward the ocean in case of emergency or excess.

Antamina's first presentation, in a full municipal theater in Huarmey four years prior to the start of mine operations, was a key moment. The company presented a video with testimonies from fishermen at a port used by BHP's Escondida mine in Chile. This purported to demonstrate that after nine years of operation, there had been no adverse impacts. The majority of attendees were from the town of Huarmey. The communities of Puerto Huarmey and Puerto Grande, located nearer to the proposed facility, were less well represented. According to an Antamina employee, the only concern in the beginning was the effect of the highway that would cross Huascarán National Park (see chapter 3). Land purchases led to litigation between the municipality of Huarmey and Antamina (e.g., disagreements over the amount of tax to be paid). As had occurred in San Marcos with the offers that had facilitated land acquisition,

Antamina personnel in Huarmey promised development in the form of employment and infrastructure. As detailed in chapter 3, expectations among farmers in Huarmey were particularly high. Council staff from the municipality of Huarmey assured me that these hopes had been fed by the mining company. The municipal officers also claimed that the previous mayor disseminated company promises such as employment, a highway from San Marcos to Puerto Huarmey, and improvement of the town's industrial wharf. Finally, they explained to me how they expected that the highway would benefit the agriculture sector:

Abel: I was president of an irrigation committee and made Antamina's offer known. The happy irrigators said, "We are going to have the paved road." We, the farmers, wanted Antamina to come.

Author: Did you see a cheaper way to get your products out?

Isaac: Yes, sure.

AB: To improve our quality of life.

A: And you did not see any problem with the highway?

AB: Not at all. For us a highway was necessary. They programmed vehicles that would transport their ore through there and gave us the option of using it with vehicles to carry *panllevar* [basic crops] for the people.

A: The highway was going to pass right by the farms?

AB: Yes, right by the farms, right there. (grammar modified)

The president of the Defense Front of Huarmey also told me that the highway would have provided employment for "its construction or at least in transport, in tire repairs, or in restaurants," providing "four thousand jobs, scholarships, microenterprises, the raising of quail and prawns, as well as loans."

Conflict arose when Antamina opted to transport the concentrate using a pipeline instead of a highway. This change destroyed any hope of paving the route from Huarmey to Aija to Recuay and made real the possibility, either by accident or intentionally, of wastewater discharge from the pipeline into the sea. The pipeline carries the concentrate to Puerto Huarmey, where ships of up to fifty tons wait to receive it. Upon reaching the port, the material is separated into solids and liquid through a process of thickening and filtering. The wet "pulp" is transported by conveyor belts three hundred meters to the dock and from there to the ship. The mineral is stored and transported in closed environments to avoid air pollution. The concentrate is stored and filtered so that residual water can eventually irrigate plants (AUDITEC 2000:27). Each day more than six thousand cubic meters of water descends to the port of Huarmey. Antamina claimed it would use oxidation ponds to treat the water and a forestation system that would irrigate 170 hectares of land adjacent to the port. The Multisectoral Technical Commission reported complaints about the risks of soil contamination by metals and particles from the concentrated ore. Some claimed that the untreated water generated odor and that during the shipment process, the ore produced dust that was carried by the wind.

According to Huarmey council members, the change of plan without consultation "created much distrust in Antamina." The changes could have been communicated better. The mayor of Huarmey, Juan Pacífico, recalled the "lack of information for the community," particularly in respect to the design modifications. This, he said, was the "responsibility" of the government. In an episode that would be long remembered by residents, Antamina presented signatures of those who had attended an event convened by the mining company, on January 16, 1999, as proof of local consent to the change in the design of the project. Addendum 3 to the environmental impact statement deemed this "information meeting" to have been a "public hearing," a definition Antamina later undertook to correct (CONAM 2001:32; K&H 1999a). The semantics were important. A public hearing would have meant endorsement of the modifications and as such would have undermined the social basis for the protests. The Defense Front of Huarmey was formed a week after the episode. Its first act was to convene a public assembly with a demand "to ignore the signatures" obtained by Antamina. Martín was the leader of this group, and for him the incident constituted the "first conflict." Unlike in San Marcos, in Huarmey there were no notorious historic family disputes with political or partisan overtones to further stoke conflicts. The mayor successfully proposed the opening of an environmental office. However, its only professional staff member resigned after two months, citing lack of support. When the socioenvironmental conflicts continued to grow, the municipality would once again seek her services.

The Multisectoral Technical Commission recognized the existence in Huarmey of a "fragmentation of organizations that threatens its capacity for consensus and participation," as well as "the division of population and polarization of attitudes in relation to Antamina" (CONAM 2001:26). As had been the case in San Marcos, a project with the dimensions of Antamina quickly demonstrated its capacity to catalyze latent conflicts. Moses, a member of a local Catholic church, told me that with the arrival of the mining company, Huarmey "was becoming the province of discord." A municipal councilor added that

Antamina had "divided the population and created distrust." As had been the case in Huallanca and San Marcos, there were many complaints in Huarmey about changes generated by the mining operation. Moses added that Antamina brought "bars, nightclubs, and prostitution." The commission documented complaints about the "cost of living, increased crime, drug addiction and prostitution," as well as a "disorderly demographic increase due to the attraction of migrants and the loss of market for some products due to its image as an allegedly contaminated area" (CONAM 2001:26).

Water, Blockages, and Mediations

Mayor Pacífico defined the strikes in terms of the expectation of reciprocity: "The show of force was to let Antamina know not to get it wrong in Huarmey and to do a better job of informing and supporting Huarmey, a town which had received it with open arms. It was also done to tell the Peruvian state to keep its eye on Huarmey because the national treasury receives money from the exports and the income tax delivers good dividends. This does not translate into benefits for the communities." As detailed in chapter 3, residents of Huarmey blockaded the Pan-American Highway—the most important trade route between the capital and the coastal cities—on two occasions during the year Antamina's operations began. The residents of the town of Huarmey were fearful of potential pollution because they extracted drinking water from underground wells. Fearing that water from the mine would destroy their crops, farmers of the lower lying areas also participated in the blockade. For their part, people in more elevated areas claimed there would be water scarcity and had high expectations around a paved road for better trading of agricultural production. The media, radio stations in particular, worked in alliance with the Defense Front of Huarmey to encourage the protests. These activities constituted direct action to obtain improvements to local roads.

The bishop of Chimbote convened a *mesa de concertación* (agreement roundtable) in Huarmey that included the participation of all interested groups and the state. According to one of the participants, the church's role as a mediator was justified on the basis of its "credibility" as a "guarantor." A group associated with the Defense Front of Huarmey demanded before the roundtable that a Comisión Técnica Multisectorial (Multisectoral Technical Commission) be formed that would "specifically address the environmental issues" linked to Antamina (CONAM 2001:12). The Multisectoral Technical Commission was chaired by the National Environmental Council (CONAM). It comprised sixteen interested "social institutions or segments" (CONAM 2001:13).[6] The Defense Front of Huarmey refused to recognize CONAM and abandoned the negotiations. The name *Multisectoral Technical Commission* had been chosen as a rhetorical strategy to deemphasize the "political" and stress instead the "technical." The latter was equated with efficiency and objectivity. However, the group's task was very political: negotiation around decisions about the impact and control of resources. The APRA political party had governed Peru from 1985 to 1990. Its term was characterized by hyperinflation, corruption, and armed violence. The Fujimori regime that followed (1990–2000) critiqued political expressions such as the demonstrations and negotiations undertaken in Huarmey as an extrapolation of APRA inefficiency or corruption. In contrast, its own leader (Alberto Fujimori, subsequently imprisoned for corruption and the ordering of extrajudicial killings) was presented as an independent and efficient technocrat. This false dichotomy has dominated political discussions on a large and small scale in Peru over recent decades.

In 2000, one year prior to Antamina entering into operation, representatives of CONACAMI traveled to the United States, met with the World Bank, and issued an alarm about mining projects in Peru. A Huarmey councilman told me, "Here the blocking of roads is the only defense mechanism left to the people once they have exhausted the sending of letters and other documents." The Pan-American Highway was blocked three times between March 2000 and June 2001. Following the third blockage, the interest groups agreed to form the Multisectoral Technical Commission to determine negotiation mechanisms, disseminate information, encourage participation, and undertake monitoring. CONAM was to be the "facilitator" of the mediation, which would be one of the first of its kind in Peru. Among the mechanisms of mediation, CONAM (2001:3) highlighted the dissemination of "information and the improvement of citizen participation" that would increase "trust" between the parties and address the complaints raised over the change in design.

Trust and social institutions can be mutually reinforcing. The former is necessary, though an insufficient condition, especially in conflict situations, for the viability of the latter. It is no accident that of the sixty-four concerns documented by the Multisectoral Technical Commission, the category *credibility* was mentioned sixteen times (in general terms and in respect of both Antamina and the government). Forty-three concerns were about what I define as "environmental impact." There were accusations against Antamina (often undocumented) for "not having honored promises and commitments made," which generated mistrust (CONAM 2001:16, 32). Antamina tried to regain Huarmey's trust through various measures, including guided tours of its facilities. In addition, the municipality implemented in its own premises a little-visited Citizen Environmental Documentation Center that included a library of mining environmental reports. The enormous asymmetry between the community and the mining company was manifest in differentiated capacities for analysis and access to information. Javier, a member of the Port of Huarmey Junta Vecinal (Neighborhood Board) and its representative at the Multisectoral Technical Committee, emphasized the need to "analyze [and] consult technicians for guidance and direction," and to "reconfirm the information" together with data cross-checking because of the high degree of suspicion. The contrast becomes more evident where there is no state to mediate.

An Antamina staff member summed up the darkest fears in Huarmey in this way: "The Defense Front of Huarmey said that there was a hidden pipeline releasing waste into the sea, that it would bring uranium, that fishing would disappear, that farmers in the valley would lose their land, because everything would be contaminated." The most delicate issue facing the Multisectoral Technical Commission was a set of eight claims for impact on the hydrological environment, which highlighted the risk, in the absence of adequate treatment of wastewater from mining operations, of "some toxic elements reaching the aquifer (and eventually in this way to the sea or sites of underground extraction for human consumption)" (CONAM 2001:16). Antamina maintained that after the water was filtered, the waste would be absorbed by the forest and through evapotranspiration would never reach the water table. The quarterly evaluation of water samples included groundwater. Once again Peruvian quality standards were not yet in place. The EIA permitted the dumping of wastewater into the sea. Antamina had to guarantee "zero discharge" (i.e., that it would not release water on the surface or underground) (CONAM 2001:21, 29). The Multisectoral Technical Commission reported that "there are no signs of contamination that exceed the MPLs for chemical or bacteriological elements in underground or marine water, except for lead in a sample of groundwater," and recommended "comprehensive monitoring" and investigating the causes (CONAM 2001:7). In other words, the commission permitted pollution, did not mention the consequences, and apparently was concerned only that it not exceed the permissible limits.

South of the port facilities, the Antamina forest irrigation project (166 hectares) aimed to receive the water from the concentrate and have it evaporated by plants. The Multisectoral Technical Commission required increasing the size to 180 hectares in order to add water evaporation and transpiration by plants, since these absorb the liquid through their roots and release it through their leaves (CAO 2006). At the request of residents, the project is currently located fifteen meters above the water table, a distance greater than originally planned. Antamina indicated that there would be no discharge to the sea and that all the liquid would go to the forest system following treatment (CONAM 2001:18). There were fears that some portion of wastewater would reach the shallow water table (twenty-two meters), affecting rivers and eventually reaching the sea.

There were two additional concerns: ships' ballast and the arrival of mining vessels. Residents of the port expressed concerns about possible contamination from the ships bringing new human and animal populations. This entailed concerns about health of the arriving crew members, the risk of discharging ballast (the seawater that a ship carries in its holds for balance), and the presence of microorganisms on the hulls of ships, which can damage the port's environmental health (CONAM 2001:20). The proposed solution was joint supervision based on transparent mutual vigilance, an approach that would dispel mistrust, as it had done in the case of the Huascarán Working Group (see chapter 3) or the joint monitoring undertaken in San Marcos. Javier, a resident of Puerto Huarmey, suggested that the replacement of the ballast be supervised by local and state representatives in a "rotating" manner that would eliminate any temptation for "corruption." Five years after the first shipment, the CAO (2006:7) acknowledged that copper concentration in the sediment of the dock had increased but they were unable to "gather further information on discharges of ballast or other effluent from cargo ships, because this information is not monitored and reported."

The local fishermen considered the company's failure to announce the arrival of the mining ships in the port as an assault. There was no siren radar and no light communication system. "The boats came in as if entering a desert," recalled one fisherman. This made it more risky for fishermen when setting to sea at night. The danger of a collision between a small boat and the mining vessels seemed very real. There were also complaints about the disappearance of artisanal fishing resources in Puerto Grande, allegedly due to explosions and noise from the company's operations. There was criticism, too, about the reduction of the fishing area and restricted access during loading times. The fishermen's boats were generally nonmotorized. The large mining vessels affected the waves and forced the fishermen to make large detours to reach their fishing grounds, incurring the associated time and opportunity costs. Antamina undertook to tow the nonmotorized boats to the side of the dock during loading periods. It also established an entry road to the dock and the port. The Multisectoral Technical Commission agreed that access routes should be available to local residents (CONAM 2001). The company was also obliged to use sirens during the day and intermittent night lights, while avoiding nocturnal noise near populated areas and communicating the loading schedule to the fishermen's associations.

Antamina monitored the quality of the static level of groundwater on a biweekly and quarterly basis. This information was compared with the quarterly DIGESA "surveillance" reporting and the biannual audit control. Antamina evaluated the air quality every three days. DIGESA prepared a report that was delivered to the CMVFAH (Comité de Monitoreo, Vigilancia y Fiscalización Ambiental de Huarmey, or the Huarmey Monitoring, Surveillance, and Environmental Monitoring Committee). This had arisen on the recommendation of the final report of the Multisectoral Technical Commission, which said it should include national government institutions (e.g., DIGESA), municipal jurisdictions, local fishermen's organizations, the Irrigation Users Board, several NGOs, and the National University of Santa (CONAM 2001). The committee evaluated the results presented by DIGESA and Antamina. CMVFAH was incorporated as a legal entity in 2002 and sought funds to undertake its own sampling and analysis. Three years later, following local elections, it received $26,000 from Antamina for logistical expenses, including counter samples (CMA 2006f:59). This Antamina financing was viewed with suspicion by the population of Huarmey (CAO 2006). Antamina continues to participate as an invited member on the commission but has no voting rights. Due to its foundation nature, the committee currently receives funds from the Presidency of the Council of Ministers, becoming a unique case in Peru. It carried out thirty-eight water surveys between 2001 and 2012 that were later shared with the National Water Authority. It has monitored marine sediments twenty-nine times since 2001 and air quality on fifteen occasions since 2003.

Rural representatives and fishermen participated on the committee with a certain degree of apathy. They complained about the time investment (the meetings lasted more than four hours) and lack of remuneration by comparison with company personnel and state officials who received salaries and per diems for travel expenses. The residents of Huarmey also criticized the abuse of technical terminology and employment of expert rhetoric, which they considered as designed to encourage their exclusion from the environmental control process. "It is tiring to hear that they are talking at a certain [higher] level," said Moses. This asymmetry of codes and information conjured a technical expert discourse as a rhetorical weapon to combat demands. Juan, an Antamina environmental expert, challenged the community: "If you say that I contaminate, show me how, where, explain it to me." He highlighted the need to share information in order to build trust, noting the aim to "have the evidence that our results are not hidden, [so] I take them out to share and to provide greater transparency." To file a criminal or civil complaint, the plaintiff needed administrative backing; that is, MEM had to admit that the company had not complied in some respect with a legal norm. As environmental lawyer Doris Balvín explained, the burden of proof lay with the community, which had to prove a cause-and-effect relationship (e.g., contaminated water led to livestock deaths). It would have been fairer had the onus been on the party that was posing risk to the environment—and was profiting financially from the activity—to prove that it was not contaminating. Local residents demanded a sustained government presence to resolve the mining conflicts. Huarmey had more success than San Marcos in drawing media and government attention. The blockade of coastal roads had national repercussions, given that these connect more than half of the country's population and government officials constantly conjure a risk of frightening away foreign investment, which in turn elevates the urgency of the mining conflict.

Postscript

Three years after the creation of the Huarmey Environmental Committee, an event exposed the deficient flow of environmental information within the project and the international pressure effectiveness for considering local parameters. In 2004, three years after beginning operations, Antamina identified changes in the condition of the irrigation water table and waited more than a year to issue its first public pronouncement (CAO 2006). The discovery coincided with claims that irrigation could be contaminating both Huarmey's bay and its domestic water supply. The diagnosis was not shared with authorities because "Antamina determined the issue was not sufficiently significant to warrant formal notifications to MEM in its 2005 quarterly reports" (CAO 2006:8).

CAO evaluated claims alleging that the port facilities had damaged the marine environment, as well as concerns about possible wastewater discharges and metal concentrates in the bay. CAO worked for six months with the "complainants" and engaged an "independent" hydrologist. It reported that although the "shipping activities do not appear to have had any negative impact on fish populations in the bay," the concentrate handling at the dock "led to sediment (increase in copper concentration) that are limited to within 250 meters of the pier." It also stated that changes in water table levels and quality below the irrigated land flowed northward, "not directly toward the bay," which would explain why "there is no evidence of contamination of the bay water resulting from the irrigation" (CAO 2006:6–7).

The problem was that Antamina's plant was designed for an application of irrigation water supply at a rate of seventy liters per second but had not considered the seasonal change in evapotranspiration. The historical average coefficient was sixty-two liters per second. The surface of the irrigation project was calculated as the average monthly evapotranspiration coefficient multiplied by seventy liters per second. The final effective planting area was 166 hectares. Evapotranspiration from April to October was less than the designed irrigation coefficient and was insufficient to absorb the seventy liters per second. Therefore, during seven months of the year, "some of the treated concentrate filtrate water could seep to the underlying groundwater," and this was shown to have occurred (CAO 2006:annex A, p. 6).

CAO (2006:annex A, p. 6) concluded, "An underestimate of seasonal effects on evapotranspiration from the irrigation plots together with limited characterization of the subsurface beneath the irrigation plots has resulted in infiltration of irrigation water below the root zone, an elevated water table beneath the irrigation plots, and degradation of groundwater quality beneath the plots from the leaching of salts in soils." Moreover, the variation in the hydraulic conditions and the increase in the gradient of the irrigation farm "have caused poor quality water in upland areas to migrate towards the Huarmey River alluvial aquifer where water is currently of good quality for irrigation and domestic uses" (CAO 2006:annex A, p. 9). Antamina committed to deliver to MIGA copies of future and past reports. Although the mining company built a reservoir that was ten times larger to store irrigation water during winter in the months when evapotranspiration decreased, the loss of confidence and the associated criticisms remained (CAO 2006). As with the experience in Huascarán National Park and the pipeline (chapter 3), it is evident that pressure on a mining company brought to bear from overseas proved effective for environmental monitoring and for promoting transparency.

Risk, Pollution, and Conflict

> *Major Walsh: It's a coincidence, it's not scientific!*
> *Scientist Claude Lacombe: Listen to me, Major Walsh, it is an event* sociologique*!*
> —*CLOSE ENCOUNTERS OF THE THIRD KIND*, FILM, 1977

Hardly a week goes by without news in international media about a natural resource threatened with destruction. In 2010, for example, the *New York Times* reported that the BP oil spill in the Gulf of Mexico had become "the largest accidental release of oil into marine waters" (Aigner et al. 2010). According to a BP document, "Officials chose, partly for financial reasons, to use a type of casing for the well that the company knew was the riskier of two options" (Urbina 2010). Seven years earlier, the head of the United States Environmental Protection Agency had declared that "fish in virtually all of the nation's lakes and rivers were contaminated with mercury, a highly toxic metal that poses health risks for pregnant women and young children," and proclaimed that "mercury is everywhere," at the same time promising more evaluations and assuring that "emissions are down and will continue to go down" (Janofsky 2004). If this is the experience of the world's largest economy, it is worth asking to what extent environmental destruction is an inevitable cost of development or industrialization. To what extent can local negative environmental impacts really be estimated when they are justified on the basis of the national interest yet harm vulnerable groups? How might these costs really be calculated in the context of a sustainable approach for local nature and its living creatures? What might contamination mean? Who might decide what the indicators are and on what basis might they make this determination? And what might the definition of a contaminated site be?

Anthropologist Mary Douglas and political scientist Aaron Wildavsky, in their now-classic book *Risk and Culture*, show how "risk perception depends on shared culture not on individual psychology" (Douglas 2004:xix [1966]). To understand these decisions, one must understand the "cultural bias to recognize moral and political issues underlying a debate about physical risks," showing "our moral and political judgment to bear openly on the basic assumptions"

(Douglas and Wildavsky 1982:195). In the 1970s, faced with growing fears of industrial contamination, risk analysis focused on the relations between politics and uncertainty. Douglas and Wildavsky analyze risk as a taboo with morally and politically charged debates, where political affiliation is the best indicator in the distribution of attitudes to danger. The choice of what to regard as a threat and what to ignore depends on which dangers one wishes to prevent (Douglas 2004:xix [1966]). The experts prioritize environmental characteristics to be evaluated when constructing parameters for contamination. The practical application results in a historical social construct imposed by a group with authority. Reflecting the influence of the contributions of Bruno Latour and many other critical science studies scholars, subsequent anthropological works have been influenced by poststructural approaches, emphasizing not only how science encompasses politics, nature, and knowledge, but also the fluidity of nature-culture boundaries (Goldstein 2017).

The sociologist Ulrick Beck (1992, 2002 [1988]) explores how in the 1980s, societies faced unprecedented technological risks of a nuclear, chemical, or genetic nature. According to Beck, the new challenges had to be faced through public criticism of specialized institutions using new rules of consultation and decision making, and industries had to demonstrate that their processes and products were safe. Beck was one of the first to question the political basis of modern industrial societies by promoting the study of how societies organize themselves to deal with the hazards that modernity brings.

Ecological economist Joan Martínez-Alier (2002) locates concerns about contamination in the last century, seeking to harmonize the "wilderness cult," which contemplates nature without touching it, and the "gospel of eco-efficiency"—referred to as "scientific industrialism" by historian Ramachandra Guha—with the aim of a continuous and balanced use of nature through "sustainable development." The "environmentalism of the poor," or the environmental justice movement of "subaltern environmental struggles" (Muradian et al. 2003:777), demands social justice for poor countries or impoverished sectors of industrialized nations who consider that their environment, health, and productive activities are being affected by agents who, for their part, claim to be delivering economic development. The critique highlights environmental causes in conflicts where subjects do not necessarily recognize themselves as environmentalists (Guha 1989; Martínez-Alier 2002:54).

Martínez-Alier (1990:13; 2002:55) locates the first environmental conflict of the last century in 1907: strikes over working conditions included pollution protests in Ashio, Japan, because of construction of a large sediment basin to store contaminated water that meant the destruction of a local community. In the 1960s, industrialized countries of the North experienced significant environmental social mobilizations. The UN Conference on the Human Environment in 1972 in Stockholm empowered these mobilizations and led to the creation of the first ministries of the environment, and to air and water quality standards around the globe—although Peru would have to wait decades to incorporate those changes (Dargent et al. 2017). In Peru the first social mobilization against ecological damage was the result of contamination to pasture, rivers, and the air by La Cerro's La Oroya smelter and refinery between 1920 and 1930 (Martínez-Alier 2002:58). The pastures became unusable and people fell ill. Local communities won a lawsuit, and La Cerro was compelled to purchase their properties. Seeking to alleviate the labor problem of decreasing yields on small agricultural parcels because of pasture impacts and livestock deaths, the company began contracting some of its workforce locally.

In the 1950s and 1960s, the south of Peru became home to the country's largest copper extraction. At the start of the millennium, Southern Peru Copper Corporation, owned by Asarco and the U.S.-owned Newmont Gold Corporation, was Peru's largest exporter and among the ten largest copper producers in the world (Martínez-Alier 2002:59). Sixty percent of national copper production was centered on the departments of Tacna and Moquegua. Southern Peru was the largest company until the entry of Antamina. The south of Peru has experienced some of the greatest impacts from mining, with the water and air quality of the sixty thousand inhabitants of Ilo affected by La Southern over more than thirty years.

In subsequent decades, state and private mining were the principal sources of environmental degradation, especially during the 1980s when the sector became recognized as the most contaminating in the country (Glave and Kuramoto 2002:529). In the 1990s, significant mining conflicts arose in the communities affected by fumes from the La Oroya smelter and those around Ilo (La Southern) in the south. A complaint heard by the International Water Tribunal in 1992 led to compliance with agreements between the population, the state, and La Southern (Balvín 2002; Loveday and Molina 2006). Several conflicts gained media attention as the new millennium began. Yanacocha was a recurring name. Among the most notorious cases was a mercury spill by this mining company in the small market town of Choropampa in mid-2000. Almost one thousand people were poisoned attempting to collect the toxic liquid, which they mistook for gold. Three years later the Tambogrande case (see chapter 1) illustrated the financial risk for a mining company when it dispenses with local participation and the "social license"—to borrow a widely used expression in the mining business—in rural areas (Gil Ramón 2010). The northern Andean cases of Quilish (2004) and Conga (2011) were each frustrated attempts to expand Yanacocha. Protests by farmers were central to stopping the projects. They reflected the competition for land and water between a large mine that generates little local employment and smallholder agriculture, which was a major source of employment for local residents.

Limiting Environmental Degradation

Globally, the early 1990s saw a period of openness toward the environmental agenda. The preparations for the 1992 Earth Summit constituted a milestone. Five years earlier, the United Nations Environment Programme had presented the report *Our Common Future*, also known as the Brundlandt Report, which introduced the now-widespread concept of sustainable development. These events impacted Latin American countries such as Colombia, which introduced a new "green" constitution, and Peru, which introduced in 1990 its Environment Code.[7] The code, developed with the collaboration of environmental NGOs, was poorly received by the business community, which claimed to have to been excluded from the preparation process (Caravedo 2003:5). Following the creation of CONAM in 1994 as the central environmental authority (its role would be subsumed fourteen years later by MINAM), natural resource public policies were more directly addressed through regulations such as the Organic Law for the Sustainable Use of Natural Resources (Law 26821), the Law on Natural Protected Areas (Law 26834), and the Law for the Conservation and Sustainable Use of Biological Diversity (Law 26839), which together came to form the basis for national environmental management (Pulgar-Vidal 2002). The redesign of the environmental framework has witnessed both progress and reversals.

In 1993, months before the creation of CONAM, MEM approved the regulations on environmental protection for metallurgical mining activities, defining four management instruments: the MPLs, the EIAs, the PAMA (see chapter 3), and the closure plans. The MPL for liquid mining effluents were approved in 1996 and fourteen years later were revised by supreme decree (10-2010-MINAM). Peruvian laws differentiated "limits" from "standards":

MPL refers to the source of the "emission" or "effluent," and the environmental quality standards refer to the environmental objectives sought for the "receiving body." For air quality, the MPL measure the emission at the source (e.g., a chimney). For water, the measure is the effluent taken—for example, at the overflow of a tailings dam. The regulation for standards and limits differentiated the effluent (liquid) from the emission (gas). Standards are measured in the environment (e.g., breathable air quality or potable water). Legally, the environmental quality standards are measures that establish the level of concentration or the degree of the elements present in the receiving body (air, water, or soil), limits that supposedly put human or environmental health beyond significant risk.

In the beginning, the ministry responsible for the sector of the source of the discharge—MEM, in the case of mining—set the authorized margins and CONAM registered them. MEM supervised mining company compliance with the mining MPL. OSINERGMIN (Organismo Supervisor de la Inversión en Energía y Minería, or the Supervisory Agency for Investment in Energy and Mining), part of MEM, was created in 2007 as a supervising, oversight, and sanctioning body in the electricity, hydrocarbons, and mining sectors, including overseeing compliance with the effluent and emissions MPL. Critics questioned both its autonomy—given its status within MEM—and its efficiency. It is important to remember that MEM has the legal mandate to promote mining. Two years later, a new water resources law established the ANA (Autoridad Nacional del Agua, or National Water Authority) to control and supervise compliance with water quality standards, including the functions of prevention, surveillance, and remediation measures in basins at risk. ANA is attached to the Ministry of Agriculture and works in coordination with the Basin Council. In addition, ANA grants mining companies the authorization to discharge effluents into water courses. Surveillance in the receiving environment had previously been the responsibility of DIGESA (in the Ministry of Health).

In 2010 the OEFA—formally created in 2008 as an agency attached to MINAM (see chapter 3)—assumed from OSINERGMIN the responsibility to evaluate and monitor environmental quality (i.e., water, air, soil, flora, and fauna) and to control and prosecute breaches in several productive sectors, including mining (medium- and large-scale mining) and energy (hydrocarbons and electricity). Since that time, OEFA has been monitoring compliance with the MPLs for liquid effluents, gaseous emissions, and particle matter from mining metallurgical activities. Environmental impact assessments generally lack evidence to show that discharges will not affect the environmental quality of the receiving body.

The regulatory framework prior to the 1990s required neither explicit environmental or social standards for mining companies nor compensation or remediation for environmental degradation. Created in 1992, MEM DGAAM was the first Peruvian environmental mining institution. Until the middle of the first decade of twenty-first century, there were no environmental parameters for mining in Peru in respect to emissions into the air of zinc, mercury, cadmium, and other basic measures. The ombudsman's office concluded then that "MPL for polluting emissions in the mining sector [were] too permissive in relation to international standards" (DP 2005:19). The World Bank (2005b:89–90) reported that Peruvian MPLs for air discharges of lead, arsenic, and particle matter were "significantly higher" than the bank's own benchmarks. The General Environment Act stated that where parameters for environmental control did not exist, those set by "institutions of Public International Law" (e.g., WHO) would serve for "reference use."[8] In the case of air quality standards, there have been three legislative milestones since 1996, and the number of parameters regulated over this period has risen from four to twelve. The values have generally become stricter; for example, the daily average for sulfur dioxide was lowered from six hundred to twenty micrograms per cubic meter. However, since 2013 the government has exempted three atmospheric basins—housing two refineries and a metallurgical complex—from the aforementioned parameter, and permitted its quadrupling. The MPL for air are unchanged since the initial approval in 1996 (Aquino 2015). Until 2015, of the 350 mining companies operating in Peru, only 16 percent (59) had fulfilled an obligation that required them to develop comprehensive plans to incorporate the environmental standards for water and the MPL for liquid effluents. At that time, 89 percent (53) were warned (SPDA Actualidad Ambiental 2015).

Coordination of the EIA with the required ANA conditions has apparently represented a step forward in environmental control. So, too, have the updated parameters contained in the new environmental quality standards for water (2008) and the 2010 MPLs established for mining effluents (Aquino 2015). Since 2008 the development of environmental quality standards and MPL has been the responsibility of MINAM. The standards approved that year included more parameters with stricter values than the 1983 benchmark. Since 2010 MINAM has been setting MPL for the discharge of liquid effluents from mining metallurgical activities. Four years later, however, the *paquetazos ambientales* (environmental packages, Law 30230), which included norms from 2013, relaxed environmental safeguards in an effort to encourage private investment, mostly in mining and hydrocarbons.[9] Law 30230 established that the approval of environmental limits was no longer an exclusive responsibility of MINAM. At present MINAM proposes the limits, but they then need approval by a vote in the Council of Ministers, which, particularly due to the presence on this body of the audited sectors—such as the minister for Energy and Mines—politicize the decision beyond the purported technical issues associated with environmental health to the point where conflict of interest arises. This law also limited the role of OEFA. For three years (2014–2017) it could only apply corrective and preventive measures—rather than fines—other than in exceptionally serious cases. Where a fine did apply, the amount was only half what it had previously been, albeit that between 2010 and 2014 the entity had only imposed twenty-eight fines (Gil Ramón 2014). In 2016 OEFA president Tessy Torres declared before Congress that due to a lower cost of incurring an infringement, the regulation had led to an increase in the percentage of environmental breaches, from 10 to 37 percent in mining and from 24 to 71 percent in hydrocarbons. The following year, after pressure from sectors of civil society, including a bill presented to parliament (269/2016/CR), article 19 of the aforementioned law was corrected and OEFA regained its mandate to issue fines in cases of contamination by extractive activities.

The pressure toward the deregulation of environmental safeguards has continued. MINAM recently proposed the elimination of EIAs for most mining exploration projects and the lowering of air and water quality standards, while displaying inaction in the implementation of land-use planning policies. This has occurred in the midst of risks of underfunding of the environmental oversight body following a lawsuit by mining companies and attacks by some mining entrepreneurs and press on legal initiatives that would protect vulnerable headwaters of river basins against extractive activities.

The state has managed the issue of the environmental impacts of mining through the EIA, PAMA, and the environmental assessment programs. A new mine must now have an EIA, and a mine started prior to 1993 must have a PAMA.[10] The EIA should be discussed in public hearings following MEM approval. The ministry supervised two semiannual environmental audits by a private service provider until 2010, when the supervision responsibility was transferred to OEFA, attached to MINAM. MEM approved the mining and hydrocarbons EIA prior to 2016, at which point the responsibility was reassigned to SENACE, also attached to MINAM. This change promised a more autonomous environmental certification.

Mining companies prefer countries where more permissive legislation enables greater profits. The World Bank (2005b:63) recognized that prior to the environmental regulations of the 1990s, "[e]ven foreign mining companies known to be rigorous in ensuring adequate environmental and social performance in their countries of origin often failed to be proactive in taking specific measures that could ensure improved environmental compliance." Globalization of communications diminishes the information gap between nations. Demands to control the environmental performance in mining projects land in the EIA. While hazards to nature can remain, the EIA does have a so-called participation component that can politically legitimize the instrument when it is validated by stakeholders and takes into account the potential victims.

Environmental Liabilities, Fears, and Distrust

An environmental conflict can originate from disagreement about the extent of the damage. The state apparatus—generally focused on expediting the generation of foreign currency through mining taxes—prefers language such as *pasivos ambientales* (environmental liabilities), where *pasivo* means, literally, "passive." This rhetoric that downplays the risk of mining to organisms and nature, all of which are exposed to the waste through erosion from rain, wind, or the constant Andean earthquakes. Official discourses frequently associate environmental damage with an undefined past, which, in the case of Peru, tends to invisibilize the fact that until the early 1990s the country's regulations had not even started to address environmental concerns. Public declarations frequently displayed this rhetoric:

> Minister for Energy and Mines Carlos Herrera: From the environmental point of view, I would divide the mining sector into three groups. One sector I refer to as environmental liabilities. These are the mines that started quite long ago in the past and finished in the past too. I think they have left liabilities that need to be collected. The second is small-scale mining, which is a social problem because miners work for subsistence and cause tremendous damage to the environment and to themselves. The third is the medium and large-scale mining, which has impact and environmental adaptation studies. . . . The one that

is least problematic for the environment is medium and large mining. I call it successful mining. However, environmental claims are always been directed at them . . .

Journalist Jaime de Althaus: . . . one still thinks of the mine as a great *socavón* [adit] full of contamination which affects communities, when it is far from being like that.

M: . . . in the past it was like that. Unfortunately, past reputation affects current activity. Failing to communicate through the press in a timely way and with sufficient breadth has been an error by the companies.[11]

The minister's rhetoric citing "successful" mining invisibilizes the enormous environmental footprints left by mining companies such as Doe Run Peru in La Oroya or the multiple firms that have exploited the main mines at Cerro de Pasco City (van Geen et al. 2012). It assumes that the dissemination of technical "truths" is sufficient. It fails to address central questions such as the legitimacy of environmental demands and the crisis of trust—and therefore of citizen representation—that occurs when a state apparatus has incentives to permit environmental degradation and leaves environmental permits and monitoring in the hands of the same ministry responsible for promoting the extractive activity. As mentioned before, it was only recently—2010 and 2016—that responsibility for the audit function and EIA approval were respectively passed to MINAM's agencies OEFA and SENACE.

The enormous environmental liabilities left by big mining in Peru increase their menace when combined with the distrust in government oversight. It was only in 1995 that the state began recording environmental liabilities from mining. Six years later it had identified 611. This excluded state-owned mines. The estimated remediation cost ($200–250 million) was considered an underestimate (World Bank 2005b:39). By 2006 the number had risen to 850, and nine years later it was 8,616. The majority (1,199) were located in the Ancash Department (see figure 23). As mentioned, large projects had to adapt to environmental standards through PAMAs, and by 2000 only eight out of the sixty-five had done so. Martín, from the Defense Front for Huarmey, invoked historic contamination dating as far back as colonial times to explain the level of distrust: "Everything stays the same. The miners arrive, they take out a mineral . . . that does not feed [us], and that's what they call investment . . . and they leave us with tailings, lagoons of sores, contaminated water. . . . Now there is a new mask. They call it cutting-edge technology . . . that does nothing for

FIGURE 23 Tailings in Ticapampa, Santa River Basin. 2014. Author's photo.

the community at all. It's good for the mining company, because what it used to mine over twenty or thirty years, it now extracts in fifteen or twelve . . . using less labor. The technology does not speak to the contamination debt left behind" (grammar modified).

Prior to the transfer of its oversight function to MINAM's OEFA in 2010, the dual role of MEM had at best led to contradictory messages and at worst represented a conflict of interest that increased mistrust. Although MEM had issued three environmental fines to mines in 2000 (a figure that rose to 111 four years later), the delay to compliance with PAMAs was evidence of doublespeak, particularly given the known impact on human health of the metallurgical processes at La Oroya. The extension of La Oroya's PAMA did, however, have the support of the local community because, unlike a mine, refineries of its kind require considerable local labor (MMSD América del Sur 2002). Fifty six percent of the fines issued by OEFA for the main extractive sectors (mining, hydrocarbons, electricity, and fishery) in the period 2010–2014 were for mining companies. They exceeded $77 million, equivalent to just 0.43 percent of the more than $20 billion in profits of the ten largest mining companies over this same period.

In the contest between definitions about environmental risks, pollution, and contamination, it is helpful to observe the context of distrust when the different criteria interact. Within the framework of "joint monitoring," "chains of custody," and the bioindicator facilities constructed by Antamina (i.e., the fish farms and the model farms), there were doubts about whether the risks to health and local livelihoods were being properly understood and if they could be accurately measured. When Antamina installed a fish farm in Ayash to demonstrate that the trout could survive, the farmers accused the company of "planting" the fish. Similarly, when, in the face of complaints about dust pollution in the same locality Antamina proposed a demonstration plot, the farmers argued that it would manipulate the experiment to cover up the environmental degradation. Mistrust and the tendency to ignore local demands were the hallmarks of many encounters between Antamina and its neighbors. Living side by side with a giant neighbor that emits dust and other substances requires a tremendous act of faith. As Lazarus, from Ango Raju, stated, "With an open pit, how can there be no contamination when there is so much dust!" The following is a dialogue I had with Pedro, an Antamina environmental expert:

Author: Returning to the issue of credibility, especially when you go to rural areas where the parameters are different and you have to translate a technical language, it could become a matter of faith: I must trust in you and I also do not trust the state.

Pedro: I do not trust the state and you tell me that you follow the state regulations. . . . I do not trust the state, nor do I trust you. . . . In these environmental committees, we do joint monitoring; they call it "monitoring together." We have people from the community, from the laboratories, and even in San Marcos the last time we had [people from] the defense front. . . . We all go take samples together and sometimes we have even brought the samples to Lima in the truck, with the people from there and they said, "Oh, you are taking the samples to Lima and you are going to change them." They imagine this gigantic conspiracy theory that manipulates everything. . . . So we do the joint monitoring with the agencies and the people. That helps educate them and we talk about the permissible limits and the government explains them, and the biologists can talk about the fish. Then people begin to understand them; it's kind of a process. . . . If you explain and communicate, you can remove some of these conflicts.

For this mining employee, the local suspicion was based on lack of knowledge. According to many farmers, the uncertainty was associated with a structural condition, as noted by Martín:

> There is a conservative sector struggling to survive against the competition of other transnationals, so they bribe presidents, congressmen, mayors, everyone, in order to save the maximum possible [money], so that the transnational, that company, could keep growing its capital. What happens when they arrive to Huarmey and Peru? They find themselves with a corrupt government . . . [with] Fujimori, with [the former presidential adviser and former intelligence chief, Vladimiro] Montesinos paying magistrates. Even Yanacocha [mine] got involved in the bribes with Montesinos.

Struggles between mining companies in the midst of the corruption of the Fujimori regime of the 1990s came to light in the media through the so-called *vladivideos*, recordings made by Montesinos of people visiting him and seeking illegal favors or exchanges.[12]

Thus, distrust at the local level was symptomatic of something taking place at a national level in the context of a long history of corruption scandals (Quiroz 2013).[13] Based on multiple surveys, Payne et al. (2002) placed Peruvians in the penultimate position of interpersonal trust in Latin America for the period 1996–2001. More recently, the Corporación Latinobarómetro (2011:18) poll for the period 1996–2011 found Peru ranked among the most distrustful countries in the region: only 18 percent of people would trust an unfamiliar third party, whereas the regional average was 22 percent. A culture of local suspicion would serve as a defense mechanism against government regulations and institutions that leave the common citizen helpless, especially in impoverished rural areas. In the face of anomie, it is preferable to protect oneself by distrusting the authorities. Seeing the owners of television networks, congressmen, businessmen, and other members of the national ruling elite receiving bribes in the armchair of the former chief of intelligence left a mark on many citizens. According to the journalist Ángel Páez of *La República*, Montesinos was known as Mr. Fixit by CIA officers stationed in Lima. If wealthy and powerful people participated in acts of corruption, many wondered how much it would take to bribe a modest local mayor. Pedro regarded this suspicion as having conditioned the relationships between local authorities and the mining company: "That is another political problem in Peru. If you are the mayor of a town, [and] if you are very close to the [mining] company, they are going to say that you are a *comprado* [bought], and if you attack the company all the time, they will say, 'That guy is a real jerk.' He won't work with us. So the mayor has to play this political game." Some authorities could find themselves trapped in a double bind (see chapter 4):

if they said "Antamina contaminates," they were called antimining, but if they did otherwise, they were branded as "bought."

Gradation, Authority, and Learning

The conflicts over contamination described in this book arose from the attempt to impose knowledge frameworks in contexts where mistrust reigned. The mechanism legitimizes the authority of the mining company or so-called governmental technical experts and ignores local development expectations and indicators of damage to livelihoods (see chapter 4). Near the operations area, the problems began when the concerns were ignored, parameters were set without real local discussion, and claims made by the community were discredited and simply given labels such as "perceptions" or "aesthetics." Mateo, from Antamina, illustrated how this inattention was later presented as a lesson learned:

Author: There is reference to the MPLs and, on the other hand, there are also degrees of effect or impact at the local level and we could talk about tolerance limits, when, for example, the animals in Ayash are affected that don't want to drink that water.

Mateo: What happened there was a particular case. We did the analysis of what we had when we started discharging. We had everything within the limits and standards, and it caused no damage. But we never considered—that is, we did not realize—that there were other parameters that in English are "aesthetics" whereas in Spanish it is like [saying] the characteristics [of] smell, taste, color. It is nothing to do with not being able to drink the water, right? . . . Let's say that you are used to Coca-Cola, then the chemistry changes and they give you Inka Cola. You will notice a change. . . . It does not mean that it is bad-quality water or that you cannot drink it, but the color changed, the flavor changed, the smell changed. Then it is a change for you, and if the change originates from the mine, it is logical for you to be scared. In this case there was a really unpleasant smell, and foam was generated because of the huge fall of water, etcetera. . . . We did all the studies . . . we started to [see] that the discharged water that had all the characteristics . . . of the same quality of water in measurable terms, because it is difficult to measure smell. . . . Before discharging we made a horse drink and then a cow. But we had no way of analyzing [the smell]! That was something that we had not imagined, but when it happened,

> we did recognize it as a direct impact. As a result, we built a water system . . . for them to drink, because they were drinking water from the river that was not potable, and it did them harm, and the animals too, with [a] drinking trough, and for the clothes [see figure 21]. So there is no impact, but additionally, we also fixed the problem of the odor and the foam. . . . It was an unexpected result.

The smell was considered a subjective characteristic, difficult to measure with parameters judged to be scientifically objective. At a public meeting in San Marcos, several experts suggested including local indicators in addition to common technical parameters such as MPLs.[14] The complicated part was creating conditions for a meaningful dialogue. The chemist Miguel Alfaro, from the NGO Vida, proposed analyzing the "reactive centatives used in mining," given that the signals analyzed "have very little to do with smell, color and foam." Another chemist proposed measuring components that correlated better with the odor in order to detect dangerous levels. New mobile "electronic nose" devices and mathematical models developed more recently have improved the monitoring of hazardous chemicals and pollutants in the environment (Wilson 2012).

It is revealing that the parameters of odor, taste, color, and water consistency that were prioritized by the local community were considered mere perceptions or aesthetic and subjective characteristics by the mining company. Changes in water near the operations area can be considered negative externalities because, as occurred in Ayash, farmers had to move their animals to other water sources, investing time and energy that could have been spent on other activities. From a cultural-economic perspective, the farmers internalized the time and energy assigned to the transfer of their animals and assumed this cost rather than compelling these creatures to drink from sources that were deemed unsafe.

In the chapter's title, the resident protests to defend his livelihood, invoking a caring relationship with his animals. The nature of this relationship means he does not force the donkey to drink from the dubious water source and expose it to harm. This protest steps away from a utilitarian rationality. The claim entails a sociocultural relationship of work and reciprocity between human and animal. The latter is as useful as an automobile, with the benefit of being a living, communicative creature that also provides company. One does not have to be an environmentalist to appreciate the farmer's point. It does not need advertising campaigns to become a humanized machine, as when cars are sold as an enhanced projection of personal image. The relationship is effortlessly understood in urban contexts, given the affection people feel for their pets, who are even certified as "emotional support animals" in some contexts. The farmer prefers to reach another water source together rather than force his animal. The environmental impact generated additional financial and opportunity costs, which the mining company sought to remedy using pipes and drinking troughs.

What does the donkey represent in the farmer's request? I would posit, "You cannot fool him!" It proclaims an affected bioindicator and an unnoticed dimension. The donkey could well represent nature without much political cultural mediation, although locally it also popularly connotes thoughtlessness and stubbornness. The farmer's subversion, using humor to reverse power categories, arises from the exclusion of the local perceptions and highlights a closed mentality of the powerful and an asymmetry of power. From the farmer's perspective, the mining company had failed to display the most intelligent behavior and were therefore invited to converse with the donkey, the symbolic Andean epitome of obstinacy and intolerant unintelligence. There is much political and cultural rebellion contained in this local caricature that probably reflects a certain technical expert racism in the face of the local evidence. The donkey symbolizes the criticism of a community member excluded from the discussion of parameters and indicators, alluding to someone who lives near the mine and has experiential knowledge about that environment, such as the farmer. It is probable that, by embodying an inhabitant distant from instrumental political interests, it is closer to a legitimate demand, suggesting a state of nature without further human and political intervention.

The value associated with the animals is comparable to the importance associated with plants in a case near the operations area. TMI (see chapter 4), which had a forest nursery project next to the Ayash River, also reported a reluctance by farmers to use the affected water for irrigation, preferring instead to bring it from other sources. Just as they would not risk their animals, so, too, they chose not to risk their plants. Both used alternative water sources. The most purely utilitarian approach would have been to begin by testing some plants with the suspect water. The genuine protest about affected livelihoods was beyond the utilitarian. It implied a cultural—deeply human—bond. Several individual behaviors became a form of collective protest. On each occasion, a consistent, and very human, cultural relationship closer to friendship was on display over and above a simple instrumentality, claimed by the farmers on behalf of nature and economy.

Among the farmers, the gradation generated confusion. The question seemed simple enough: Is there contamination or not? A member of the San

Marcos Environmental Committee, annoyed at the dumping of tailings into the Ayash River, was unable to understand why Antamina "did not admit that it had affected something" and criticized its "lack of definition." Two of Antamina's technical experts insisted that "the river flows," taking with it and washing away the discharged substances, and that the appropriate language was *afectación* (affectation) rather than "contamination." There are two cultures at odds here: a so-called technical culture, which places value on shades or degrees, and a local dichotomous culture—contaminated or clean—when faced with environmental impact. The latter could be comparable to considerations in a laboratory setting, when a sample minimally exposed to an extraneous or hazardous material is considered contaminated because its composition has been altered. How much of an alien substance would any of us be willing to accept in our next cup of coffee? Pedro commented on the complexity of referring to contamination as a continuum category when the farmers opted for a discrete division, based on indicators such as smell, color, and consistency, under a context of distrust:

> Contamination is the word we use in English. More than contamination, [the word we use] is pollution. But what people have to understand is that every human activity has an impact and that there can be impact without damage, and the MPLs are designed to prevent damage. And it's impossible to run a mine without an impact. It's impossible to have a town without an impact, and the people in Ayash themselves impact their environment, they impact their plants, their animals, they crap in their front yards, pee and throw trash in their river, they have their cattle walking around there.

Antamina typically referred to changes in the water in the context of the MPLs, insisting—albeit in a somewhat contradictory way—that it did not modify the water's "quality." As one of its experts stated at a public meeting in San Marcos, "About the smell and color in the Ayash River, it is true, even though the water quality has not been altered, certain characteristics have changed in the river. It's not just color and smell, it's also foam." Similarly, another Antamina environmental official told me,

> The environmental impact study says we're going to work for the long term; we won't have negative impacts on the environment. That doesn't mean that occasionally you're not going to have some muddy water. So when you have

> some muddy water, then they say, "Oh, you are contaminating, you're screwing up the world, everything is going to be really bad." I think we ourselves are guilty of saying, "Nothing will change, everything is going to be the same," and we probably put the wrong message forward. We should have said, "There's not going to be a negative impact overall in the long term to the environment. However, from time to time the water gully is going be different. It's going to look different, it's going to smell different. It will be different because you have a huge mine up there." But we ourselves weren't careful on how these messages were delivered.

Although it may seem contradictory, the use by technical personnel of the concept of degrees is strategic for a mining company that formally denies a contaminating impact. This discourse can be puzzling, as the following statement made by an Antamina environmental expert in Huarmey shows: "The company maintains its policy of zero contamination; [however], with a minimum contamination, what can be done, right? [It means] we have to improve the systems more." The mining company would claim that a sample is within the permitted parameters. Nevertheless, other aspects in the surroundings of the project were ignored. They included smell, color, or appearance (e.g., foam), and it was to these that people and animals reacted. Their exclusion increased the level of mistrust in mining or state experts, as well as in the measurement systems and the authority of the so-called technical processes presented as closed social constructs. That is to say, the determination of whether a river is contaminated will depend on the MPL threshold, which, it must be remembered, will vary according to which authority sets them (e.g., the Peruvian government, the Canadian government, or the World Bank). Moreover, the reductionist threshold of a permissible limit does not take into account the different possible effects of larger cumulative impacts on nature, including its living beings.

Doubts can also be generated by the manner in which the measurements are taken, especially when the emitter knows in advance the location and timing of the sample. Likewise, as an environmental expert from a Lima-based NGO pointed out, an "illusion" of low-level impact could be created by the use of larger flows of water during the measuring process. This harks back to the claim by Antamina that the river flow would wash away the emissions. The mining company's monitoring stations were known to the farmers. Apparently, if discharge took place when it rained, or if the testing was conducted a considerable time afterward, the concentration decreased and was diluted. Seven years after Antamina began to operate, a standard was set that prohibited the mixing of freshwater from the environment with wastewater in order to reach the MPL.[15] The degree of impact could correspond to a scale of compensation, although this would imply a strategic and legal risk for a mining company, which could lead to direct compensation. Antamina undermined local confidence by insisting that the impact of the mine was not harmful to nature, in circumstances in which for many farmers, a change to the characteristics of the environment was equivalent to contamination of that environment.

The joint monitoring and public meetings to discuss environmental issues show that Antamina indeed recognized the complicated social and political local landscape. Antamina admitted that "interaction with diverse social groups with dissimilar interests is a complexity that is difficult to approach with a predetermined conception," accepting that they had "made learning one of [their] best virtues," and emphasizing that the knowledge of the company should be transmitted "in the most didactic way possible" (CMA 2002:56). Local environmental monitoring was recognized as a collective exercise that provided prestige and had been established in various locations since the late 1990s, such as in the Vicos community in Carhuaz (Ancash). Municipal and state recognition of monitoring groups could reduce costs (Kuramoto et al. 2002). Since 2008, the regulation of citizen participation in mining draws on the fact that the General Law on the Environment and its regulations recognize *vigilancia ciudadana* (citizen monitoring) and the right to environmental monitoring.[16] However, there is a legal vacuum because the Law of the Right to Prior Consultation for Indigenous and Native Peoples does not require or regulate environmental monitoring committees (Sanborn et al. 2016:58).

I spoke with a lawyer who represented Antamina on the monitoring commission in Huarmey, who insisted that he did not understand why the mining company had to participate in the committee when it was complying with the law. Antamina was a "permanent guest member" without a voice or a vote. I told him that his question would probably be more understandable in an ideal context where the citizens trusted their authorities without questioning their performance, decisions, and legitimacy. Local residents participating on the commission questioned the scarce state representation, the actions of the mining company, and the environmental auditors. Pedro stressed the company's intention to participate in local processes but recognized cultural differences and different communication capabilities:

> We have to integrate into this culture and do what we can to build capacity to understand environmental issues, etcetera. . . . We are out there, in the field, doing environmental monitoring . . . everything we do is an opportunity to talk with people and teach them what we are doing, because most of the concerns come from lack of communications. People see Antamina, it's like a giant spaceship that has landed up there in the mountains. This $2.3 billion spaceship has landed next door, and the people are worried about us. . . . There are a lot of issues as a result of lack of communication. . . . If you are behaving yourself, you are following the laws, the rules, etcetera; beyond that, what we need to do is to communicate.

This cultural exchange implied a mutual learning. For the mining company, it meant at least recognizing that it needed personnel seeking to translate the social, cultural and environmental complexity.

> Pedro: One thing that became very apparent in the early days was that we could not separate the environment from the community. They are interlinked, [they are] interdependent . . .
>
> Author: Especially in rural areas.
>
> P: They are very tied to the environment there. Even though they might themselves pollute their own environment. . . . They just have not realized that their pollution is causing damage. So when a peasant from San Marcos or Ayash throws his Coca-Cola bottles into the river, he does not think it is causing any damage. . . . We realized early on that we had to work very closely between environment and the community relations, and that kind of ties into the politics as well. . . . Our philosophy was to listen to anyone who was willing to work with us. To communicate and get involved and be out there. . . . We really made an effort to talk and learn, and be in as many places. . . . Now that we have a group within my department of environment and safety called "socio-environmental." . . . They are full time in the field, attending meetings, talking to people, going out with peasants if there is an environmental issue that concerns them. That's what they do full time: they talk to people. . . . We have dragged the government in. . . . So we do capacity building, we get the people involved; it's all about working with people, all about relationships. . . . They [the residents] never dealt with a mining company [of this magnitude] before, and we had never dealt with the town of Ayash before. Therefore, we both had to learn and unfortunately that took some time. . . . First, establish mechanisms

> as quickly as possible for communication. . . . Another lesson learned is that I do not think we really knew what we were getting into . . . we did not know that we would have thirty people in the Environment, Health, and Safety Department and [the person in charge of Corporate Affairs] did not know that he would have thirty people in his area . . . it took time to develop this, and in that time we lost some ground. . . . It is a learning process. . . . We waited too long to do things and then we had some conflicts. Until we had the *mesa de trabajo* [working group], the *mesa de desarrollo* [development roundtable], and the environmental committee of Ayash—until we established the mechanisms for communication and for involvement—we did not do as many things as we should and as quick as we should. (grammar modified)

To what extent can throwing a bottle of Coca-Cola into the river be compared to the impact of a giant mine? The definition of scales and degrees is central to the definition of environmental risk. The harm produced by the mining project constitutes a relatively new type of risk for residents, and on an immensely greater scale.

The mining company was aware of the benefit of improving their social relationships. This learning was essential at the beginning of the project, which depended on external financing. "We want to get along with the communities . . . [because] it makes good business sense. If we are friends with the communities . . . and if they make us look good, they can have some benefits, right? They [residents] can be our best security, if we are worried about terrorists, etcetera . . . we are going to hear about that. . . . It is better than any security force in the world, isn't it?" commented Pedro. The mining company was not always as open as it tried to present itself. It learned that old approaches with little dialogue were counterproductive to a good relationship with its neighbors. It was slow to learn the lesson of increasing participation and improving communication in order to prevent conflicts. The episode of the Antamina pipeline spill in the Cajacay District (see chapter 3) revealed flaws in the structure of communication between the company and local residents, both at the time of the event and in the face of subsequent unsatisfied demands for compensation.

Conclusion

More than once I heard an Antamina official use the following example: "Think of the glass of water you always drink. Now we change the smell and color and we assure you that you can drink it the same." This could encapsulate the dilemma that arises when acts of faith are required but the context is one of distrust. The faith required was, of course, exaggerated considering Peru's history of government and corporate corruption, over and above the legacy of mining contamination. The generalized skepticism brought many things into question: environmental risk and exposure assessments, local representation and participation, state institutions and their interaction with mining companies, and the legitimacy of the monopoly on definitions and parameters. On the assumption of this lack of faith in the system and between the subjects, the periodic multi-actor environmental assessments or "joint monitoring" evidenced concern about impacts and attempted to build trust.

The communities opted not to risk their nursery plants by attempting to irrigate them with water from the affected river. They did not want to endanger what they referred to affectionately as their *plantitas* (little plants). Yet that same smallholder was capable of emptying garbage into the river without considering this a jolt to the balance of coexistence. Of course cyanide discharged by a large mine is not the same as a plastic bottle thrown away by a local resident, so it is not surprising, then, that a large-scale impact is perceived as dangerous by people whose livelihoods are vulnerable and that this generates resistance. In Huarmey the risk of contamination from the fishmeal plant was probably considered by the fishermen to be manageable since it did not prevent them setting out to sea. In each case the local organizations were ill-equipped to manage all the scientific environmental details. In Huarmey the Multisectorial Technical Commission concluded that the information gap "limit[s] them to participat[ing] in a more proactive way in the debate on environmental issues" (CONAM 2001:28). The discourse of the so-called technical Western expertise exercised a virtually impermeable hegemony over other knowledge. In a more urban context, it is normal for citizens to trust in the monitoring undertaken by the state to ensure environmental health, albeit cities still contain polluted landscapes, and in many cases this condition is more prevalent when associated with marginalized populations, reflecting race or class issues.

A culture of hazard exposure prevention would involve exchanging culturally learned concepts. Antamina staff employed from overseas were surprised to find, widespread among the local labor force, what they considered to be a weak culture of prevention in occupational health and safety practices. A mining official commented on the frustration this caused: "We employ workers who have no safety culture, who mishandle things, who just look at the wires sticking out of the wall that could electrocute them at any moment, but they are used to it and don't care" (grammar modified). Local employees were probably more concerned with short-term savings, such as the cost cutting reflected in poorly installed live cables. This is consistent with local practices in which additional preventive payments are regarded as unnecessary costs or luxuries and not part of the investment.

On one of my journeys to Huallanca, seated among a busload of drowsy passengers, I noticed the driver's eyelids were also lowering with such frequency that he easily could have taken us all into the next dimension. I woke my neighbor to verify that I was not in a nightmare. He attempted to allay what he considered to be an exaggeration from my side: "This driver does this route every day, he can even do it in his sleep!" On that occasion it was true. We arrived safely in the middle of the collective dream, nuanced by my friendly greetings to keep the overconfident driver awake. This vignette is consistent with my travel experience in Peru, a country with one of the worst road accident records in the region.[17] The cultural pattern of carelessness or insufficient preparation in the face of hazards is rooted in daily practices across the country, including more affluent groups where the lack of investment in safety is even more inexcusable.[18] A similar criticism could be made of the culture of putting out social fires, which subordinates actions in the social realm that might prevent later explosive protests (see chapter 2). The mining company learned that the cost of the burned socioenvironmental prairie and the associated loss of confidence was high and difficult to recover from.

Antamina provided industrial safety standards training to its workforce. Mining is a hazardous enterprise, and companies seek to raise security awareness in order to prevent tragedies. It is therefore worth asking how much the mining company should be obliged by law to invest in environmental health safety for the neighboring areas it impacts given that its activity raises short and accumulated long-term socioenvironmental hazards. The degrees of these risks are different in each mining project. A more realistic analysis would require a case-by-case discussion for combining transparent, real-time monitoring, together with the provision of public information on a daily basis, with data collected under a neutral procedure. This system could also be participatory so as to assure its legitimacy in the eyes of the affected groups. Evaluations should be integrated into larger spatial-temporal studies on the socioecosystem, including accumulated and aggregated impacts across the region. These could use instruments such as remote sensing images, which could, for example, demonstrate the effect of mining over a decade on human health, vegetation cover, harvests, and the hydric balance of basins and microbasins.

Despite various advances, the institutionalization of environmental enforcement has been weak and has been threatened in Peru at various times, especially through the recent deregulation of environmental safeguards. This panorama reflects pressure from business sectors that accuse the state of *tramitología* (procedure-ology, or excessive procedures and overregulation) and of creating excessive compliance costs for investors, which creates a less attractive investment by comparison with other countries. The socioenvironmental conflicts reflected a struggle between the power of authorities and the knowledge of local communities. There is both an environmental receiver and a social receiver. The parameters for the latter are very subtle and vary from community to community, especially when the point is reached at which the animals no longer drink, and this starts to effect the household economy. The mining company referred to the odor, taste, and appearance of the water as "aesthetic characteristics." The connotation was that these attributes were superficial—notwithstanding the measurable socioeconomic impacts such as the time necessary for transfer of the animals to alternative water sources—implying additional, but uncounted, transport and opportunity costs. Given that pollution risks are defined differently by different groups, an economic valuation for compensation should discuss externalities established as cultural constructs. The monitoring parameters of ministries and mining companies do not necessarily coincide with the characteristics of a river that are prioritized or perceived as negative externalities by local residents. Nor can a perfect equivalence with local activities and valuations of nature outside the realm of the market be assumed. The valuation may contain elements of legitimate subjectivity that cannot be quantified in the existing markets. This dimension includes, for example, sacred sites, such as attempting to mine beneath a cemetery or a cathedral.

Listening and learning require resources. It is useful to reflect on to the extent to which the accusation of contamination would explain conflicts, researching the cultural and political assumptions that were debated, including the possible motivations that underpinned the environmental definitions and the context of their formulation. The conflicts included discussions of transaction and monetization in the face of local demands. The demands made by the communities prompted better understanding of their rights and how to claim them, allowing a better connection with the state and with the nation. This crisis of representation was reflected in the testimonies of residents from San Marcos and

Huarmey, who sought consultation in the process of environmental decision making and who typically referred to their "authorities"—such as mayors—in distant terms. The demand was frequently for an environmental monitoring committee with paid technical personnel who were independent of the government and the mining company.

This chapter has shown how the contested field of environmental risk demarcation in conflictive, distrustful mining scenarios revealed power and strategies in the asymmetric negotiation contests for participation in defining contamination scenarios. The advances and limits of the regulations and the monitoring proposals evidenced the constraints of imposed models that generated situations of social critique and demands for more political participation. These processes have enabled multiple lessons, as discussed in the conclusion.

Conclusion

Reassessing Stratagems, Struggles, and Citizenship

IN THIS CLOSING CHAPTER, I WANT TO REVIEW AND EXPOSE FINDINGS AND RELATIONSHIPS that were not much highlighted before in order to complete the argument of the book. After painting the big picture, I will elaborate on several conditions in which strategies reshape political landscapes, and how the mining sociotechnologies responded to frictions at the Antamina project. I will also expound on the exploration of the encounters of risk cultures under mining expansion. Finally, I will discuss the instrumentality of protests and the economic and ethical nature of mining conflicts.

This book strived to broaden the range of studies of development and conflicts by investigating the emergence and shape of citizenship conflicts arising from the expansion of the Peruvian mining frontier, under the context of privatization regimes for natural resources and promises of socioenvironmentally responsible development. The elusive distance between policies and plans, contrasted with ground realities for host communities, fueled confrontational scenarios. The fine-grained examination of the strategies applied during dialectical and asymmetrical interactions, and the associated negotiations in the history of the entrance of the large-scale, transnational Antamina mining apparatus into a complex Andean region, reveals demands for citizen participation through negotiations between the company, the government, and the communities. These resulted in evictions, design changes, and participatory processes while marginalized groups coalesced in order to confront and address environmental degradation and asked for benefits. Many residents expected fair participation as a consequence of a complete reciprocity, having contributed positively to the mining project—in the case of Huallanca, through the provision of a construction corridor, or in the cases of Huaripampa and Ango Raju, through the ready sale of land. The ethnographic approach unpacks the interaction of legal and institutional arrangements at local, regional, national, and international layers. By comparing diverse communities involved with the same mining project, I have shown how demands for participation were constructed and eviscerated by the mining and state apparatuses of governance regimes in processes that illustrate how imposed and unequal development proposals could generate scenarios for political maturation and social action, and how citizenship could arise through conflict.

At the heart of the research is the EIA, a requirement that arose in Peru in the early 1990s as part of the promotion of mining investment amid state encouragement of investment of foreign capital across all economic sectors. The book reveals how the EIA has become a central discussion instrument in mining projects and how it connects global corporations with marginal groups. The EIA, as one of the sociotechnologies of power, is presented as heralding a modern business culture under a rhetoric of objective and participatory professionalism, using purportedly public consultations that present it as a tool capable of predicting and preventing or mitigating negative impacts. The highly specialized language of the EIA, coupled with limited mechanisms for real local participation, means that in practice the document is mainly an agreement between the state and the company and its financiers. In different localities I found no direct references to the EIA, an unsurprising result given that the document was not designed for local supervision.

Different degrees of resistance and negotiation emerged in the face of displacement impacts, environmental risks, and development expectations. I have examined demands for development in the context of a neoliberal model, where the state cedes spaces to mining companies and civil society organizations amid steps forward and backward in regulatory frameworks. The demand—fundamentally economic—for paved roads described in several chapters of the book emerged from groups clamoring to connect to the rest of the country and the national economy, as well as to participate and become visible before the nation. It constituted a call for tangible democracy, for real citizen participation. Discussions about governance and participation are increasingly central to mining and development debates. We can appreciate them in protests related to territoriality, such as the cutting of access to grazing routes due to the establishment of mining operations, complaints about ineffective experimental agricultural projects begun without consultation, and the blockades in Bagua invoking ILO 169, which resulted from attempts to operate in Indigenous territories without having the basic social licenses in place.

The extraterritoriality, when added to the fact that the mine generally imported its food and labor—contrary to local expectations based on precedents such as Contonga—fed a local uneasiness. Until the 1980s, mining companies built town squares, health centers, and schools in their camps—as in the case of Huanzalá in Ancash—which residents were, to a certain extent, able to access and thus obtain benefits from the health and education services on offer. In these cases, the miners created a small island of modernity that was valued by local residents as a possible source of employment or better services than the state could provide. In the context of local expectations and demands, the mining model has become perceived locally as closer to a near enclave. This perception exacerbates resentment in communities against the billionaire neighbor that fails to share the benefits over the short term. The presence of the mine also prompted the return of individuals, including leaders such as the mayor of Huallanca and members of environmental committees, all drawn by the prospect of an economic boom. The opening of Antamina revealed socioeconomic complexities across various impacted sites, catalyzing old family and economic rivalries while aggravating social divisions.

Mining Strategies

> *Sell not virtue to purchase wealth, nor Liberty to purchase power.*
>
> —BENJAMIN FRANKLIN, 1738

Time becomes a critical cost for business. The increasing ease and speed of communications precipitates events. The haste to finish the infrastructure and save personnel and logistical costs catalyzes social interactions since it truncates opportunities for exchange and communication. Each additional day carries a cost and increases the risk of failure in the effort to obtain the start-up finance. Given the possibility that inadequate time for the initial phases might cast a shadow over future developments or even jeopardize the viability of a project, a greater initial allocation of time should be viewed more as an investment for the long-term operations of a project rather than as a mere cost.

Initially, to alleviate disputes, the mining company opted for the "firefighting" approach. This model was visible in the resettlement process, some damages payments, the attempts to provide compensation for contamination and dead animals, or the hiring of affected individuals to perform labor. Antamina's tactics relied on the legitimacy provided by the approved EIA and private audits overseen by MEM, with the subsequent addition of joint monitoring and support to the formation of local environmental monitoring committees. Strategically, the mining company took environmental samples in the presence of residents and interested groups. The committees allowed Antamina to appease claims in the short term by minimizing contacts that could have resulted in clashes with traditional local leaders. The company recognized the need for political negotiation, discussing the "matters of concern" (Latour 2004), including the indicators and the authority to define what environmental risk and degradation meant.

Antamina admitted the political dimension present in the measurement of impacts and reliability, involving itself in joint monitoring to prevent conflicts, which included establishing local bioindicators such as fish farms or model plots. The approach was ultimately accompanied by compensation for damages, such as the installation of drinking troughs and a potable water system in Ayash. The pattern of seeking to build trust based on shared control and mutual vigilance—as reflected in the samples sent to various laboratories accompanied by stakeholder representatives—was similar to that seen in the creation of the Huascarán Working Group. "Chain of custody," repeated the mining company, exposing generalized mistrust. Neighbors of the mine highlighted the absence of a shared baseline. Neither Huarmey nor San Marcos possessed a publicly available inventory of the quality of soil, air, and water that predated Antamina. The EIA had virtually no local data on which to develop a health baseline. The absence of the state in the relationship was again evident. The state's promotion of mining has evidenced incoherence through its virtual neglect of local demands for transparency in environmental information. However, the experience of the local environmental committees alleviated conflicts, at least in the short term.

The groups that cause pollution question the need for more socioenvironmental risk regulation, whereas local residents and organized civil society request stricter regulations to prevent hazards. Indeed, the state is the main regulator and recipient of requests for regulation of such threats. Peru has recently seen the introduction of the so-called environmental packages. There have been rhetorical battles fought over the reversals of socioenvironmental safeguards, which benefit companies and reduce the prevention of negative environmental impacts. Among those involved there is a lack of simple consensus about the definitions of socioenvironmental risks in these public policies, resulting in clashes over the validity of knowledge and information.

The current consensus is oriented toward greater accountability, with faith placed in an "audit culture" (Strathern 2000) in which purportedly nonmeasurable impacts such as the odor in the water in Ayash could be invisibilized. Making use of reductionist pretensions about nature, the preference is to ignore possible restrictions inherent in monitoring. The role of the auditors is a topic that should be revised in more detail in the different contexts that apply, especially in terms of plurality in participation and neutrality. Given the complicity over recent decades of major consulting firms (e.g., the role of Price Waterhouse in covering up Enron's accounts), it is relevant to ask how we might better audit the auditors. Furthermore, how can their neutrality be guaranteed when they are contracted by firms operating inside the mining business network?

Tactics, Instrumentality, and Protests

A leader of the Defense Front of Huarmey assured me that the World Bank, on recognizing that Antamina was going to "ruin the fishing, ecology, agriculture, and the foundations of the houses," would force the company to "make the road to take the mineral through the most impacted area: San Marcos and Huarmey." A central discussion in ecological economics concerns how a negative externality should be "internalized" through absorption by the polluting agent in the form of compensation paid (Martínez-Alier 2002). This situation assumes that among those involved there is an ideal cultural shared attunement, skills parity, perfect information, and probably chimerical notions of irreconcilable ontological planes of natural values (de la Cadena 2010; Li 2015). An auditor engaged by the investors reported that the people of San Marcos had highlighted "environmental issues and employment expectations" as central concerns (CMA 2001c:11). Personnel from an NGO in San Marcos explained to me how Antamina tried to resolve socioenvironmental conflicts in Ayash by hiring the most affected residents "to do anything." The company was messaging the possibility of short-term employment as a means of buying silence in the aftermath of some environmental protests.

Local environmental "aesthetic characteristics" have socioeconomic implications. Local residents use indicators that reflect concerns about nature in a more comprehensive relationship, where they live and work with their animals, breathe the same impacted air, and drink the affected water shared with their livestock, crops, and fishery. The population required credibility from the authorities in charge of monitoring. Even though the mining company unsurprisingly provided assurances that the water was potable, it is difficult to imagine that residents and their animals would have drunk from a source that had changed color, taste, and consistency. They considered the mining company's rhetoric to be insufficient, based on the gradation and relativity of the compliance with the MPLs, and that the national parameters were more permissive than those in force internationally.

The socioenvironmental risks of extractive activities in Peru date back to pre-Hispanic times. During the colonial period, genocide was a byproduct of the activity. More recent events include mercury spills from Yanacocha in Choropampa, the Camisea gas pipeline, and the Antamina ore pipeline in Cajacay, as well as multiple oil spills in the Amazon. In the 1980s, large-scale mining in Peru was recognized as the most polluting economic activity (Glave and Kuramoto 2002). However, it employed more local labor than it does at present, and generated fewer violent protests. According to an Antamina staff member, people previously "did not care about the contamination, because they thought the benefit was worth it." The progressive mechanization of the industry meant less local employment in the large mines that exploit the deposits using the open-pit system. Under this invasive model, each day begins with a great explosion that immediately starts producing significant impacts on nature. Layers of soil are exposed to gases in the air that produce reactions and then release dust that is then carried by the wind or rain to the rivers.

In cases such as Contonga and La Oroya, local residents have condoned environmental degradation caused by the extractive project because of its short-term economic benefits, especially employment. Their participation in the defense of the La Oroya metallurgical complex—recognized as one of the most contaminated sites in the world—illustrates how people could lend support to a contaminating company when their jobs or subnational fiscal transfers are at stake, even at the expense of their medium and long-term health. When in 2004 the Doe Run company refused to comply with the timetable for its environmental responsibilities and threatened to withdraw, local residents joined in solidarity with the company and attacked state authorities. Eleven years later, the residents blocked roads and demanded that the complex return to full operation following a seven-year partial hiatus. Faced with the paralysis of the complex, the mayor of La Oroya commented, "Mining is so important for La Oroya that when the metallurgical complex operated and contributed with through taxes, the municipality [annually] received 30 million soles [$9.4 million] for mining royalties and canon. . . . Now we receive just 870 thousand soles [$272,000]. . . . [The complex] is, ironically, our main source of life" (Sánchez 2015). It is probable that in such cases a considerable sector of a local community will consider itself no longer dependent directly on the environmental services for its productive activities, and also barely be aware of the magnitude of the accumulated damage to its health. Gaining long-term employment with a mining company can enable people to abandon agricultural activities, educate their children, and ultimately get their families out of poverty. The mined area and surroundings can, however, be left with high-level environmental degradation that includes accumulated negative externalities traveling through the air or in water and streams, exposing agricultural livelihoods and other life forms to health hazards on a larger scale. Some socioecosystems run the risk of being harmed by short-term activities motivated by impoverished, subsistence-oriented groups or extractive companies that seek immediate gains.

In Huarmey, surprisingly, while contamination by the local fishmeal plants was acknowledged in the mine's EIA and local residents became increasingly more aware of the environmental risks, local environmental protests over Antamina's port and the hazards in the sea excluded the fishmeal facilities. So, too, did the subsequent joint monitoring program. The *sanguaza* (grease and organic waste from the industrial processing of fishmeal) obstructs the oxygen necessary for the photosynthesis of marine plants. Smoke from the fishmeal chimneys pollutes the air. These industries enjoyed wide local support, probably because they were a source of stable and long-term employment. "Formerly, there . . . was pollution, there were fishing companies and nobody said anything. Now you see the commitment, not only to claim from Antamina, but a moral commitment to do so also from the fishing companies," said a Puerto Huarmey leader as he remarked on the change in local environmental expectations. This apparently strategic approach would explain, at least partially, some of the complaints in Huarmey and San Marcos and the absence of major protests about the gigantic tailings deposits (750 meters long and up to 15 meters high) accumulated during the 1970s and 1980s near the town of Ticapampa along the Santa River on the road to Huaraz (see figure 23 and map 4).

Along the spectrum of expectations, pollution could become a category negotiable through compensation, as signaled by Moses, a member of the Catholic Church in Huarmey: "Some think that foreign capital is harmful and contaminates. Another sector is in favor of it, and there are others in the middle: they recognize the damage, but they think that companies should do sustainable *obras*. In view of the material injury [suffered] . . . they should leave something behind through projects" (grammar modified). As the mayor of Huarmey told me, "An environmental impact implies a distortion that creates conflicts, trauma. . . . That's why we demand that there be *obras* of social impact [works of infrastructure] and that these help to alleviate the effects on the inhabitants." A swap of contamination for development would suppose the hope of employment and of infrastructure in the context of a reduced economic reproduction base through, for example, the sale of agropastoral land. It is essential to explore in each context how development and pollution are interwoven in discourses and in social practices. The complaint can become a political weapon in the demand for compensation. In a short-term logic, the pollution-development transaction seems to work. Environmental degradation in Huarmey caused by the fishmeal plant appeared to be of little concern if it provided employment and the artisanal fishery was viable. La Oroya is probably the epitome of the exchange of mining pollution for development, especially where the latter is defined as employment. Justified environmental claims can be accompanied by local development demands, occasionally fed by mining companies. The incompleteness of the asymmetric reciprocity in the population displacement—which permitted the rapid sale of land for relatively low prices—is what encouraged the request to the billionaire company for a "big gift." This gift would help to socially legitimize the neighbor's wealth, consistent with the sponsorship rationale of Andean festivals or the ethnological "big man." The local debates about the contract penalty paid by Antamina and its distribution illustrates how works, or big gifts, are demanded for local development as a right to compensation for socioenvironmental impact and as a mechanism to legitimize power status through symbols of generosity.

The mining company sought to undermine the environmental claims by portraying them as false accusations with the sole purpose of compensation. "The environment was never an issue in itself, but it became a negotiation mechanism," said Mateo, an Antamina Community Relations executive. To him the environmental protests were simply a political weapon to demand benefits: "People complain about the environment because they see it as a tool to negotiate with Antamina and get money." Explaining contamination protests as solely utilitarian becomes insufficient in the absence of a complete and neutral environmental analysis. Legitimate complaints about impacts that put livelihoods at risk can constitute "weapons of the weak" (Scott 1985) to demand development, seeking also to satisfy expectations of reciprocity and well-being.

Complaints about the deterioration of the natural environment can also become a mechanism for requesting state presence. The mayor of Huarmey stressed that the monitoring committee required "laboratories and technicians specialized in environmental matters," and for that, state resources (human and financial), since the ministerial reports were insufficient. He added that this committee should be the one "to lead the monitoring on behalf of the population." In order to avoid conflicts of interest, the material support could not come from Antamina. Demands for state involvement can be interpreted as a request by people for greater participation in national affairs to improve their status as citizens. This reveals a degree of empowerment that stands in contrast with earlier periods—for example, prior to the Agrarian Reform, when those living on the estates faced conditions approaching slavery.

"The only way to influence capitalism is through the environment," said a former mayor of Huarmey. The politics of shame constituted an effective resource for local negotiation, as exemplified through letters to the World Bank and blockades of highways. These protests evidence abuses in asymmetric power relationships through attempts to embarrass companies and investors, to the point of creating a risk to the investment, particularly at the point of securing the initial finance. The environmental protest was useful for attracting the attention of groups or networks with greater capabilities. The direct action may use the news media, as happened in the blockades of the Pan-American Highway in Huarmey. The threat of publicizing disputes through the media brought pressure to bear. The letter from the people of San Marcos to the World Bank complaining about pollution and resettlement embodied such a threat. As occurred in Huarmey and San Marcos, protests before the media and global actors as a tactic in the politics of shame can strengthen local causes by attracting networks with greater skills and knowledge. This strategy is also used by NGOs, as we saw when TMI intervened in the threat to Huascarán National Park. The evidence indicates that coloring a protest green increases the possibility of gaining global allies.

Economy, Ethics, and Conflict

The World Bank has declared "learning by mistakes" to be one of its principles. This is in addition to the well-known slogan "learning by doing."[1] These experiences explain, for example, how the bank's operational directives privileged land-for-land compensation over money. The different groups demonstrated a form of strategic learning in which they chose the tactics best suited to achieving their goals. At the start of the Antamina project, the citizens of Ancash were far from equipped to manage tools such as the referendums that their peers would later wield in Tambogrande. Antamina's mining apparatus learned that allocating most of the resources under the label of development to, for example, experimental agricultural or livestock laboratories in San Marcos was of little use economically and politically. The intervention of the World Bank and its supposed political culture that required defining the economic viability of the projects encouraged different groups to discuss development visions. The narratives analyzed in this book are part of the learning process for the different groups involved in mining conflicts.

This research empirically demonstrates how understanding social and economic relationships in practice requires exploring beyond isolated individualities and abstract markets. The case study analyzed shows the economy embedded in the social networks that define it. The definitions of regulations and individual motivations played a significant role in the economic discussions. This condition resulted in competition for benefits and in debates about how to define negative externalities, such as those related to the risk of contamination and population displacement. This book has shown how, through greening alliances and using the mechanism of the politics of shame, local communities reincorporated ethical discussions into the economic debate. Through battles over definitions and rhetoric, ethical and moral elements were redefined. The discursive resource becomes central during the design of a billion-dollar mining project urged to secure its financial component. In the power struggles that were part of the conflicts examined in this book, the highlighting of the ethical and social basis of the activities that had economic impacts was a fundamental political strategy. So we see the mining company proclaiming its role in national development, or the local insistence that mineral wealth is national patrimony that should bring benefits that are subject to a fair redistribution. We also find environmentalists arguing that putting Huascarán National Park at risk was an attack on the global community.

The ethic of reciprocity, central to Andean rural transactions, helps to explain the claims and protests. In *Moral Economy of the Peasant*, James Scott (1976) expands on his central thesis about the origins of social revolutions as a violation of a peasant "moral economy" constructed as fair prices by states and elites. This work helps to explain the root causes of the conflicts over development and population displacement presented in this book. The communities neighboring Antamina were more willing to legitimize asymmetric reciprocity through a "big gift" perceived mostly as a *gran obra* of infrastructure for the collective and as jobs for the individual. The claims escalated when the population perceived that the mining company was breaching reciprocity following the initial collaboration by community members to accelerate the sale of land or the displacement of families in the operations area. Although Antamina has not directly recognized them, projects such as the coliseum for bullfighting represented the provision of big gifts. The company has preferred to officially report them as part of its "corporate social responsibility," seeking to play down any obligation of reciprocity and avoid the appearance of the "paternalistic" behavior that it had condemned.

Discussions about what was socially and environmentally sustainable shaped a process in which each group promoted its own interpretations. Information was a crucial resource. In the accelerated resettlement process, Antamina benefited from the limited local participation. This probably accelerated land sales and relocation. Paying lip service to World Bank standards functioned as a ploy by the mining company to accelerate the project. The nebulous nature of some of the bank's guidelines enabled Antamina to interpret them to its own advantage. As we saw with the displacement process and debates over Huascarán National Park, the guidelines lacked implementation guidance that could be tailored to local contexts and practices. Unexpectedly, the scant openness to social participation that was on display—at least formally through policies and commissions sent to the operations—was driven by financial groups and multilateral organizations. This was accepted by the mining company only after debates held internally with those who still believed in an older mining paradigm. Internal disputes in Antamina, visible during the displacement process or in the definition of so-called development projects, show that a mining corporation should not be assumed to be an internally homogeneous or monolithic entity. Although to an external audience this conglomerate might present a united face or single position, it is in fact a social organization composed of subjects in competition, each with individual and probably mutable motivations.

This conclusion is consistent with studies on state apparatus (e.g., Ferguson and Gupta 2002; Scott 1998). The old mining paradigm had privileged the company interacting almost exclusively with the state and only very indirectly with neighboring communities.

Tracing the origins of cultural assumptions and the motivations becomes fundamental in understanding how cultural disagreements shape conflicts between NGOs, the state, local residents, development agencies, and international corporations. Much of the friction reflected misunderstandings about "expectations of modernity" (Ferguson 1999) based on demands fueled by informal verbal offers (e.g., by the media and representatives of the mining company), which led to local interpretations that were difficult to satisfy. This situation became particularly complicated when oral promises were made, such as to purchase land. Expectations in a mining area begin with the tender for the concession, long before the mining company has direct contact with local residents. The government administers ownership of the underground assets on behalf of the nation and can grant them in concession as a right of exploitation without transferring ownership of the surface lands. These conditions generate tension between the license holder and the landowners, as manifested in the involuntary resettlement. The ownership of the subsoil resources—a national patrimony across almost the entire planet—is the basis of the demands for participation in the benefits that come from the mining of those resources.

"Do you think humanity can live peacefully under capitalism?" was the question posed to Noam Chomsky at the end of a conference in Berkeley (Junkerman 2002). In his response, the political analyst, academic, and activist invoked the words of Mahatma Gandhi when asked what he thought about Western civilization: "Maybe it would be a good idea." Chomsky added that behind the system were powerful groups that impede a real and more equitable capitalism. Can communities and their billionaire mining neighbors become friends? Corporate social responsibility makes sense for mining businesses; it is an investment for the company and could contribute to the social legitimacy of projects located in areas of socioenvironmental, economic, and political vulnerability. The start of a mining project is probably the most socially sensitive stage since the experience powerfully impacts the future levels of trust. Given the company's size and capacity, Antamina could have organized this phase better. The protests about involuntary resettlement and design changes show how a transnational mining company can be vulnerable to the demands of investors when there are local confrontations and these threaten the start-up finance. The state's regulations proved insufficient, and the mining company responded with an imprecise and voluntary corporate social responsibility program, as part of "corporate social technologies" designed to manage its public image (Rogers 2012). The need to secure investments led to programs to improve the appearance of the mining company's management of socioenvironmental issues. This strategy was an attempt to mitigate local concerns and anticipate subsequent efforts to strengthen legal frameworks. In general, large businesses work with rhetorics under which voluntary social responsibility will suffice for dealing with socioenvironmental issues in order to prevent legislation changes. Freewill models of corporate responsibility have evidenced clear limits in the mediation between mining companies and communities. The limitations are exacerbated by their discretionary nature, which tends to favor the companies. Evidently, the question of how much will be enough to cover local expectations of reciprocity always remains unanswered. Furthermore, the evidence shows how illusory it has become to imagine corporations as entirely transparent and accountable institutions (Kirsch 2014).

The challenge for the state is almost a chimera, as it includes updating regulations, having a presence of its own, addressing local demands for the redistribution of benefits while guaranteeing socioenvironmental health, and mediating transparently in the relations between citizens and the mining companies—all in the context of the need to overcome a news media that tends to criticize social protests and stigmatize them as unjustified antimining or anti-investment movements, a favor that is returned by the mining companies through the placement of advertising. It is necessary to investigate further to what extent and in which locations mining may or may not be compatible with diversified and sustainable development, as well as to understand the extent to which some groups could act as a barrier to more socioenvironmentally sustainable models, and why. Some approaches conclude that capitalism has historically demonstrated its incompatibility with sustainability (Kirsch 2014). Other perspectives point toward proposals for scientifically informed and socially validated models of ecological-economic zoning to try to reconcile activities in some spaces, apart from more conservationist models of no-go zones exempt from extractive activities.

In Peru the blocking of a road can lead to the establishment of a dialogue roundtable. Arguably, mining conflicts have been an occasion to make claims for improvements in the status of citizenship, seeking mechanisms of participation—including consent—that are meaningful in decisions where risks are local. The rise of the consensus building and development roundtables in places affected by mining is an example. The demands have increased for prior and periodic consultations with informed consent and effective participation, where local agents can influence the decisions that affect them. The peculiarities that have come to light as a result of the global expansion of mining and their social struggles reflect processes of negotiation, ideally enhancing our understanding of the relationships between nature and the beings who inhabit it. Understanding negotiations with local participation calls for research ready to unpack behaviors and institutions at multiple scales, assuming that an ontological compatibility would probably only appear in an ideal plane.

The participation of communities and the definition of nature in the EIA continue to constitute challenges that will probably only be partially met, especially if we assume insurmountable ontological differences. Mining legislation in Peru related to socioenvironmental protections had limitations and experienced setbacks over recent years. The challenge presented by the expansion of the mining frontier in countries, such as Peru, with deep inequalities and large vulnerable populations becomes particularly complex, given urgent demands for the satisfaction of basic living conditions and a redistribution of the benefits from a national legacy. The power claimed by the central government to appropriate the final decision about the feasibility of exploiting subsoil resources—above possible mechanisms of prior consultation and local consent—continues to be central to disputes between issues of national sovereignty and local citizen participation. The central government maintains that it personifies the nation, and, accordingly, it makes the final decisions about nature and natural resources in representation of the citizens. The communities that neighbor mining projects demand significant involvement in a decision that directly affects their vulnerable livelihoods. In the logic of state and business, a participatory process that includes local prior consent would suppose the risk of veto for the utilization of a national resource. In any case, crucial moments such as the approval of the exploration permit and the concession—where only "technical" permits such as MEM's environmental tick-off are generally required—become key points in the construction of social expectations and can sow the seeds of later disputes.

Peru's mining protests can be construed as a reappropriation of the expanded definition of citizenship and national and international governmental participatory tools, reinforced by global demands for representation and exemplified in mechanisms such as the development roundtables. This "deep democracy" (Appadurai 2001) in the horizontal form of social networks was possible to different degrees. We see it in San Marcos through the letters that attracted the World Bank's attention, in TMI's demand for conservation of Huascarán National Park, and in Huarmey, through the use of road blockades that drew the government's attention as a result of media coverage. These actions were in tune with the approach for citizenship demands in Northern Hemisphere countries and constituted local struggles to share in the benefits of the privatization of mining. The demands of local groups were strengthened by international connections in the context of investors obliged to respond to their shareholders, who in turn were seeking to protect their investment. The way in which "grassroots movements are finding new ways to combine local activism with horizontal, global networking" in a kind of ideal "democracy without borders" (Appadurai 2001:25, 42) is something only time will tell.

This book has illustrated how important it is to be able to engage in and manage legal and scientific discourses in order to participate, albeit in a limited fashion, in negotiations for access to and impact on nature. The environmental committees and the so-called development roundtables have constituted primary spaces for participation in decisions that affect local communities. Thus, the presence of new mines has promoted debate about more direct local participation scenarios, something that was relatively unexpected at the beginning of the contemporary expansion of the mining frontier. The mining battles examined in this research form a network of direct actions activated by particular demands. On aggregate these activities can also be interpreted as requests for access to a more complete and equitable citizenship that demands a more genuine participation. If we follow the definition of a social movement by Alain Touraine (1989), it would be necessary to evaluate historically to what extent the mining claims could be part of a larger social movement in Peru. Not every protest implies a social movement, since the latter requires an organized and ideological expression capable of disputing the predominant system of social organization. The social networks and direct action processes analyzed here have demanded better living conditions and greater participation in the nation, and have constituted mobilizations that have drawn mostly on temporary alliances, while seeking to resolve immediate and localized claims. The processes elucidated also remind us that outcomes could have unfolded differently, since neither a single nor an automatic path for shaping citizenship battles appears to exist.

ABBREVIATIONS

AMIDEP	Asociación Multidisciplinaria de Investigación y Docencia en Población (Multidisciplinary Association for Research and Teaching in Population)
ANA	Autoridad Nacional del Agua (National Water Authority)
APRA	Alianza Popular Revolucionaria Americana (American Popular Revolutionary Alliance)
BHP	Broken Hill Proprietary Ltd.
CAO	Compliance Advisor Ombudsman (an office of the World Bank Group's IFC and MIGA)
CODELCO	Corporación Nacional del Cobre (National Copper Corporation [Chile])
CONACAMI	Confederación [former Coordinadora] Nacional de Comunidades Campesinas Afectadas por la Minería (National Confederation of Communities Affected by Mining)
CONAM	Consejo Nacional del Ambiente (National Environmental Council)
DIGESA	Dirección General de Salud Ambiental del Ministerio de Salud (General Directorate of Environmental Health)
EIA	environmental impact assessment
EM	Energía y Minas (Ministry of Energy and Mines)
FIDA	Fondo de Inversiones para el Desarrollo de Ancash (Ancash Development Investment Fund)

GRADE	Grupo de Análisis para el Desarrollo (Group for the Analysis of Development)
GDP	Gross Domestic Product
GNP	Gross National Product
IDB	Inter-American Development Bank
IFC	International Finance Corporation (of the World Bank)
IMF	International Monetary Fund
INEI	Instituto Nacional de Estadística e Informática (National Institute of Statistics and Informatics)
INRENA	Instituto Nacional de Recursos Naturales (National Institute of Natural Resources)
MEM	Ministerio de Energía y Minas (Ministry of Energy and Mines)
MIGA	Multilateral Investment Guarantee Agency (of the World Bank)
MINAM	Ministerio del Ambiente (Ministry of the Environment)
MPL	maximum permissible limits
NGO	nongovernmental organization
OEFA	Organismo de Evaluación y Fiscalización Ambiental (Evaluation and Environmental Supervision Office)
OSINERGMIN	Organismo Supervisor de la Inversión en Energía y Minería (Supervisory Agency for Investment in Energy and Mining)
PAMA	Programa de Adecuación y Mitigación Ambiental (Environmental Remediation and Management Program)
PETT	Proyecto Especial de Titulación de Tierras y Catastro Rural (Special Land Titling and Cadastre Project)
SENACE	Servicio Nacional de Certificación Ambiental para las Inversiones Sostenibles (National Service for Environmental Certification for Sustainable Investments)
SNMPE	Sociedad Nacional de Minería, Petróleo y Energía (National Society of Mining, Petroleum, and Energy)
TMI	The Mountain Institute

NOTES

Introduction

1. This book refers mainly to metallic minerals.
2. According to the Peruvian Office of the Ombudsman (DP 2006a:1), a conflict is defined as including at least one of the following: "threat to the life, personal safety, or health of people, damage to public or private property, impediment of free movement, impediment to the exercise of the functions of an authority, or the paralyzation of the provision of public services."
3. The EIA aims to predict environmental and social impacts in order to mitigate them, including guidelines for monitoring reports (McManus 2002).
4. As this book deals with conflictive scenarios, the identity of each interviewee is protected by the use of a first name pseudonym, other than individuals whose identity is apparent because of their public pronouncements.
5. Legislative Decrees 613, 662, and 757.
6. The three basic instruments were the EIA for new operations and extensions of greater than 50 percent of the production or size of the plant, PAMAs (Programas de Adecuación y Mitigación Ambiental, or Environmental Remediation and Management Programs) for mines in operation, and external audits by private companies.
7. Paradoxically, of the 257 legal stability agreements between 1993 and 2002 related to tax revenue collection, 46 percent were modified at the request of companies, in many cases invoking repealed incentives (Campodónico 2005; SUNAT 2002:11).
8. CONAM was formed by one representative from the universities, one from the national professional associations, one from the regional governments, one from the environmental NGOs, one delegate from the municipal governments, two businessmen (secondary and tertiary sectors), and three state representatives.

9. The mining company could simply deposit the compensation in the Banco de la Nación (State Bank). This mechanism—considered confiscatory or expropriatory—has rarely been implemented but is available to a mining company to apply pressure when it seeks to purchase land (see chapter 2).
10. On June 5, 2009, 33 people died (23 police officers and 10 private citizens) and another 205 were injured close to the Amazon town of Bagua during a clash between the police and Indigenous demonstrators that came to be known as the Baguazo. The protests arose in the context of a decree to implement the U.S.-Peru Free Trade Agreement, which allowed extractive industries—such as timber, oil, and mining—to enter territories with neither proper consultation nor the consent of Indigenous communities, each required under ILO Convention 169.
11. For a critical ethnographic review of the 1969 Agrarian Reform, see Mayer (2009). For an overview of Peru's historical changes since independence, see Contreras and Cueto (2007).
12. The index is based on twenty-five items, excluding oil and precious metals. The base year is 2000. The measure includes the rise in the nominal price of copper fueled by Chinese demand in the context of the weakening dollar.
13. The historian Alfonso Quiroz (2013) estimated the average annual cost of corruption during that decade to be $2.04 billion. An anticorruption attorney, Pedro Gamarra, claimed that this led to losses of $6 billion, of which the state was only able to recover $184 million by 2010 (Romero 2010). In 2001 a survey reported that 32 percent of people supported privatization whereas 49 percent preferred state ownership (Boza 2003:6). The following year, support for privatization had fallen to just 22 percent, while 60 percent supported state ownership. In 2007 another survey showed a narrower result in the national capital, where support of privatization was most obvious: 48 percent rated privatization as "very negative / negative," while 46 percent felt it was "very positive / positive" (IOP 2007:4).
14. In the first four years of operation, following its founding in 2010, OEFA (Organismo de Evaluación y Fiscalización Ambiental, or the Evaluation and Environmental Supervision Office) opened 729 cases against 132 mining companies for potential environmental damage. These claims represented 56 percent of cases opened across all sectors: mining, hydrocarbons, electricity, and fisheries. Fines exceeded $77 million (Convoca 2015:15).
15. Large mines in Peru are usually foreign-owned and process more than five thousand metric tons of ore daily, using the open pit method. Medium (350 to 5,000 tons per day) and small mines (less than 350 to 25 tons per day) use underground tunnels. Large- and medium-scale mining is defined, in a legal sense, solely by their volume of production. Artisanal mining covers less than 1,000 hectares and exploits up to 25 tons per day (INEI 2005).
16. For an overview of how ethnographic efforts are facing the challenge of unpacking the global ethnographically, see Gingrich (2002) and Golub (2014).
17. Political ecology studies show "cultural practices—whether science, or 'traditional' knowledge or discourses, or risk, or property rights—are contested, fought over,

and negotiated," as Watts (2003:259) indicates. Part of the debate seeks to harmonize natural sciences and more humanistic disciplines. The ethnographies of poststructuralist cultural political ecology—influenced by the works of Michael Foucault—privilege the study of how language is shaping politics in the discursive polyphony of the subjects (Escobar 1996). These efforts study the connections between power discourses—enunciated and practiced—for control of the environment and societies.

18. The statement came the same day of the lamentable events occurred in the vicinity of the town of Bagua in June 2009 (see n. 10).
19. Kuipers et al. (2006) compared the impact on water quality of 183 hard rock mines operating in the USA since 1975, finding that the initial predictions of the environmental impact statements systematically underestimated the actual impacts later registered, and overestimated the effectiveness of mitigation actions (Kirsch 2014).
20. This company had been previously (1901–1914) known as Cerro de Pasco Mining Company. In 1915 it was renamed Cerro de Pasco Corporation and later Cerro de Pasco Copper Corporation.
21. Graeber (2005:170) argues that the "neoliberal vision of 'globalization' is pretty much limited to the free flow of commodities, and actually increases barriers against the flow of people, information and ideas." Thus, the border force between the USA and Mexico has almost tripled in size following the signing of NAFTA. Jobs are currently more static than in the nineteenth century, when a passport was not required (Edelman and Haugerud 2004:98).
22. See World Bank publications such as *Opportunities for All* (2005a) and *An Opportunity for a Different Peru* (Guigale et al. 2007).
23. Based on responses by household heads to a question about their mother tongue, the 2007 census estimated Peru's Indigenous population to number four million (Sanborn et al. 2016:7).
24. The nation-state system came into crisis after the privatization of diverse state spheres, as manifest in the use of violence by nongovernmental groups and in the intervention of multilateral agencies (e.g., the World Bank or IMF), or in NGO activists and citizen mobilizations appropriating different means of political action.
25. Dagnino (2006) details the emergence since the 1980s, in different national historical contexts, of the redefinition of the neoliberal version of citizenship—promoting individual integration into the market—in Latin America as a political reference developed as a strategy or a project to create new political participation, cultural inclusion, equal rights, and more everyday democratic processes.
26. Tarrow (1999:792) locates the pluralisation of the term *social movements* in the twentieth century, after scholarship and social change abandoned the confinement of the singular reference to the working class. It became applied to a variety of "uninstitutionalized groups of unrepresented constituents engaged in sequences of contentious interaction with elites or opponents." This book follows that path while discussing protest mobilizations, direct action networks, and other social claim acts, all manufacturing a repertoire of aggregated strategies in contentious politics.

27. Unless otherwise noted, the translations of personal testimonies and of official Peruvian documents are my own.
28. The Peruvian state includes three levels of government: national, regional, and local. There are twenty-four departments and a Constitutional Province of Callao, and each of these units has its own regional government. Testimonies, both in the media and informal settings, commonly use the word *region* to refer to a department. The local level includes 196 provincial municipalities and their 1,676 district-level peers, as well as 2,611 of a special type of municipalities called *municipalidades de centro poblado*, for small towns. The latter are created by the provincial municipalities, and their funding comes from the provincial and district municipalities.

Chapter 1

1. A good starting point for understanding Andean lake mythology is the literature of José María Arguedas and Ciro Alegría and the ethnographies of Efraín Morote and Luis Millones. The giant serpents inhabiting Andean lakes were called *amarus* (Allen 1988; Morote 1988). Legends about *mukis* are also common in the Andes. These goblins inhabit mining passages and offer riches from the mountain if the miners give tribute, or illness if they do not.
2. In Peru's southern Quechua, *apu* means "lord," a term reserved for the most powerful sacred places, such as certain mountains (Allen 1988:257).
3. Law Decree 674.
4. Bastida, Waelde, and Warden-Fernández's (2005) book is a recommended volume for more information on the subject.
5. Klohn Crippen Consultants Limited is a Canadian company founded in 1957. SVS Ingenieros S.A. was incorporated in Peru in 1985. Each presents itself as a multidisciplinary engineering company (CMA 2002).
6. Later expansions of Antamina included terrain in the province of Huamalíes (Huánuco Department).
7. Antamina subsequently defined a "sphere of social intervention" consisting of twenty districts. The approximate population of the immediate area was 115,000. The extended area consisted of thirty districts.
8. The review "Human Ecology of the Andes" (Gil Ramón 2017) details the evolution of studies on Andean verticality.
9. Antamina subsequently included Callejón de Conchucos, the Huarmey, and the Callejón de Huaylas (CMA 2001b:5).
10. There are six types of "canon" fiscal transfers to local governments in Peru: mining, hydroelectricty, gas, fishing, forest, and oil (Canon Law 27506). Each entails a state revenue redistribution to regional, provincial, and municipal governments in which the respective extractive activity is located. The mining canon—hereafter mostly referred to as canon—represents 50 percent of net income tax to mining industries (see chapter 4). Since 2001 its distribution to regional and local governments has been influenced by population projections and poverty rates (reflecting

infrastructure and basic needs). Demographic density previously defined the distribution (World Bank 2005b:132). Ten percent of the mining canon is allocated for the municipal government(s) where the concession is located; 25 percent is for municipalities in the local province; 25 percent is for the regional government (20 percent out of this 25 percent is allocated to fund research at state universities in the department); and the remaining 40 percent is for the municipal government(s) in the department, considering a poverty index. The main rethoric of these schemes claims to share and decentralize resource windfalls while attempting to gain local acceptance to the extractive industries, since the local authorities could access—albeit through bureaucratic barriers—significant sums for infrastructure or services (Loayza and Rigolini 2016).

11. According to the 2007 census, the district population of San Marcos was 11,204 and the rural percentage had diminished to 72 percent, probably reflecting migration to the town, among other places.
12. A hacienda refers to a landed estate in Latin America (Mayer 2002:336).
13. The contemporary peasant community, recognized by the 1969 Agrarian Reform, derives from two structures: the pre-Hispanic *ayllus* (social unit and corporate kinship) and those of more recent formation encouraged by tax benefits and land rights. The peasant community is the most important organization in the Peruvian Andes, covering several types of communal structures, which are defined by the condition of being co-owners of land and by the assignment of communal tasks (e.g., cleaning of canals and construction of premises).
14. The most recognized historic reference to the defense fronts dates from 1978, when the Defense Front of the People of Loreto was founded in response to a failure by the government to deliver its offer of funding through the oil canon. The group included hundreds of organizations of various types (Santos and Barclay 2002).

Chapter 2

1. The Land Law, complemented by other regulations, followed a Mexican precedent, which had transformed the Constitution in that country and provoked a debate about the inalienability of peasant communities (Glave and Gil Ramón 1998). This Mexican experience proved to be more controversial than would be the case in Peru. Two decades later, and in contradiction of the Land Law, MEM decreed (Supreme Decree 001-2015-EM) that the consent of the communal board—an organ of lower rank than the Communal General Assembly—was sufficient to authorize the use of surface lands by a mining company.
2. Other relevant guidelines, approved after the establishment of Antamina, include the IDB's (Inter-American Development Bank) (1998) *Operational Policy on Involuntary Resettlement* (OP-710) and the IFC's (2012 [2006]) *Performance Standards on Environmental and Social Sustainability*.
3. The Law of the Right to Prior Consultation to Indigenous or Native Peoples (Law 29785), approved in 2011, which in practice excluded precisely the Andean

peasant communities where the majority of mining deposits are located, generated debate about with whom the consultation should be conducted. Two years later the Ministry of Culture published a general reference guide that lacked specific lists of communities. This detail had to wait another three years, before being published in 2015 (Sanborn et al. 2016).

4. This book refers mostly to Operational Directive 4.20 and 4.30, which were in force at the time of the Antamina population displacement process. Both were replaced, respectively, in 2002 and 2005.
5. The five-page "Socioeconomic Annex II Resettlement Plan" of the environmental impact statement provided little more than a list of topics. It mentioned the need to minimize disruption and the number of people affected, as well as offering to consider their sociocultural conditions and their housing options. It noted that wealth and assets would be replaced in kind, including compensation or rehabilitation to a standard of living "minimum equal" to the previous "level." It also stated there would "be employment opportunities, access to natural resources and public services" (KS 1998a; 1998b:36–37).
6. The *compromiso previo* (prior commitment) guidelines contained in a 2003 Supreme Decree and Antamina's own code of conduct would each subsequently become part of the documentation for subcontractors and temporary workers, allegedly seeking progress in the project's social aspects.
7. I collaborated in the design of the GRADE (1999) study to evaluate the opening of the Antamina project in San Marcos.
8. By 2000, Antamina had complied with the obligations recognition contracts through "extra judicial transactions" ($5,000) or the inclusion in the "Plan Acelerado de Reubicación" (Accelerated Resettlement Plan), leaving four cases unresolved, including the Ango Raju community (GRADE 2000). Antamina subsequently stated that many claims were reduced through the offer of programs to repair damage to the livelihoods of the most affected families, including support projects (e.g., agricultural technical assistance) that were outsourced to other organizations.
9. GRADE (2000:29) defined four categories that took into account a multiplicity of social institutions for using pastoral land and proposed a gradation for the compensation.
10. The assessment also identified nine additional cases of families affected to a minor degree and needing special compensation and two cases for further review (GRADE 2000). Six years after the displacement began, Antamina reported that twelve families were still to be resettled and fifteen families were awaiting compensation (CMA 2004:47). Another five families had been resettled and fourteen compensated with productive investments to improve their living conditions. Additionally, seven families were in the process of relocation and one was negotiating compensation.
11. Subsequent probusiness testimonies ensured Milpo's efforts to incorporate codes of business conduct.

12. Salomon and Niño-Murcia (2011) as well as Mayer (2002:129)—for Tupicocha and Tangor, respectively—provide further information about the importance of public acts as reciprocity symbols and venues for legitimizing corporate entities in Andean contexts.
13. Ethnographic accounts of mining in Bolivia show how rural dwellers identified mercantile relationships as negative and unnatural because of their impersonal nature and fixed value accounting, something at odds with the values of solidarity and reciprocity that are considered functional with monetary scarcity. The mercantile mining relationships were associated with negative or demonic figures, in opposition to functional and supportive behaviors, including Catholic teaching (Nash 1993 [1979]; Taussig 1980).
14. In economic theory, perfect information implies a state where each market participant has "complete up-to-date information about products and prices" and thereby can make "perfectly rational choices" (Law 2018). In most cases, agents have to make relatively fast decisions in complex scenarios, bounded by imperfect information.

Chapter 3

1. In 2005, TMI had approximately seventy international personnel and fifty staff based in the United States. The annual budget was approximately $3.5 million (TMI 2005:4).
2. Corinne Schmidt's (1999) thesis in policy studies addresses important aspects of early disputes related to the plan for roads that would impact the park.
3. The pipeline costs identified in the environmental impact statement can be grouped into five categories: easement, topography, time (delays or interruptions), the potential impact on populated areas, and road construction and its impact when crossing the park. Antamina was obliged to build a highway in any case, in order to transport goods and services to the mine and to provide routes for maintenance and protection within the park.
4. The EIA report insufficiently addressed the risk of road accidents, especially for the central route. In 1998, around the time of the EIA, Ancash Department recorded the seventh highest number of traffic accidents in Peru (PNP 2012).
5. For example, the community of Chaquitambo—including several private landowners—refused to sell their property but agreed that Antamina could utilize six meters of their collectively owned land, with the community maintaining its crops. The contract prohibited the planting of trees and stipulated that Antamina could excavate on the land at any time and pay compensation to the community in an amount equal to the value of an annual harvest. The municipal government also leveraged the negotiations by obtaining company support for a request to the state for electrification of the town in return for access to the highway that Antamina sought.
6. Many countries require a separate social-impact study complementary to the EIA, offering environmental and social issues to be evaluated in a more comprehensive and integrated manner (World Bank 2005b:78). The first Peruvian mining regu-

lation to mention social issues dates from 1993. Nonbinding EIA guidelines that included a "socio-economic environment" requirement have existed since 1995. A 2001 decree mandated a nonbinding social impact study as part of the EIA and included a model format. Two years later, MEM promulgated the prior commitment decree, which it modified in 2009 to include provision by the mining company of declarations on sustainable development, local employment, timetables, plans, and obligations in respect to investment levels. A 2014 regulation introduced the requirement for a social management plan with some goals and indicators. The OEFA became responsible for monitoring these plans (Aquino 2015).

7. Ministerial Resolution 728-99-EM.
8. Ministerial Resolution 596-2002-EM.
9. Supreme Decree 028-2008-EM and Ministerial Resolution 304-2008-EM.
10. Since a mining concession does not automatically authorize the development of site activities, the consultation for mining occurs prior to these activities: exploration, exploitation, *concesión de beneficio* (benefit concession) of the chemical and physical procedures of the operation to extract the marketable part of the ore, and its transportation (Sanborn et al. 2016).
11. Supreme Decree 040-2014-EM.
12. Ministerial Resolution 057-2017-MINAM.
13. Supreme Decree 028-2008-EM.
14. For instance, in 1997 INRENA had approved the Chilean Lucchetti company's heavily criticized EIA to build a noodle factory in the ecologically sensitive marshes of Villa, one of the last protected areas in Lima. The factory closed in 2003 after a scandal that involved bribery in exchange for judicial favors in the legal dispute over the permit for the operations (Quiroz 2013).
15. Ríos's public trajectory embodies a radical case of a contingent rhetoric of appearance within the cast of conflicts. In 2009 he was sentenced for having received a bribe to change his party allegiance in congress. Five years later he was elected regional president—renamed "regional governor" in 2015—of Ancash and organized a public cash collection to pay his civil damages. In 2016 he was sentenced to five years in prison for unlawful acts committed during his tenure as mayor of Huaraz (1999–2000).
16. The committee remains in operation and works independently of the municipality of Huarmey. It is the only committee in Peru that receives direct financial support from the Office of the Prime Minister. This support aims to guarantee its work while promoting separation from the mining company, whose impact it is monitoring.
17. Supreme Decree 028-2008-EM.

Chapter 4

1. The Ashaninka leader made these remarks in reference to the multibillion dollar Camisea gas project located on land belonging to his Amazon Indigenous group (*Caretas* 2004).

2. For Kruijt and Vellinga (1979) and Flores Galindo (1993 [1974]), the mining economy of La Cerro was mostly isolated from the rest of the region, implying an enclave (Mallon 1983:181). According to Flores Galindo (1993:33 [1974]), La Cerro maintained "autonomy" because "the laws did not apply to it," and it destroyed the small and medium-sized owners and affected trade through having its own commercial system (Long and Roberts 1984).
3. The relationship between the government of Velasco and Southern Peru Copper Corporation in Cuajone was markedly different because of the exceptional advantages this U.S. company enjoyed. In 1969, just prior to the government approving stricter regulations, the state and La Southern had signed an agreement to exploit Cuajone. In 1974 and 1976, agreements were signed protecting Cuajone from state intervention. The mine began to operate in 1977 and produced 40 percent of the country's copper.
4. In 1996 the company agreed to stop discharging tailings into local rivers and pay an estimated $500 million in compensation. A second lawsuit in 2004 followed public pressure and forced BHP to settle and transfer 52 percent of shares to a development trust, which cost the company $3 billion dollars in lost revenue (Kirsch 2014:10).
5. According to the state's privatization commission, or COPRI (Commission for the Promotion of Private Investment, now Promotion Agency for Private Investment, or ProInversión), the largest portion of the funds derived from privatization (31 percent, or $1.36 billion) was directed to politicized social spending during electoral campaigns, including food donations and the construction of schools and *lozas deportivas* (sport concrete pitches suitable for five-a-side soccer) (Campodónico 2005).
6. Unlike the United States, Europe, and a good part of the rest of the region, capital gains in this stock exchange were exempt from income tax. That exemption remained in effect as of 2018.
7. A mining concession requires state permissions prior to extractive activities. MEM (2017) estimates that mining exploration and production units covered 1.28 percent (1.65 million hectares) of Peru's territory in 2016. The majority of national territory (63 percent) is protected from mining, as it is reserved for other uses (e.g., urban development).
8. The UNDP (2016:219) Multidimensional Poverty Index found that 10 percent of the population was living in multidimensional poverty, with an additional 12 percent "near" this state, and another 2 percent in "severe" multidimensional poverty.
9. Poverty rates are based on expenditure rather than income because the former tends to remain more stable and because household surveys report spending with greater accuracy. Vásquez (2012) argues that the poor become invisible when there are discrepancies between the one-dimensional official INEI claim of a fourteen-point reduction (from 42 percent to 27 percent between 2004 and 2007) and the reduction of 4 percent (44 to 39 percent) registered by the Multidimensional Poverty Index. Vásquez estimates that in 2011 the proportion of the population

experiencing multidimensional poverty was 39 percent, some 12 percent above the monetary poverty estimated by INEI (27 percent).

10. Based on Peruvian population census, Loayza and Rigolini (2016) found that mining districts had higher average consumption per capita and lower poverty rates than districts that were otherwise similar. Nevertheless, these optimistic effects severely diminished with distance from mining centers. Furthermore, consumption inequality within mining districts was higher than in their comparable nonmining peers. Based on national surveys, Agüero et al. (2017) estimate that, in general, redistribution of canon in mining districts increased math test scores, adult employment, and health outcomes. Nevertheless, the net effect on these test scores became negative for the extremely canon-rich municipalities. Furthermore, although public employment increased—probably reflecting a clientelistic approach—the redistribution had a weak impact on reducing overall unemployment.
11. In the period 2004–2011, the state had foregone $1.59 billion because of this arrangement (Mendoza and de Echave 2016:102). The unpaid royalties of Antamina (35.6 percent), Yanacocha (18.7 percent), and Cerro Verde (18.5 percent) represented 72.8 percent of the amount.
12. The $162 million collected for the year 2006 only represented one-tenth of the increase in profits from 2005 to 2006. Half of the increase in profits could have represented the starting point for the negotiation (Campodónico 2006b).
13. Between 2007 and 2016, mining amounted to an average of 63 percent of exports (MEM 2017).
14. The Gini coefficient measures inequality degrees in distribution, such as income, on a range of zero, where there is perfect equality, to one, where a single individual holds all the wealth (Scott and Marshall 2005b).
15. The major subcontracted companies were Antamina Operaciones (15 percent, or 1,006 employees), Spie Capag (13 percent, or 869 employees), and the food vending company Sodexho (9 percent, or 624 employees). Both Spie Capag and Sodexho were French enterprises.
16. The Chinese state model is also relevant, although its relatively recent presence in Peru has not been without criticism for socioenvironmental impacts and conflicts (Ray et al. 2017). By 2016, Chinese investment represented more than 30 percent of the portfolio of projects in the mining sector.
17. Welker (2014:12) locates the establishment of the corporate responsibility industry in the 1990s as a reaction to transnational advocacy and direct action networks opposing multinational and international development agencies, such as the World Bank or the IMF.
18. The "prior commitment" Supreme Decree 042-2003-EM required mining companies to act "with respect towards local institutions, authorities, culture, and customs" in a "continuous dialog." It urged mining companies to "preferably promote local employment." Nevertheless, the regulation did not specify metrics to monitor these commitments.

19. The works of the anthropologist John Murra and the historian María Rostorowski are valuable resources for understanding the Inca reciprocity system as used to legitimize their invasions.
20. In rural areas, almost 25 percent of the population considered environmental contamination to be the main problem that municipal investment should address (MIM 2012:27).
21. As reflected in table 1, in 2007, six years after the mine entered into operation and a year after the multiplication of canon transfers to the municipality of San Marcos (see figure 14), according to official censuses—not exempted from credibility issues, as noted in this chapter—and following a national trend, the percentage of households in San Marcos with at least one unsatisfied basic need reduced from 91.5 to 64 percent since 1993. The figure also decreased in Chavín de Huántar, Huallanca, and Huarmey for this period (INEI 2018). Whereas in 1993 the neighboring San Marcos and Chavín de Huántar had been almost on par in terms of the population percentage suffering at least one unsatisfied basic need, the difference amplified between 1993 and 2017, from 2.4 to 12.3 percent. For the intercensus period 1993–2017, San Marcos led the reduction of this vulnerable population with 54.6 percent, followed by Chavín de Huántar (44.7 percent), Huallanca (40.5 percent), and Huarmey (15.6 percent). Nevertheless, with the exception of Huarmey in 1993 (52.6 versus 56.8 percent), these districts fare worse than the aggregated national estimates for this time. This divergence in trajectories was probably reflecting the fact that San Marcos led the national ranking of canon transfers, and over the decade commencing 2006 had received more than $400 million (see figure 14). Also, to a certain extent, it could reflect the increase in the aforementioned temporary municipal employment in San Marcos, among other possible factors, including so-called development projects.
22. The three governors of Ancash between 2007 and 2017 have been sentenced to prison for irregular use of public funds. Several mayors of San Marcos have also been accused of corruption. The mayor elected for the period 2007–2010 died in an unexplained road accident one year before finishing his term. Between 2012 and 2014, two mayors were recalled because of nepotism. Javier Medina, the third mayor during the 2011–2014 period, faced imprisonment for accusations of fraud against the municipality of San Marcos. In 2017 the mayor elected for 2015–2018 was already facing investigations of bribery.

Chapter 5

1. The socioenvironmental impact in Huallanca primarily involved changes in the urban architecture, and this produced the demands and the compensation examined in chapter 4.
2. A Canadian firm, EcoMetrix (2005), contracted by Antamina, concluded that four lagoons had been damaged by the mining company between 1998 and 2005. These lagoons were included in the company's monitoring program. Yanacocha, Canrash,

and Shahuanga were affected by the turbidity of the runoff from the site during construction. The Pajoshccocha Lagoon received the effluent of treated wastewater from the pioneer Antamina camp in Contonga, closed in 2000. Contonga mine reopened in 2004, and Antamina withdrew this lagoon from its evaluations. Nor did it include Shahuanga, because, according to EcoMetrix (2005:2.4), "There was just a small turbidity column in the lagoon for a short period in 2000."

3. EcoMetrix (2005:3.6, 3.8) indicated that the depth decreased one to two meters in the part of the Canrash Lagoon "that was cloudy during the construction of the highway." It added that in 2004 "the total dissolved concentrations of the main metals were below detection levels in the lagoon" and that in general the lagoon "had an exceptionally good water quality and showed no signs of water runoff from the highway." Optimistically, it did not expect the "changes in some sediment chemistry parameters to influence the overall health of the lagoon."
4. RD-0372-2001-DIGESA-SA.
5. In Huarmey I noticed similar impacts on houses near the terminal, and I heard concerns about daily explosions that occurred as part of the construction process for the port.
6. Participants included Antamina, the municipality of Huarmey, the National University of Santa, four ministries, the Catholic Church, the General Directorate of Captains and Ports, the Neighborhood Board of Puerto Huarmey, the Board of Irrigation Users, and the Associations of Shipowners and Artisanal Fishermen of Puerto Huarmey, among others.
7. Legislative Decree 613.
8. Law 28611.
9. Supreme Decree 054-2013-PCM and 060-2013-PCM.
10. From 1993, PAMAs had set the temporary goals in cases where a mine discharged material prior to the establishment of the corresponding parameters. Until at least 2005, with the exception of Hydrogen Potential (pH), the projects that began before 1993 had PAMAs with equal and even more permissive standards than those that applied to new projects (World Bank 2005b:89). The negative cost was transferred to the population and the environment.
11. TV show *La Hora N*, June 21, 2001.
12. The U.S. journalist Lowell Bergman (2005) reported how these recordings "reveal how deeply involved Montesinos was in the protracted battle between French, Australian, and American mining companies in the mid- to late 1990s for control of Yanacocha, Peru's largest gold mine."
13. In 1962, the sociologist William White conducted a "survey of values" among 508 seniors from state and elite private schools in Lima and found only one common trait: lack of trust. When asked whether they could trust others, only 34 percent answered affirmatively. In a comparable investigation in the United States, the figure was 79 percent (Whyte and Flores 1963).
14. "Third Public Meeting of Environmental Issues," April 21, 2002.
15. Supreme Decree 002-2008-MINAM.

16. Supreme Decree 028-2008-EM and Law 28611.
17. Between 1998 and 2005, Peruvian police registered between seventy thousand and eighty thousand traffic accidents annually (PNP 2006:2). For the 2003–2005 period, the number of fatalities for every ten thousand vehicles in Peru was twenty-nine, compared to fourteen in Colombia and seven in Chile (DP 2006b:5).
18. In 2002 the luxurious Lima nightclub Utopía was destroyed by fire, with many of its occupants trapped. The internal finishes were not fire resistant, the floor was covered with rubber, and the premises lacked extinguishers. On the night of the incident, caused by a pyrotechnic display, the venue was hosting double its authorized capacity. The administrator was sentenced to seven years in prison and was the only one convicted among dozens of accused.

Conclusion

1. I thank Yale University professor Michael Dove for this detail.

REFERENCES

Adams, Richard. 1959. *A Community in the Andes: Problems and Progress in Muquiyauyo.* University of Washington Press, Seattle.

Agrawal, Arun. 2005. *Environmentality: Technologies of Government and the Making of Subjects.* Duke University Press, Durham, NC, and London.

Agüero, Jorge, Carlos F. Balcázar, Stanislao Maldonado, and Hugo Ñopo. 2017. "The Value of Redistribution: Natural Resources and the Formation of Human Capital Under Weak Institutions." *Avances de Investigación* 28. GRADE, Lima.

Aigner, Erin, Joe Burgess, Shan Carter, Joanne Nurse, Haeyoun Park, Amy Schoenfeld, and Archie Tse. 2010. "Tracking the Oil Spill in the Gulf." *New York Times,* August 2. New York. http://www.nytimes.com/interactive/2010/05/01/us/20100501-oil-spill-tracker.html.

Aldana, Susana. 1999. "La crisis y el derrumbe minero siglo XVII." In *Historia de la minería en el Perú,* edited by José A. del Busto, pp. 175–205. Compañía Minera MILPO S.A., Lima.

Allen, Catherine J. 1988. *The Hold Life Has: Coca and Cultural Identity in an Andean Community.* Smithsonian Institution Press, Washington, D.C.

Allison, Lincoln. 2003. "Participation, Political." In *The Concise Oxford Dictionary of Politics,* edited by Iain McLean and Alistair McMillan, pp. 391–392. Oxford University Press, Oxford.

AMIDEP (Asociación Multidisciplinaria de Investigación y Docencia en Población). 1997a. "Censo de la población residente en el área de influencia de la mina Antamina." CMA. AMIDEP, Lima.

———. 1997b. "Estudio socioeconómico del área de influencia de la mina, línea de transmisión, mineroducto y puerto del proyecto minero de Antamina." CMA. AMIDEP, Lima.

Appadurai, Arjun 2000. "Grassroots Globalization and the Research Imagination." *Public Culture* 12(1):1–19.

———. 2001. "Deep Democracy: Urban Governmentality and the Horizon of Politics." *Environment and Urbanization* 13(2):23–43.

Aquino, Pavel. 2015. *Recomendaciones para el fortalecimiento de la evaluación del impacto ambiental de las actividades mineras en el Perú.* DAR, Lima. http://dar.org.pe/archivos/publicacion/pu_161_estudio_mineras.pdf.

Arellano-Yanguas, Javier. 2011. *¿Minería sin fronteras? Conflicto y desarrollo en regiones mineras del Perú.* Instituto de Estudios Peruanos, Pontificia Universidad Católica del Perú (PUCP), and Universidad Antonio Ruiz de Montoya, Lima.

Asociación Ancash. 2004. *Memoria anual 2003.* Asociación Ancash, Lima.

Assadourian, Carlos Sempat. 1982. *El sistema de la economía colonial: Mercado interno, regiones y espacio económico.* Instituto de Estudios Peruanos, Lima.

Assadourian, Carlos Sempat, Heraclio Bonilla, Antonio Mitre, and Tristan Platt. 1980. *Minería y espacio económico en los Andes, siglos XVI-XX.* Instituto de Estudios Peruanos, Lima.

Aste, Juan. 2000. "La gestión del impacto ambiental y social de la actividad minero metalúrgica." In *El rostro de la minería en las comunidades del Perú*, edited by CONACAMI, pp. 92–98. CONACAMI, Lima.

AUDITEC S.A.C. (Empresa de Auditoría e Inspectoría Sociedad Anónima Cerrada). 2000. "Informe de fiscalización minera: Normas de conservación del medio ambiente. Compañía Minera Antamina S.A.-U.P. Antamina (II Semestre)." CMA. San Marcos Environmental Committee, Peru.

Auty, Richard M. 1993. *Sustaining Development in Mineral Economies: The Resource Curse Thesis.* Routledge, London.

———. 2000. "How Natural Resources Affect Economic Development." *Development Policy Review* 18(4):347–364.

Ballard, Chris, and Glenn Banks. 2003. "Resource Wars: The Anthropology of Mining." *Annual Review of Anthropology* 32:287–313.

Balvín, Doris. 2002. *Medio ambiente, minería y sociedad: Una mirada distinta.* Asociación Civil Labor, Lima.

Barham, Bradford, Stephen G. Bunker, and Denis O'Hearn (editors). 1994. *States, Firms, and Raw Materials: The World Economy and Ecology of Aluminum.* University of Wisconsin Press, Madison.

Bastida, Elizabeth, Thomas W. Waelde, and Janeth Warden-Fernández. 2005. *International and Comparative Mineral Law and Policy: Trends and Prospects.* Kluwer Law International, The Hague.

BCP (Banco de Crédito del Perú). 2006. "La minería en el Perú." Report. División de Mercado de Capitales del BCP, Lima.

Bebbington, Anthony J., and Jeffrey T. Bury. 2009. "Institutional Challenges for Mining and Sustainability in Peru." *Proceedings of the National Academy of Sciences* 106(41):17296–17301.

——— (editors). 2013. *Subterranean Struggles: New Dynamics of Mining, Oil, and Gas in Latin America.* University of Texas Press, Austin.

Beck, Ulrich. 1992. *Risk Society: Towards a New Modernity*. Sage Publications, London.

———. 2002 [1988]. *Ecological Politics in an Age of Risk*. Polity Press, Malden, Massachusetts.

Benavides, Marcela, and Guida Gastelumendi. 2001. *Responsabilidad social empresarial: Un compromiso necesario*. Centro de Investigación de la Universidad del Pacífico (CIUP), SASE Servicios para el Desarrollo, and Perú 2021, Lima.

Bergman, Lowell. 2005. "Montesinos' Web: Special Investigation." *Frontline/World*. Electronic document, http://www.pbs.org/frontlineworld/stories/peru404/web.html.

Blaikie, Piers, and Harold Brookfield. 1987. *Land Degradation and Society*. Methuen, London.

Bonilla, Heraclio. 1974. *El minero de los Andes: Una aproximación a su estudio*. Instituto de Estudios Peruanos, Lima.

Botts, Steven, Frida Caballero, and Jorge Recharte. 2001. "Antamina and Huascarán National Park: A Case Study in Mining, Conservation, and Sustainable Development." CMA, PNH, and TMI. Electronic document, https://santabarbaraconsultants.com/_wp/wp-content/uploads/2014/01/Huascaran-National-Park-AQP.pdf.

Bouillon, Cesar P. 2003. "Inequality, Exclusion, and Poverty in Latin America and the Caribbean: Implications for Development." Paper presented at the EC/IDB Seminar on Social Cohesion in Latin America and the Caribbean, Brussels, June 5–6.

Bouillon, César P., Mayra Buvinic, and Carlos M. Jarque.2004. *Building Social Cohesion in Latin America and the Caribbean*. IDB, Washington, D.C.

Boza, Beatriz. 2003 "The Standing of Competition Authorities vis-a-vis Civil Society." Paper presented at the International Competition Network conference, Mérida, June 23–25.

———. 2006. *Canon minero: ¿Caja chica o palanca para el desarrollo?* CAD, CIES, and SNMPE, Lima.

B&R (Barrenechea y Rosemberg Asociados). 1998a. "Resettlement as an Opportunity for Progress of the Family." CMA, Lima.

———. 1998b. "From Resettlement to Sustainable Development: Identification of Project Initiatives." CMA, Lima.

Brosius, J. Peter. 1999. "Analyses and Interventions: Anthropological Engagements with Environmentalism." *Current Anthropology* 40(3):277–309.

Brown, Kendall. 2012. *A History of Mining in Latin America: From the Colonial Era to the Present*. University of New Mexico Press, Albuquerque.

Bryant, Raymond. 1992. "Political Ecology: An Emerging Research Agenda in Third World Studies." *Political Geography* 11:12–36.

Bunker, Stephen. 1985. *Underdeveloping the Amazon: Extraction, Unequal Exchange, and the Failure of the Modern State*. University of Illinois Press, Urbana.

Burger, Richard L. 1992. *Chavín and the Origins of Andean Civilization*. Thames and Hudson Ltd., London.

Bury, Jeffrey. 2004. "Livelihoods in Transition: Transnational Gold Mining Operations and Local Change in Cajamarca, Peru." *Geographical Journal* 170(1):78–91.

Byron, Reginald. 2002. "Identity." In *Encyclopedia of Social and Cultural Anthropology*, edited by Alan Barnard and Jonathan Spencer, p. 292. Routledge, London.

CAD (Ciudadanos al Día). 2005a. *Canon minero 2005: Situación y perspectivas.* CAD No. 39. CAD, Lima.

———. 2005b. *Canon minero en Ancash 2005.* CAD No. 12. CAD, Lima.

Campodónico, Humberto. 2005. "Es hora de revisar los contratos de estabilidad tributaria." *La República*, September 15. Lima.

———. 2006a. "El óbolo minero: Otro retroceso." *La República*, November 24. Lima.

———. 2006b. "Bolsa de Valores de Lima (BVL): Ganancias de capital deben pagar impuesto a la renta." *La República*, December 30. Lima.

Cantuarias, Felipe. 2004. "La responsabilidad social en la minería: Un avance." Electronic document, http://www.snmpe.org.pe/pdfs/ResponsabilidadSocialFelipeCantuarias.pdf, accessed December 20, 2006.

Cano, Jannet, and Manuel Otárola. 2017. "Las exportaciones de minerales en el Perú de cara al bicentenario: análisis económico, proyección estadística y perspectivas para el mediano plazo." *Review of Global Management* 3(2):56–66.

CAO (The World Bank Group's Office of the Compliance Advisor Ombudsman of the IFC and MIGA). 2001. *Preliminary Audit Review of MIGA in Relation to Compañía Minera Antamina S.A.* CAO, Washington, D.C.

———. 2006. *Final Assessment Report: Complaint Regarding the Antamina Mining Project in Huarmey, Peru.* CAO, Washington, D.C.

Caravedo, Baltazar. 1998. *El impacto social de las empresas mineras en el Perú.* Instituto de Estudios Energético Mineros (IDEM), Lima.

———. 2003. "¿Cómo promover la responsabilidad social empresarial? La experiencia peruana." *Papeles de Ética, Economía y Dirección* 8:1–16.

Cárdenas, Mercedes. 1999. "Minería y metalurgia preinca." In *Historia de la minería en el Perú*, edited by José Antonio del Busto, pp. 17–57. Compañía Minera MILPO S.A, Lima.

Caretas [Lima, Peru]. 2004. "Las lecciones de Camisea: Manual al vuelo de cómo sacar adelante un multimillonario proyecto de desarrollo." Vol. 1835, August 12. Lima.

Castillo, Pedro. 2013. "IV Cenagro y las comunidades del país: su presencia es innegable." *La Revista Agraria* 155:12–13.

CEPRI-Centromin (Comité Especial de Privatización-Centromin). 1996. "Bases del concurso. Concurso Público Internacional: Promoción de la inversión privada en Antamina." CEPRI-Centromin, Lima.

Cernea, Michael M. 1999. "Why Economic Analysis Is Essential to Resettlement: A Sociologist's View." In *The Economics of Involuntary Resettlement: Questions and Challenges*, edited by Michael M. Cernea, pp. 5–49. World Bank, Washington, D.C.

———. 2003. "For a New Economics of Resettlement: A Sociological Critique of the Compensation Principle." *International Social Science Journal* 55(1):37.

Chirif, Alberto. 2015. "Los 20 años del Convenio 169 de la OIT en el Perú. ¿Algo que celebrar?" *Servindi*, April 23. Electronic document, http://servindi.org/actualidad/128507.

CLAS (Comunidades Locales de Administración de Salud) San Marcos. 2001. *Programa de Salud Local.* Ministerio de Salud-CLAS San Marcos, San Marcos.

CMA (Compañía Minera Antamina S.A.). 1999a. "Información básica: Situación actual de las familias reubicadas." Oficina de Desarrollo Comunitario, San Marcos.
———. 1999b. "Oferta de reubicación." CMA, San Marcos.
———. 1999c. "Situación actual de las familias reubicadas." Oficina de Desarrollo Comunitario, San Marcos.
———. 2000. "Se firmó contrato para construir mineroducto." *Antamina en Acción* 6, February.
———. 2001a. *Ambiente, salud y seguridad industrial en Antamina*. EH&S–CMA, Lima.
———. 2001b. *Balance de la gestión social 2000-CMA*. Lima: CMA.
———. 2001c. "Programa de Monitoreo y Control Ambiental, Zona Yanacancha: Informe trimestral para el Comité de Medio Ambiente de San Marcos (February–June, 2001)." CMA-Departamento de Medio Ambiente, Lima.
———. 2001d. "Programa de Monitoreo y Control Ambiental, Zona Yanacancha: Informe trimestral para el Comité de Medio Ambiente de San Marcos (July–September, 2001)." CMA, Lima.
———. 2001e. "Primer taller participativo sobre medio ambiente: Proceso de consulta." Workshop presented by CMA, EH&S, and Social Capital Group, Lima, February 2.
———. 2002. *Reporte de sostenibilidad 2001 de CMA*. CMA, Lima.
———. 2003a. "Augusto Baertl deja presidencia de Antamina." Electronic document, http://www.antamina.com/noticias/noticias_01.html.
———. 2003b. *Reporte de sostenibilidad 2002: De la licencia social al capital social*. CMA, Lima.
———. 2004. *Reporte de sostenibilidad 2003: Información y comentarios acerca de una operación minera, social y ambientalmente responsable*. CMA, Lima.
———. 2005a. "Antamina en cifras." Electronic document, http://www.antamina.com/01_antamina/CMA.html.
———. 2005b. "Fondo de Inversiones para el Desarrollo de Ancash (FIDA)." Presentation by CMA, Lima, August 18.
———. 2006a. *Código de conducta: Manual de políticas y procedimientos*. CMA, Lima.
———. 2006b. "Cuatrocientos ochenta millones de soles por concepto de canon minero." *Desde Conchucos: Antamina Informa* 3.
———. 2006c. "Informe trimestral de monitoreo ambiental: Segundo trimestre del 2006 (April–June)." CMA, Lima.
———. 2006d. "Pago complementario." Electronic document, http://www.antamina.com/04_social/pago_complem.html, accessed November 22, 2006.
———. 2006e. "Plan de monitoreo ambiental." Departamento de Medio Ambiente CMA, Lima.
———. 2006f. *Reporte de sostenibilidad 2005*. CMA, Lima.
———. 2007. "Antamina." Electronic document, http://www.antamina.com/01_antamina/antamina.html.
———. 2009. "Antamina manifiesta su disposición para continuar diálogo con comunidad de Ango Raju." Electronic document, https://www.antamina.com/noticias/antamina-manifiesta-su-disposicion-para-continuar-dialogo-con-comunidad-de-ango-raju/.

———. 2010. "San Marcos ya cuenta con un Centro de Producción de reproductores de cuyes." Electronic document, https://www.antamina.com/noticias/san_marcos_ya_cuenta_centro_produccion_reproductores_cuyes_2/.

———. 2013. *Reporte de Sostenibilidad 2012 Antamina*. CMA, Lima.

———. 2015. *Sustainability Report 2014*. CMA, Lima.

———. 2016. *Sustainability Report 2015*. CMA, Lima.

CODELCO (Corporación Nacional del Cobre). 2006. *Memoria anual 2006*. CODELCO, Santiago. https://www.codelco.com/flipbook/memorias/memoria2006/pdf/memoria.pdf.

———. 2015. "Presencia mundial." Electronic document, https://www.codelco.com/cgi-bin/prontus_imprimir.cgi?_URL=http%3A//www.codelco.com/prontus_codelco/site/artic/20110225/pags/20110225155417.html.

Collier, Paul, and Anke Hoeffler. 2000. "Greed and Grievance in Civil Wars." Working Paper No. 2355. World Bank, Washington, D.C.

Columbus, Christopher. 1906 [1503]. "Letter of Columbus on the Fourth Voyage," July 7. In *The Northmen, Columbus and Cabot, 985–1503: The Voyages of the Northmen; The Voyages of Columbus and of John Cabot*, edited by Julius E. Olson and Edward G. Bourne, pp. 387–418. Charles Scribner's Sons, New York. Online facsimile edition: www.americanjourneys.org/aj-068/.

Comaroff, Jean. 1985. *Body of Power, Spirit of Resistance: The Culture and History of a South African People*. University of Chicago Press, Chicago.

CONAM (Concejo Nacional del Medio Ambiente). 2001. *Informe final de la Comisión Técnica Multisectorial encargada de proponer mecanismos de participación ciudadana respecto a responsabilidades ambientales de la Compañía Minera Antamina en la zona de Huarmey*. CONAM, Huarmey.

Contreras, Carlos, and Marcos Cueto. 2007. *Historia del Perú contemporáneo: Desde las luchas por la independencia hasta el presente*. Instituto de Estudios Peruanos, Lima.

Convoca. 2015. *Excesos sin castigo: El rastro ambiental de las industrias extractivas en el Perú*. Convoca, Lima. https://issuu.com/convocape/docs/libro_final_12.

CooperAcción. 2016. *Noveno informe cartográfico sobre concesiones mineras en el Perú. Base de datos 2016*. Electronic document, http://cooperaccion.org.pe/informes/noveno-informe-cartografico-sobre-concesiones-mineras-en-el-peru-base-de-datos-mayo-2016/.

Corkery, Aiden. 2005. "Manhattan se va luego de pérdida de sesenta millones de dólares con Tambogrande-Peru." *Business News Americas*, February 8. Santiago. https://www.bnamericas.com/es/noticias/Manhattan_se_va_luego_de_perdida_de_US*60mn_con_Tambogrande.

Corporación Latinobarómetro. 2011. *Informe de prensa Latinobarómetro 1995–2011: Perú*. Corporación Latinobarómetro, Santiago. http://www.latinobarometro.org/documentos/LATBD_INFORME_LATINOBAROMETRO_Peru_1995_2011.pdf.

Corvetto, Aníbal. 1996. "Testimonio: Transferencia de concesiones mineras. Otorgado por CENTROMIN a CMA." Concession agreement, September 6. Lima. https://www.proyectosapp.pe/RepositorioAPS/0/0/JER/PACENTROMIN/Antamina/Contrato.pdf.

Crónica Viva. 2001. "Paro regional contra Antamina: Huarmey." April 16. Lima.
Crowley, Jack A., Rock H. Currier, and Terry Szenics. 1997. "Huanzalá Mine, Huallanca District." *Mineralogical Record* 28(4):47–54.
CVR (Comisión de la Verdad y Reconciliación). 2003 *Informe final*. CVR, Lima.
Dager, Joseph. 1999. "Minería en la independencia y temprana república. 1800–1840." In *Historia de la minería en el Perú*, edited by José Antonio del Busto, pp. 265–285. Compañía Minera MILPO S.A., Lima.
Dagnino, Evelina. 2006. "Meanings of Citizenship in Latin America." *Canadian Journal of Latin American and Caribbean Studies* 31(62):15–51.
Danielson, Luke. 2006. *Architecture for Change: An Account of the Mining Minerals and Sustainable Development Project*. Global Public Policy Institute, Berlin. https://pubs.iied.org/pdfs/G00975.pdf.
Dargent, Eduardo, José C. Orihuela, Maritza Paredes, and María E. Ulfe (editors). 2017. *Resource Booms and Institutional Pathways: The Case of the Extractive Industry in Peru*. Palgrave Macmillan, London.
Davis, Bob. 2005. "Seeking Latin America Growth." *Wall Street Journal*, February 23. New York.
de Echave, José. 2001. *Construyendo un proceso de toma de decisiones frente a operaciones mineras*. CooperAcción-Acción Solidaria para el Desarrollo, Lima.
———. 2005. "Peruvian Peasants Confront the Mining Industry." *Socialism and Democracy* 19(3):117–127.
de Echave, José, Alejandro Diez, Bruno Revesz, Ludwig Huber, Martín Tanaka, and Xavier Ricard Lanata. 2009. *Minería y conflicto social*. IEP, CIPCA, CBC, and CIES, Lima.
de la Cadena, Marisol. 2010. "Indigenous Cosmopolitics in the Andes: Conceptual Reflections Beyond 'Politics.'" *Cultural Anthropology* 25(2):334–370.
de la Cruz, Ricardo. 2011. "Diferencias entre regalías y canon en Perú." *Diario Gestión*, January 6. http://www.miningpress.com/nota/266686, accessed November 1, 2015.
Dewind, Adrian. 1975. "From Peasants to Miners: The Background to Strikes in the Mines of Peru." *Science and Society* 39(1):44–72.
DeWind, Josh. 1987. *Peasant Become Miners: The Evolution of Industrial Mining Systems in Peru, 1902–1974*. Garland, New York.
Diario Gestión. 2013. "Antamina se defiende: Cobre no llegó al agua y trabajos de remediación ya terminaron." June 4. Lima.
Díaz, Juan. 2006. *Nuevo Mapa de Pobreza del Fondo de Cooperación para el Desarrollo Social (FONCODES) 2006*. FONCODES, Lima.
Dietz, Thomas. 2001. "Policy Analysis." In *Encyclopedia of Global Change: Environmental Change and Human Society*, edited by Andrew Goudie and David J. Cuff, Vol. II, pp. 259–264. Oxford University Press, Oxford.
Dore, Elizabeth. 1988. *The Peruvian Mining Industry: Growth, Stagnation, and Crisis*. Westview Press, Boulder, Colorado.
———. 2000. "Environment and Society: Long-Term Trends in Latin American Mining." *Environment and History* 6:1–29.
Douglas, Mary. 2004 [1966]. *Purity and Danger: An Analysis of Concept of Pollution and Taboo*. Routledge, London.

Douglas, Mary, and Aaron Wildavsky. 1982. *Risk and Culture: An Essay on the Selection of Technological and Environmental Dangers*. University of California Press, Berkeley.

Dourojeanni, Marc J., and Carlos F. Ponce. 1978. *Los parques nacionales del Perú*. INCAFO and CIC, Madrid.

Dove, Michael R. 1999. "Writing for, Versus About, the Ethnographic Other: Issues of Engagement and Reflexivity in Working with a Tribal NGO in Indonesia." *Identities* 6(2–3):225–253.

Dove, Michael R., and Daniel M. Kammen. 2015. *Science, Society and the Environment: Applying Anthropology and Physics to Sustainability*. Routledge, New York.

DP (Defensoría del Pueblo). 2005. "Minería, desarrollo sostenible y derechos ciudadanos: Una aproximación inicial desde la Defensoría del Pueblo." Working paper. DP, Lima.

———. 2006a. *Conflictos sociales conocidos por la Defensoría del Pueblo al 30 de septiembre del 2006*. Report No. 31. DP, Lima.

———. 2006b. *Pasajeros en riesgo: La seguridad en el transporte interprovincial*. Defense Report No. 108. DP, Lima.

———. 2017. *Reporte mensual de conflictos sociales No. 155, enero 2017*. DP, Lima.

Echevarría, Evelio. 1981. "Early Mountaineering in Peru." In *Yuraq Janka: Guide to the Peruvian Andes. Part I: Cordilleras Blanca and Rosko*, edited by John F. Ricker, pp. 3–7. Alpine Club of Canada and American Alpine Club, Banff and New York.

EcoMetrix. 2005. *Resumen del programa de monitoreo de efectos ambientales de Antamina para el emplazamiento de la mina, 1998 a 2005*. Ecometrix, Brampton, Ontario.

Economist. 1995 "South American Mining: The New El Dorado." *Economist* 336(7930): 59–61.

———. 2005a. "160 Years On: It Is Time to Rebase our Commodity-Price Index." *Economist* 374(8413):72. https://www.economist.com/finance-and-economics/2005/02/10/160-years-on.

———. 2005b. "Mining in Peru: Halting the Rush Against Gold. Big Mining and Its Increasingly Radical Opponents." *Economist* 374(8412):47–48.

Edelman, Marc, and Angelique Haugerud. 2004. "Development." In *A Companion to the Anthropology of Politics*, edited by David Nugent and Joan Vincent, pp. 86–106. Blackwell, Malden, Massachusetts.

——— (editors). 2005. *The Anthropology of Development and Globalization: From Classical Political Economy to Contemporary Neoliberalism*. Blackwell, Malden, Massachusetts.

Eggert, Roderick G. 2001. "Mining and Economic Sustainability: National Economies and Local Communities." Report commissioned by the MMSD project of IIED. https://pubs.iied.org/pdfs/G00952.pdf.

El Comercio. 1995. "Se espera demanda de 20 mil nuevos trabajadores mineros para próximos años." September 13:E08. Lima.

———. 1996a. "En próximos 10 años invertirán US$ 15 mil millones en minería." November 3:A16. Lima.

———. 1996b. "Crece la inversión extranjera en el Perú. En los últimos tres años aumentó en 253.91%, según la Comisión Nacional de Inversiones y Tecnologías Extranjeras." October 13:E01. Lima.

———. 1997. "Casi se triplican las reservas de Antamina." February 2:E02. Lima.

———. 1998. "Antamina todavía está buscando financiar el yacimiento." September 17:E01. Lima.

———. 1999. "Antamina: Inversión esperanzadora." July 12:A23. Lima.

———. 2001a. "Nuevo coloso. Antamina incrementará el Producto Bruto Interno en cerca de 1.8%." June 1:B03. Lima.

———. 2001b. "Protesta desmedida. Bloquean tránsito en Panamericana Norte." June 20:A10. Lima.

———. 2006. "Empresa minera genera canon. Antamina transfiere 480 millones de soles a Ancash." April 21:A01. Lima.

———. 2018. "Anemia afecta a cuatro de cada diez niños menores de tres años a nivel nacional." August 20. Lima. https://elcomercio.pe/juntos-contra-anemia/ultimas/prevalencia-anemia-mayor-sierra-selva-pais-noticia-548620.

Escobal, Javier, and Carmen Ponce. 2008. *Dinámicas provinciales de pobreza en el Perú 1993–2005*. Working Paper 11. Rimisp, Santiago.

Escobar, Arturo. 1991. "Anthropology and the Development Encounter." *American Ethnologist* 18(4):658–682.

———. 1995. *Encountering Development: The Making and Unmaking of the Third World*. Princeton University Press, Princeton, New Jersey.

———. 1996. "Constructing Nature: Elements for a Poststructural Political Ecology." In *Liberation Ecologies: Environment, Development, Social Movements*, edited by Richard Peet and Michael Watts, pp. 46–68. Routledge, London.

———. 1998. "Whose Knowledge, Whose Nature? Biodiversity, Conservation, and the Political Ecology of Social Movements." *Journal of Political Ecology* 5:53–76.

Espinosa, Lorena, and Oscar Aybar. 2016. *Formas de organización, relaciones intracomunitarias y beneficios recibidos de la Compañía Minera Antamina en Huaripampa*. Master's thesis, Pontifical Catholic University of Peru, San Miguel.

Evans, Geoff, James Goodman, and Nina Lansbury (editors). 2002. *Moving Mountains: Communities Confront Mining and Globalisation*. Palgrave, London.

Ferguson, James. 1994. *The Anti-Politics Machine: "Development," Depoliticization, and Bureaucratic Power in Lesotho*. University of Minnesota Press, Minneapolis.

———. 1999. *Expectations of Modernity: Myths and Meanings of Urban Life on the Zambian Copperbelt*. University of California Press, Berkeley.

———. 2002. "Development." In *Encyclopedia of Social and Cultural Anthropology*, edited by Alan Barnard and Jonathan Spencer, pp. 154–160. Routledge, London.

Ferguson, James, and Akhil Gupta. 2002. "Spatializing States: Toward an Ethnography of Neoliberal Governmentality." *American Ethnologist* 29(4):981–1002.

Flores Galindo, Alberto. 1993 [1974]. *Los mineros de la Cerro de Pasco, 1900–1930: Un intento de caracterización social*. Obras Completas I. Fundación Andina and SUR Casa de Estudios del Socialismo, Lima.

Flores Ochoa, Jorge A. (editor). 1977. *Pastores de puna: Uywamichiq punarunakuna*. Instituto de Estudios Peruanos, Lima.

Forero, Juan. 2005. "Latin America Fails to Deliver on Basic Needs." *New York Times*, February 22. New York.

Fortun, Kim. 2001. *Advocacy After Bhopal: Environmentalism, Disaster, New Global Orders*. University of Chicago Press, Chicago.
Foucault, Michael. 1980. *The Archaeology of Knowledge*. Harper and Row, New York.
Franklin, Benjamin. 2004 [1733–1758]. *Poor Richard's Almanack*. Barnes & Noble, New York.
Gálvez, Carlos. 1999. "Los tesoros del conquistador: Minería en la primera mitad del siglo XVI." In *Historia de la minería en el Perú*, edited by José Antonio del Busto, pp. 85–125. Compañía Minera MILPO S.A., Lima.
García, Alan. 2007. "El perro del hortelano." *El Comercio*, October 27. Lima.
Gil Ramón, Vladimir R. 2005. *Strategies in Local Conflicts with a Transnational Mining Corporation in Peru: The Antamina Case, 1996–2003*. PhD dissertation, Yale University, New Haven, Connecticut.
———. 2009. *Aterrizaje minero: Cultura, conflicto, negociaciones y lecciones para el desarrollo desde la minería en Ancash, Perú*. Instituto de Estudios Peruanos, Lima.
———. 2010. Review of *Tambogrande: Mangos, Murder, Mining*, by Ernesto Cabellos and Stephanie Boyd. *Visual Anthropology* 23:65–67.
———. 2014. "Is Environmental Deregulation in Peru's Best Interest?" *Al Jazeera*, August 12. Doha, Qatar. http://www.aljazeera.com/indepth/opinion/2014/08/environmental-deregulation-per-2014812111722135954.html.
———. 2017. "Human Ecology of the Andes." In *Oxford Bibliographies in Ecology*, edited by David Gibson. Oxford University Press, New York. https://www.oxfordbibliographies.com/view/document/obo-9780199830060/obo-9780199830060-0175.xml.
Gingrich, Andre. 2002. "When Ethnic Majorities Are 'Dethroned': Towards a Methodology of Self-Reflexive, Controlled Macrocomparison." In *Anthropology, by Comparison*, edited by Andre Gingrich and Richard G. Fox, pp. 225-248. New York: Routledge.
Glave, Manuel, and Vladimir R. Gil Ramón. 1998. "La reforma de la propiedad de los recursos naturales agrícolas y su impacto sobre la organización social y la toma de decisiones en el campo." Working paper. GRADE, Lima.
Glave, Manuel, and Juana Kuramoto. 2002. "Minería, minerales y desarrollo sustentable en el Perú." In *Minería, minerales y desarrollo sustentable en América del Sur*, edited by Equipo MMSD América del Sur, pp. 529–591. CIPMA, IDRC, and IIPM, London.
Godoy, Ricardo. 1985. "Mining: Anthropological Perspectives." *Annual Review of Anthropology* 14:199–217.
Goldstein, Donna M. 2017. "Commentary: Science, Politics, and Risk: Catastrophic Asia from the Perspective of a Brazilianist Anthropologist." *Journal of Asian Studies* 76(2):481–497.
Golte, Jürgen, and Marisol de la Cadena. 1983. "La codeterminación de la organización social andina." *Allpanchis* 19(22):7–34.
Golub, Alex. 2014. *Leviathans at the Gold Mine: Creating Indigenous and Corporate Actors in Papua New Guinea*. Durham, NC: Duke University Press.
GPC (Grupo Propuesta Ciudadana). 2012. "Programa minero de solidaridad con el pueblo 2006–2011: Aporte voluntario en Áncash, fondo minero Antamina." GPC, Lima.

GRADE (Grupo de Análisis para el Desarrollo). 1999. "Gran minería y la comunidad." GRADE, Lima.

———. 2000. "Evaluación del proceso de reubicación y del programa de postreubicación en Antamina: Informe final." GRADE, Lima.

———. 2001. "Notas complementarias al informe final (evaluación del proceso de reubicación y del programa de postreubicación en Antamina)." GRADE, Lima.

Graeber, David. 2005. "The Globalization Movement: Some Points of Clarification." In Marc Edelman and Angelique Haugerud, *The Anthropology of Development and Globalization: From Classical Political Economy to Contemporary Neoliberalism*, pp. 169–172. Blackwell, Malden, Massachusetts.

Greenpeace. 2003. *Noranda: Desde Canadá a la Patagonia, una vida de crímenes*. Greenpeace, Amsterdam.

Gregory, Steven. 2008. "Infrapolitics." In *A Companion to the Anthropology of Politics*, edited by David Nugent and Joan Vincent, pp. 282–302. John Wiley & Sons, Malden, Massachusetts.

Grillo, Ralph D., and Roderick L. Stirrat (editors). 1997. *Discourses of Development: Anthropological Perspectives*. Berg, Oxford and New York.

Grupo Allpa. 2012. *Memoria institucional, 1997–2012*. Grupo Allpa, Lima.

GTH (Grupo de Trabajo Huascarán). 2000. "The Huascarán Working Group: A Conflict Resolution Experience in a Biosphere Reserve." GTH, Huaraz.

GTH and INRENA. 2000. "Antecedentes del grupo de trabajo Huascarán." GTH, Huaraz.

Guaman Poma de Ayala, Felipe. 2004 [1615/1616]. *El primer nueva corónica y buen gobierno*. The Royal Library, Copenhagen. http://www.kb.dk/permalink/2006/poma/info/en/frontpage.htm.

Gudeman, Stephen, and Alberto Rivera. 1990. *Conversations in Colombia: The Domestic Economy in Life and Text*. Cambridge University Press, Cambridge.

Guerra, Margarita. 1999. "La minería entre 1950 y 1998." In *Historia de la minería en el Perú*, edited by José Antonio del Busto, pp. 315–347. Compañía Minera MILPO S.A., Lima.

Guha, Ramachandra. 1989. *The Unquiet Woods: Ecological Change and Peasant Resistance*. Oxford University Press, Delhi.

Guigale, Marcelo M., Vicente Fretes-Cibils, and John Newman. 2007. *An Opportunity for a Different Peru: Prosperous, Equitable, and Governable*. World Bank, Washington, D.C.

Habermas, Jürgen. 1996. *Between Fact and Norm: Contributions to a Discourse Theory of Law and Democracy*. Cambridge, MA: MIT Press.

Hamilton, Lawrence S. (editor). 1998a. *Mountain Protected Areas Update: June 1998*. Electronic document, http://www.mtnforum.org/resources/library/hamil98b.htm, accessed March 3, 2004.

———. 1998b. *Mountain Protected Areas Update: September 1998*. Electronic document, http://www.mtnforum.org/resources/library/hamil98c.htm, accessed September 24, 2000.

Harvey, David. 2003. *The New Imperialism*. Oxford University Press, Oxford.

Hein, Jayni Foley, and Caroline Cecot. 2017. "Mineral Royalties: Historical Uses and Justifications." *Duke Environmental Law & Policy Forum* 28:1–30.

Hernández, Francisco. 1999. "La minería en el Tahuantinsuyo." In *Historia de la minería en el Perú*, edited by José Antonio del Busto, pp. 59–83. Compañía Minera MILPO S.A., Lima.

Hirschman, Albert O. 1958. *The Strategy of Economic Development*. Yale University Press, New Haven, Connecticut.

———. 1978. "Exit, Voice, and the State." *World Politics* 1(31):90–107.

Hoffman, Kelly, and Miguel A. Centeno. 2003. "The Lopsided Continent." *Annual Review of Sociology* 29:363–390.

Humphreys, Macartan. 2005. "Natural Resources, Conflict, and Conflict Resolution." *Journal of Conflict Resolution* 49(4):508–537.

Humphreys, Macartan, Jeffrey D. Sachs, and Joseph E. Stiglitz (editors). 2007. *Escaping the Resource Curse*. Columbia University Press, New York.

Ian Thomson Consulting. 1999. "Revisión y evaluación del programa de reubicación, plan de desarrollo de la comunidad y programa de relaciones con la comunidad de Compañía Minera Antamina." CMA. Ian Thomson Consulting, Vancouver.

IBC (Instituto del Bien Común). 2015. *La gran deuda del Estado frente a las comunidades*. Electronic document, http://www.ibcperu.org/noticia/titulacion-la-gran-deuda-del-estado-frente-a-las-comunidades/.

IDB (Inter-American Development Bank). 1998 "Operational Policy on Involuntary Resettlement (OP-710)." Prevailing Reference Document: GN-1979-3. IDB, Washington, D.C. https://www.iadb.org/en/about-us/about-us-7.

IDMA (Instituto de Desarrollo y Medio Ambiente). 2004. "Balance de la labor institucional IDMA 2004." IDMA, Lima. http://www.idmaperu.org/info-idma-2004.pdf.

IFC (International Finance Corporation). 2012 [2006]. "Performance Standards on Environmental and Social Sustainability." IFC, Washington, D.C. https://www.ifc.org/wps/wcm/connect/topics_ext_content/ifc_external_corporate_site/sustainability-at-ifc/publications/publications_handbook_pps.

ILO (International Labour Organization). 1989. "Convention Concerning Indigenous and Tribal Peoples in Independent Countries (ILO No. 169)." https://www.ilo.org/dyn/normlex/en/f?p=NORMLEXPUB:12100:0::NO::P12100_ILO_CODE:C169.

Incháustegui, Juan. 1999. "Para la agenda del desarrollo nacional." *El Comercio*, August 24: A15. Lima.

INEI (Instituto Nacional de Estadística e Informática). 2005. *Perú: Compendio estadístico 2005*. INEI, Lima.

———. 2017. *Evolución de la pobreza monetaria del Perú, 2007–2016*. INEI, Lima.

———. 2018. *Perú: Mapa de Necesidades Básicas Insatisfechas, 1993, 2007 y 2017*. INEI, Lima. https://www.inei.gob.pe/media/MenuRecursivo/publicaciones_digitales/Est/Lib1588/.

Ingold, Tim. 2003. "Introduction to Culture." In *Companion Encyclopedia of Anthropology: Humanity, Culture and Social Life*, edited by Tim Ingold, pp. 329–349. Routledge, New York.

INRENA (Instituto Nacional de Recursos Naturales). 2003. *Parque Nacional Huascarán. Plan Maestro 2003–2007*. INRENA, Lima.

INRENA and SPDA (Sociedad Peruana de Derecho Ambiental). 2002. *Compendio de legislación de áreas naturales protegidas*. INRENA and SPDA, Lima.

IOP (Instituto de Opinión Pública-PUCP). 2007. *Boletín Estado de la Opinión Pública: Empresa 2*. Electronic document, http://repositorio.pucp.edu.pe/index//handle/123456789/15768.

IPE (Instituto Peruano de Economía). 2017. "El valor agregado de la minería en el Perú." IDEM, Lima.

Janofsky, Michael. 2004. "E.P.A. Says Mercury Taints Fish Across U.S." *New York Times*, August 25. New York.

Johnston, David. 2007. "How to Evaluate the Fiscal Terms of Oil Contracts." In *Escaping the Resource Curse*, edited by Macartan Humphreys, Jeffrey D. Sachs, and Joseph E. Stiglitz, pp. 53–88. Columbia University Press, New York.

Junkerman, John (director). 2002. *Power and Terror: Noam Chomsky in Our Time*. Siglo, Tokyo.

Kahatt, Karim. 2003. "Financiamiento y medio ambiente: El impacto de los aspectos ambientales en las políticas crediticias de las instituciones financieras." *Thémis. Revista de Derecho* 46:255–278.

Kapelus, Paul. 2002. "Mining, Corporate Social Responsibility and the 'Community': The Case of Rio Tinto, Richards Bay Minerals and the Mbonambi." *Journal of Business Ethics* 39(3):275–296.

Kaplan, David. 1998. "Gift Exchange." In *The Dictionary of Anthropology*, edited by Thomas Barfield, pp. 224–225. Blackwell, Oxford and Malden.

Karl, Terry L. 1997. *The Paradox of Plenty: Oil Booms and Petro-states*. Berkeley: University of California Press.

Katona, Jacqui. 2002. "Mining Uranium and Indigenous Australians: The Fight for Jabiluka." In *Moving Mountains: Communities Confront Mining and Globalisation*, edited by Geoff Evans, James Goodman, and Nina Lansbury, pp. 195–206. Palgrave, London.

K&H (Knight Piésold Consultores S.A. and Hallam Knight Piésold Ltd.). 1998. *Addendum 2 del EIA para el Proyecto Antamina*. CMA, Lima. http://intranet2.minem.gob.pe/web/archivos/dgaam/estudios/antamina/addendum2/AddendumII.PDF.

———. 1999a. *Addendum 3 del EIA para el Proyecto Antamina (Volumen I)*. CMA, Lima. http://intranet2.minem.gob.pe/web/archivos/dgaam/estudios/antamina/addendum3/Addendum3.PDF.

———. 1999b. *Addendum 3 del EIA para el Proyecto Antamina (Volumen II)*. CMA, Lima. http://intranet2.minem.gob.pe/web/archivos/dgaam/estudios/antamina/addendum3/Anexo2.pdf.

Kirsch, Stuart. 2014. *Mining Capitalism: The Relationship Between Corporations and Their Critics*. University of California Press, Oakland.

Kriesberg, Louis. 1999. "Social Conflict." In *The Social Science Encyclopedia*, edited by Adam Kuper and Jessica Kuper, pp. 122–125. Routledge, London.

Kruijt, Dirk, and Menno Vellinga. 1979. *Labor Relations and Multinational Corporations: The Cerro de Pasco Corporation in Peru (1902–1974).* Van Gorcum, Assen.

Krupa, Christopher, and David Nugent (editors). 2015. *State Theory and Andean Politics: New Approaches to the Study of Rule.* University of Pennsylvania Press, Philadelphia.

KS (Klohn Crippen—SVS S.A. Ingenieros Consultores). 1998a. *Estudio de Impacto Ambiental: Compañía Minera Antamina.* CMA, Lima. http://intranet2.minem.gob.pe/web/archivos/dgaam/estudios/antamina/estudioantamina.htm.

———. 1998b. *Estudio de Impacto Ambiental: Addendum 1.* CMA, Lima.

Kuipers, Jim, Ann S. Maest, Kimberley A. MacHardy, and Gregory Lawson. 2006. *Comparison of Predicted and Actual Water Quality at Hardrock Mines: The Reliability of Predictions in Environmental Impact Statements.* Earthworks, Washington, D.C.

Kuramoto, Juana. 2000. *Las aglomeraciones productivas alrededor de la minería: El caso de la Minera Yanacocha S.A.* UN, Santiago de Chile.

Kuramoto, Juana, Zoila Martínez, Edgardo Llerena, and Gabriel Quijandría. 2002. *Participación comunitaria en el monitoreo de las actividades mineras: Los casos de Vicos y de San Mateo de Huanchor.* GRADE, APGEP-SENREM, and USAID-CONAM, Lima.

Laite, Julian. 1980. "Miners and National Politics in Peru, 1900–1974." *Journal of Latin American Studies* 12:317–340.

———. 1984. "Migration and Social Differentiation Amongst Mantaro Valley Peasants." In *Miners, Peasants and Entrepreneurs,* edited by Norman Long and Bryan Roberts, pp. 107–139. Cambridge University Press, Cambridge.

Laite, Julian, and Norman Long. 1987. "*Fiestas* and Uneven Capitalist Development in Central Peru." *Bulletin of Latin American Research* 6(1):27–53.

Larson, Brooke. 1995. "Andean Communities, Political Cultures, and Markets: The Changing Contours of a Field." In *Ethnicity, Markets, and Migration in the Andes: At the Crossroads of History and Anthropology,* edited by Brooke Larson, Olivia Harris, and Enrique Tandeter, pp. 5–54. Duke University Press, Durham, North Carolina.

Latour, Bruno. 2004. *Politics of Nature: How to Bring the Sciences into Democracy.* Harvard University Press, Cambridge, Massachusetts.

Law, Jonathan. 2018. "Perfect Information." In *A Dictionary of Finance and Banking.* Oxford University Press, Oxford. https://www.oxfordreference.com/view/10.1093/acref/9780198789741.001.0001/acref-9780198789741-e-7283?rskey=ebmGuO&result=1.

Lechtman, Heather. 1984. "Andean Value Systems and the Development of Prehistoric Metallurgy." *Technology and Culture* 25(1):1–36.

Li, Fabiana. 2015. *Unearthing Conflict: Corporate Mining, Activism, and Expertise in Peru.* Duke University Press, Durham, North Carolina.

Loayza, Norman, and Jamele Rigolini. 2016. "The Local Impact of Mining on Poverty and Inequality: Evidence from the Commodity Boom in Peru." *World Development* 84:219–234.

Long, Norman, and Bryan R. Roberts. 1984. *Miners, Peasants, and Entrepreneurs: Regional Development in the Central Highlands of Peru.* Cambridge University Press, Cambridge and New York.

Love, David A., Alan H. Clark, and J. Keith Glover. 2004. "The Lithologic, Stratigraphic, and Structural Setting of the Giant Antamina Copper-Zinc Skarn Deposit, Ancash, Peru." *Economic Geology* 99(5):887–916.

Loveday, James, and Oswaldo Molina. 2006. "NGOs, the Extractive Industries and Community Development: The Case of NGO Labor in Peru." ODI, London. http://www.odi.org.uk/rapid/projects/ppa0104/docs/CS8_Oswald_Molina_Environment.pdf.

Macleod, Murdo J. 1997. "Aspects of the Internal Economy of Colonial Spanish America: Labour; Taxation; Distribution and Exchange." In *The Cambridge History of Latin America. Vol. 2: Colonial Latin America*, edited by Leslie Bethell, pp. 219–264. Cambridge University Press, Cambridge.

Mallon, Florencia E. 1983. *The Defense of Commmunity in Peru's Central Highlands: Peasant Struggle and Capitalist Transition, 1860–1940.* Princeton University Press, Princeton, New Jersey.

Markham, Clements Robert. 1872. *Reports on the Discovery of Peru.* Berkeley: Printed for the Hakluyt Society.

Martínez-Alier, Joan. 1990. "La interpretación ecologista de la historia socioeconómica: Algunos ejemplos andinos." *Revista Andina* 8(1):9–46.

———. 2002. *The Environmentalism of the Poor: A Study of Ecological Conflicts and Valuation.* Edward Elgar, Northampton.

Mauss, Marcel. 1990 [1950]. *The Gift: The Form and Reason for Exchange in Archaic Societies.* Routledge, London and New York.

Mayer, Enrique. 1992. "Peru in Deep Trouble: Mario Vargas Llosa's 'Inquest in the Andes' Reexamined." In *Rereading Cultural Anthropology*, edited by George E. Marcus, pp. 181–219. Duke University Press, Durham, North Carolina.

———. 2002. *The Articulated Peasant: Household Economies in the Andes.* Westview Press, Boulder, Colorado.

———. 2009. *Cuentos feos de la Reforma Agraria.* Instituto de Estudios Peruanos, Lima.

McManus, Phil. 2002. "Environmental Impact Assessment." In *Encyclopedia of Global Change: Environmental Change and Human Society*, edited by Andrew Goudie, pp. 376–378. Oxford University Press, Oxford.

MEF (Ministerio de Economía y Finanzas). 2017. "Portal de Transparencia Económica." Electronic document, www.mef.gob.pe/es/portal-de-transparencia-economica.

Mejía, Maurilio. 2002. "La carretera de Aija a Huarmey." *Nuestra Época: Para una sola voz, un mismo pueblo. Una revista para Huarmey y Aija* 3:15.

MEM (Ministerio de Energía y Minas del Perú). 2007. *Anuario Minero 2006.* MEM, Lima.

———. 2017. *Anuario Minero 2016.* MEM, Lima.

Mendoza, Armando, and José de Echave. 2016. *¿Pagaron lo justo? Política fiscal peruana en tiempos del boom minero.* Oxfam and CooperAcción, Lima.

Mendoza, Juan. 1999. "Integración." *El Comercio*, September 4:B03. Lima.

MIM (Mejorando la Inversión Municipal). 2012. *Boletín MIM Informa: Ancash*, no. 8. MIM, Huaraz.

MINAM (Ministerio del Ambiente del Perú). 2015. "Mesa de diálogo de Cajacay (Áncash)." *Diálogo*. Informative Bulletin 1:10–11.

MMSD (Mining, Minerals and Sustainable Development). 2002. *Breaking New Ground: Mining, Minerals and Sustainable Development*. Earthscan, London.

MMSD América del Sur. 2002. *Minería, minerales y desarrollo sustentable en América del Sur*. CIPMA, MMSD, IDRC-CRDI, and MPRI/IIPM, London.

Moir, Lance. 2001. "What Do We Mean by Corporate Social Responsibility?" *Corporate Governance* 1(2):16–23.

Morote, Efraín. 1998. *Aldeas sumergidas: Cultura popular y sociedad en los Andes*. Centro de Estudios Rurales Andinos "Bartolomé de las Casas," Cusco.

Mumford, Jeremy Ravi. 2012. *Vertical Empire: The General Resettlement of Indians in the Colonial Andes*. Duke University Press, Durham and London.

Muradian, Roldan, Joan Martínez-Alier, and Humberto Correa. 2003. "International Capital Versus Local Population: The Environmental Conflict of the Tambogrande Mining Project, Peru." *Society and Natural Resources* 16:775–792.

Murra, John. 1975. *Formaciones económicas y políticas del mundo andino*. Instituto de Estudios Peruanos, Lima.

Nash, June. 1993 [1979]. *We Eat the Mines and the Mines Eat Us: Dependency and Exploitation in Bolivian Tin Mines*. Columbia University Press, New York.

North, Douglass C. 1990. *Institutions, Institutional Change and Economic Performance*. Cambridge University Press, Cambridge.

OEFA (Organismo de Evaluación y Fiscalización Ambiental). 2013. "Resolución Directoral No. 262–2013-OEFA-DFSAI." OEFA, Lima.

Oliver-Smith, Anthony. 1996. "Anthropological Research on Hazards and Disasters." *Annual Review of Anthropology* 25:303–328.

Ong, Aiwa. 1987. *Spirits of Resistance and Capitalist Discipline: Factory Women in Malaysia*. State University of New York Press, Albany.

Orlove, Benjamin. 1977. *Alpacas, Sheep, and Men: The Wool Export Economy and Regional Society of Southern Peru*. Academic Press, New York.

Ortiz, Joaquín. 1997. "Impulsar el desarrollo: Entrevista con Alberto Pandolfi." *El Comercio*, June 9. Lima.

Ostrom, Elinor. 1990. *Governing the Commons: The Evolution of Institutions for Collective Action*. Cambridge University Press, Cambridge.

Payne, J. Mark, Daniel Zovatto G., Fernando Carrillo, and Andrés Allamand. 2002. *Democracies in Development: Politics and Reform in Latin America*. IDB and International Institute for Democracy and Electoral Assistance, Washington, D.C. Distributed by Johns Hopkins University Press, Baltimore, Maryland.

Peet, Richard, and Michael Watts (editors). 1996. *Liberation Ecologies: Environment, Development, Social Movements*. Routledge, London.

Pigg, Stacy. 1997. "Found in Most Traditional Societies: Traditional Medical Practitioners Between Culture and Development." In *International Development and the Social Sciences: Essays on the History and Politics of Knowledge*, edited by Frederick Cooper and Randall Packard, pp. 259–290. University of California Press, Berkeley.

PNP (Policía Nacional del Perú). 2006. *Anuario estadístico policial*. PNP, Lima.

———. 2012. *Anuario estadístico*. PNP, Lima.

PNUD (Programa de las Naciones Unidas para el Desarrollo). 2005. *Informe sobre desarrollo humano Perú 2005: Hagamos de la competitividad una oportunidad para todos*. PNUD, Lima.

Porter, Joe. 1994. "Saving Mining Is a Good Business." *Engineering and Mining Journal* 195(10):66–69.

Portocarrero, Felipe, Cynthia Sanborn, Sergio Llusera, and Viviana Quea. 2000. *Empresas, fundaciones y medios: La responsabilidad social en el Perú*. CIUP, Lima.

Pratt, Jane. 1998. "An Example of the Network in Action on Antamina Mine and Peru's Huascarán National Park." *Mountain Protected Areas Update*, June. http://www.mtnforum.org/resources/library/hamil98c.htm, accessed January 12, 2004.

———. 2001. "Corporations, Communities, and Conservation: TMI and Antamina Mining Company." *California Management Review* 43(3):38–43.

Pulgar-Vidal, Manuel. 1999. "Actividad minera y comunidades: Bases para un mejor entendimiento." International Congress of Mining Legislation, October 14, Lima.

———. 2002. "Recursos naturales y lucha contra la pobreza: ¿Una articulación posible? Una aproximación desde el derecho ambiental y el concepto de sostenibilidad." In *Perú: El problema agrario en debate (SEPIA IX)*, edited by Manuel Pulgar-Vidal, Eduardo Zegarra, and Jaime Urrutia, pp. 21–82. SEPIA, CIES, CARE Perú Puno, and OXFAM, Lima.

———. 2006. "Conflictos sociales: La lógica perversa del conflicto y sus insuficientes respuestas." *Ideele* 179:44–46.

Pulgar-Vidal, Manuel, and Adriana Aurazo (editors). 2003. *Mejorando la participación ciudadana en el proceso de evaluación de impacto ambiental en minería*. SPDA, Lima.

Pulido, Víctor. 1991. *El libro rojo de la fauna silvestre del Perú*. INIAA, WWF-US, US Fish and Wildlife Service, Lima.

Quiroz, Alfonso W. 2013. *Historia de la corrupción en el Perú*. Instituto de Estudios Peruanos, Lima.

Rahnema, Majid. 1992. "Participation." In *Development Dictionary: A Guide to Knowledge as Power*, edited by Wolfgang Sachs, pp. 127–144. Zed Books, London.

Raimondi, Antonio. 1873. *El Departamento de Ancachs y sus riquezas minerales*. Imprenta El Nacional, Lima.

Rappaport, Roy A. 1993. "Distinguished Lecture in General Anthropology: The Anthropology of Trouble." *American Anthropologist* 95(2):295–303.

Ray, Rebecca, Kevin Gallagher, Andres López, and Cynthia Sanborn. 2017. *China and Sustainable Development in Latin America: The Social and Environmental Dimension*. Anthem Press, London.

Renn, Ortwin, Thomas Webler, and Peter M. Wiedemann (editors). 1995. *Fairness and Competence in Citizen Participation: Evaluating Models for Environmental Discourse*. Kluwer Academic, Dordrecht.

Ricker, John F. 1981. *Yuraq Janka: Guide to the Peruvian Andes. Part I: Cordilleras Blanca and Rosko*. Alpine Club of Canada and American Alpine Club, Banff and New York.

Rizo-Patrón, Paul. 1999. "La minería entre 1900 y 1950." In *Historia de la minería en el Perú*, edited by José Antonio del Busto, pp. 315–347. Compañía Minera MILPO S.A., Lima.

Robles, Román. 2003. "Efectos de la minería moderna en tres regiones del Perú." *Revista de Antropología* 1(1):31–70.

Rogers, Douglas. 2012. "The Materiality of the Corporation: Oil, Gas, and Corporate Social Technologies in the Remaking of a Russian Region." *American Ethnologist* 39(2):284–296.

Romero, César. 2010. "Fujimorismo robó US$ 6 mil millones." *La República*, April 14. Lima.

Rosales, Cecilia. 2001. "Buenos augurios: Toledo sostiene que la producción de Antamina beneficiará al país." *El Comercio,* November 15:A04. Lima.

Rosales, Efraín. 2005. "Veinte heridos deja movilización en Huaraz contra mineras." *La República*, March 8. Lima.

Ross, Michael. 1999. "The Political Economy of the Resource Curse." *World Politics* 51:297–322.

———. 2001. *Extractive Sectors and the Poor.* Oxfam America, Washington D.C.

———. 2006. "A Closer Look at Oil, Diamonds, and Civil War." *Annual Review of Political Science* 9:265–300.

———. 2007. "How Can Mineral Rich States Reduce Inequality?" In *Escaping the Resource Curse*, edited by Macartan Humphreys, Jeffrey D. Sachs, and Joseph E. Stiglitz, pp. 237–255. Columbia University Press, New York.

Rouse, Michael J., and Usher Fleising. 1995. "Miners and Managers: Workplace Cultures in a British Columbia Coal Mine." *Human Organization* 54:238–248.

Rousseau, Jean-Jacques. 1997 [1761]. *Julie, Or, The New Heloise: Letters of Two Lovers Who Live in a Small Town at the Foot of the Alps Works.* University Press of New England, Hanover.

Sachs, Jeffrey D., and Andrew M. Warner. 1995. "Natural Resource Abundance and Economic Growth." Development Discussion Paper 517a. Harvard Institute for International Development, Cambridge, Massachusetts.

Sahlins, Marshall. 1963. "Poor Man, Rich Man, Big-Man, Chief: Political Types in Melanesia and Polynesia." *Comparative Studies in Society and History* 5(3):285–303.

———. 1972. *Stone Age Economics.* Aldine-Atherton, Chicago.

Salas, Guillermo. 2002. "Dinámica social, reciprocidad y reestructuración de sistemas de acceso a recursos: Las familias pastoras de Yanacancha y la presencia del Proyecto Antamina." Licentiate thesis, Pontifical Catholic University of Peru, San Miguel.

Salomon, Frank, and Mercedes Niño-Murcia. 2011. *The Lettered Mountain: A Peruvian Village's Way with Writing.* Duke University Press, Durham, North Carolina.

Sanborn, Cynthia A., Verónica Hurtado, and Tania Ramírez. 2016. "Consulta Previa in Peru: Moving Forward." Report prepared for Americas Society/Council of the Americas. CIUP and Americas Society/Council of the Americas, Lima. http://www.as-coa.org/sites/default/files/2015_CP_PERU_June_29.pdf.

Sánchez, Martín. 2015. "A La Oroya le interesa la inversión minera." *Perú 21*, August 14. Lima. https://peru21.pe/opinion/oroya-le-interesa-inversion-minera-192177-noticia/.
Santos, Fernando, and Frederica Barclay. 2002. *La frontera domesticada: historia económica y social de Loreto, 1850–2000*. Fondo Editorial PUCP, Lima.
Sawyer, Suzana. 2004. *Crude Chronicles: Indigenous Politics, Multinational Oil, and Neoliberalism in Ecuador*. Duke University Press, Durham, North Carolina.
Schmidt, Corinne A. 1999. "Public Participation, Environmental Policy, and Transnational Mining in Peru." Masters thesis, Johns Hopkins University, Baltimore, Maryland.
Schmink, Marianne, and Charles H. Wood. 1992. *Contested Frontiers in Amazonia*. Columbia University Press, New York.
Scott, James C. 1976. *Moral Economy of the Peasant: Rebellion and Subsistence in Southeast Asia*. Yale University Press, New Haven, Connecticut.
———. 1985. *Weapons of the Weak: Everyday Forms of Peasant Resistance*. Yale University Press, New Haven, Connecticut.
———. 1998. *Seeing Like a State: How Certain Schemes to Improve the Human Condition Have Failed*. Yale University Press, New Haven, Connecticut.
Scott, John, and Gordon Marshall. 2005a. "Enclave." In *A Dictionary of Sociology*. Oxford University Press, Oxford. http://www.oxfordreference.com/views/ENTRY.html?subview=Main&entry=t88.e720.
———. 2005b. "Gini coefficient." In *A Dictionary of Sociology*. Oxford University Press, Oxford. http://www.oxfordreference.com/views/ENTRY.html?subview=Main&entry=t88.e932.
Scurrah, Martín (editor). 2008. *Defendiendo derechos y promoviendo cambios: el Estado, las empresas extractivas y las comunidades locales en el Perú*. OXFAM International, Lima.
Sen, Amartya. 2002. "How to Judge Globalism." *American Prospect* 13(1):2–6.
SERNANP (Servicio Nacional de Áreas Naturales Protegidas por el Estado). 2017. "Mapa de Áreas Naturales Protegidas." http://www.sernanp.gob.pe/documents/10181/165150/Mapa%20publicacion%20Pag%20web%202017-02-24.pdf/af8e3ba3-9a1a-4a71-ad78-4db3fc9a2ef6.
Sheahan, John. 1999. *Searching for a Better Society: The Peruvian Economy from 1950*. Pennsylvania State University Press, University Park.
SPDA (Sociedad Peruana de Derecho Ambiental) Actualidad Ambiental. 2015. "Mineras y su resistencia a adecuarse a límites máximos permisibles y a estándares de calidad ambiental." https://www.actualidadambiental.pe/mineras-y-su-resistencia-a-adecuarse-a-limites-maximos-permisibles-y-a-estandares-de-calidad-ambiental/.
Speart, Jessica. 1995. "A Lust for Gold. Cyanide Heap Leaching Mining Pollution in the Western U.S." *Mother Jones* 20(1). https://www.motherjones.com/politics/1995/01/lust-gold/.
Spielberg, Steven (director). 1977. *Close Encounters of the Third Kind*. Columbia Pictures, Los Angeles.

Strathern, Marilyn. 2000. *Audit Cultures: Anthropological Studies in Accountability, Ethics, and the Academy.* Routledge, London.

SUNAT (Superintendencia Nacional de Administración Tributaria). 2002. "Estimación del efecto de los convenios de estabilidad jurídica sobre la recaudación." SUNAT, Lima.

Szablowski, David. 2002. "Mining, Displacement and the World Bank: A Case Analysis of Compañía Minera Antamina's Operations in Peru." *Journal of Business Ethics* 3(39):247–273.

Tarrow, Sydney. 1999. "Social Movements." In *The Social Science Encyclopedia*, edited by Adam Kuper and Jessica Kuper, pp. 792–794. Routledge, New York.

Taussig, Michael T. 1980. *The Devil and Commodity Fetishism in South America.* University of North Carolina Press, Chapel Hill.

Thorp, Rosemary, and Geoffrey Bertram. 1978. *Peru, 1890–1977: Growth and Policy in an Open Economy.* Columbia University Press, New York.

Tilly, Charles. 1995. "Citizenship, Identity and Social History." *International Review of Social History* 40:1–17.

TMI (The Mountain Institute). 1996. *Implementing the Mountain Agenda: A Report from The Mountain Institute.* TMI, Franklin, West Virginia.

———. 2002. *Annual Report 2002.* TMI, Washington, D.C.

———. 2005. *Annual Report.* TMI, Washington D.C.

Torres, Víctor. 2014. "Grupos económicos y bonanza minera en el Perú." *Apuntes* 41(75):171–210.

Touraine, Alain. 1989. *América Latina: Política y sociedad.* Espasa Calpe, Madrid.

Tsing, Anna. 2000. "Inside the Economy of Appearances." *Public Culture* 12(1):115–144.

———. 2005. *Friction: An Ethnography of Global Connection.* Princeton University Press, Princeton, New Jersey.

UNDP (United Nations Development Programme). 2016. *Human Development Report 2016: Human Development for Everyone.* UNDP, New York.

Urbina, Ian. 2010. "BP Used Riskier Method to Seal Well Before Blast." *New York Times*, May 26. New York. http://www.nytimes.com/2010/05/27/us/27rig.html.

Valera, Guillermo. 1998. *Las comunidades en el Perú: Una visión nacional desde las series departamentales.* Instituto Rural del Perú, Lima.

van Geen, Alexander, Carolina Bravo, Vladimir R. Gil Ramón, Shaky Sherpa, and Darby Jack. 2012. "Lead Exposure from Soil in Peruvian Mining Towns: A National Assessment Supported by Two Contrasting Examples." *Bulletin of the World Health Organization* 90:878–886.

Vanclay, Frank, and Daniel A. Bronstein (editors). 1995. *Environmental and Social Impact Assessment.* Wiley, Chichester.

Vásquez, Enrique. 2012. "El Perú de los pobres no visibles para el Estado: La inclusión social pendiente a julio del 2012." Working Paper. CIUP, Lima.

Watts, Michael. 2003. "Political Ecology." In *A Companion to Economic Geography*, edited by Eric Sheppard and Trevor Barnes, pp. 257–274. Blackwell, Malden, Massachusetts.

Welker, Marina. 2014. *Enacting the Corporation: An American Mining Firm in Post-Authoritarian Indonesia.* University of California Press, Berkeley.
Whyte, William F., and Graciela Flores. 1963. *Los valores y el crecimiento económico en el Perú.* Minerva, Lima.
Wilson, Alphus Dan. 2012. "Review of Electronic-nose Technologies and Algorithms to Detect Hazardous Chemicals in the Environment." *Procedia Technology* 1:453–463.
Wilson, Fiona. 2004. "Towards a Political Economy of Roads: Experiences from Peru." *Development and Change* 35(3):525–546.
Wolf, Eric. 1971. "Introduction." In *National Liberation: Revolution in the Third World,* edited by Norman Miller and Roderick Aya, pp. 1–13. Free Press, New York.
Wolfe, Gerald. 2006. "El aporte de Antamina al desarrollo del Perú." Presentation by Gerald Wolfe, Lima. http://www.canadaperu.org/Antamina2006.pdf, accessed December 22, 2006.
World Bank. 1990. "Operational Directive 4.30: Involuntary Resettlement." World Bank, Washington, D.C.
———. 1991. "Operational Directive 4.20: Indigenous Peoples." World Bank, Washington, D.C.
———. 1996. *The World Bank Participation Sourcebook.* World Bank, Washington, D.C.
———. 2005a. *Opportunities for All: Peru Poverty Assessment.* World Bank, Washington, D.C.
———. 2005b. *Wealth and Sustainability: The Environmental and Social Dimension of the Mining Sector in Peru.* World Bank, Washington, D.C.
Zambrano, Américo. 2017. "La farsa del INEI." *Hildebrandt en sus trece* 349:9–11.
Zavaleta, Nilda. 1998a. "El desarrollo de Antamina." *El Comercio,* September 21:E01. Lima.
———. 1998b. "Las otras inversiones canadienses en Antamina." *El Comercio,* September 21:E02. Lima.

INDEX

ABOUT THE AUTHOR

Vladimir R. Gil Ramón is faculty at the Environmental Development Master's Program and the Department of Social Sciences at the Catholic University of Peru (PUCP), as well as an adjunct associate research scientist at the Earth Institute Center for Environmental Sustainability at Columbia University.

FSC
www.fsc.org
MIX
Papier | Fördert gute Waldnutzung
FSC® C083411

Kolibri 360 GmbH
Ferdinand-Jühlke-Straße 7
99095 Erfurt, Deutschland
produktsicherheit@kolibri360.de